THE ZYPREXA PAPERS

by

Jim Gottstein

Table of Contents

Dedication

This book is dedicated to William S. (Bill) Bigley.

Ch. 1.Out Of The Blue

TUESDAY, NOVEMBER 28, 2006

It was just a normal day before Dr. David Egilman called me out of the blue on November 28, 2006. The days are short that time of year in Anchorage, Alaska, and it was getting dark by mid-afternoon. Dr. Egilman told me he had been hired as an expert witness by one of the law firms representing patients who had taken Zyprexa and contracted diabetes or other metabolic problems. He wanted to know about documents relating to Zyprexa I might have. In truth, he was feeling me out to see whether I might be willing to subpoena him, so he could legally send me secret documents. These documents revealed the pharmaceutical company Eli Lilly (Lilly) had from the beginning suppressed information showing Zyprexa caused these life-threatening conditions. In addition, they showed Lilly had illegally marketed this powerful and dangerous drug for use in children and the elderly. He wanted me to then send them to Alex Berenson, a reporter for *The New York Times* with whom he was already working on a Zyprexa exposé.

In fact, as I was to learn later, Mr. Berenson discovered I had already been involved in litigation concerning Zyprexa when he came across a report on the Web written by Dr. Grace Jackson in 2003 for a case of mine, titled "An Analysis of the Olanzapine Clinical Trials— Dangerous Drug, Dubious Efficacy" (Jackson Zyprexa Report). Zyprexa is the brand name for olanzapine. Berenson suggested to Dr. Egilman that I might be willing to subpoena him.

The Jackson Zyprexa Report was expert testimony in a case in which I was representing Faith Myers, who was resisting efforts by the Alaska Psychiatric Institute (API) to drug her with Zyprexa against her will. To write the report, Dr. Jackson had used documents from the Food and Drug Administration (FDA) pertaining to the approval of Zyprexa, which had been obtained by investigative journalist Robert Whitaker through a Freedom of Information Act (FOIA) request. These documents had been used by Mr. Whitaker in his landmark 2002 book, *Mad in America: Bad Science, Bad Medicine, and the Enduring Mistreatment of the Mentally Ill.* That book had been the impetus for me to found the Law Project for Psychiatric Rights (PsychRights), whose mission is to mount a strategic litigation campaign against forced psychiatric drugging and electroshock. As part of this mission, PsychRights is further dedicated to exposing the truth about these drugs and stopping the courts from being misled into ordering people to be drugged and subjected to other brain- and body-damaging "treatments" against their will.

I personally got caught up in the mental health system in 1982 when, at the age of twenty-nine, I had a psychotic break (went crazy) from lack of sleep and was locked up in API for thirty days. I was told I would have to take mind-numbing Thorazine-like drugs for the rest of my life. When I told them I had graduated from Harvard Law School (which I had), I was considered delusional. Those who believed I was a lawyer said I would never practice law again. However, my mother, who was the Executive Director of the Alaska Mental Health Association, steered me to a terrific psychiatrist, Robert Alberts, who said anyone who doesn't get sleep will become psychotic, and I just needed to learn how to keep from getting into trouble. He prescribed a sleeping pill for when all else failed. Sleeping pills are very addictive and problematic, so I only take them if needed to avoid becoming psychotic. I often go a year or more without taking one. I had one more brief hospitalization in 1985 when I didn't act aggressively enough with sleeping pills to get sleep. Since then, I have been able to keep on top of things and was lucky not to have been made into a permanent mental patient by the mental illness system. These experiences started my advocacy for people diagnosed with serious mental illness.

Before *Mad in America* came out, I had pretty much known neuroleptic drugs were harmful rather than helpful but didn't feel I could do much about it. In addition to being a terrific read, *Mad in America* was, to me, a litigation roadmap for challenging forced psychiatric drugging on the basis that it isn't in the patient's best interest. These drugs have been marketed as "antipsychotic" even though for most people, they do not have any antipsychotic properties. Instead, they suppress people's brain activity so much they can no longer be much trouble—at least temporarily. "Neuroleptic," which means "seize the brain," was one of the first names given to this class of drugs, which includes Thorazine, Haldol, and Navane. The other name was "major tranquilizer," which was to contrast them with the "minor tranquilizers" such as Valium, Xanax, and Klonopin. Thus, I use the term "neuroleptic" because it is the most accurate description. "Antipsychotic" is marketing hype.

Faith Myers had been on the neuroleptic Navane for more than twenty years when she came to Alaska and was switched to Risperdal, a newer neuroleptic, because her psychiatrist became concerned she might get Tardive Dyskinesia and wrongly believed that would not happen with Risperdal. As psychiatrist Lee Coleman describes in his terrific book *Reign of Error: Psychiatry, Authority, and Law,* Tardive Dyskinesia is a result of neuroleptic-induced brain damage, causing the patient to have rhythmic smacking of the lips, sucking and chewing movements of the mouth, protrusion of the tongue, grimacing, and in some cases, bizarre movements of the arms and legs. Many people associate this with mental illness, but it is a result of the drugs and is usually irreversible.

Faith had been functioning well all those years on Navane, raising two children as a single mother and holding jobs, including running a day care center. The psychiatrist's plan was to add Risperdal and then gradually reduce the Navane. Faith testified to the problems caused by taking Risperdal and Navane at the same time:

> I was having a lot of—seeing lights, dizziness, it was hard to drive sometimes. When I would drive, I might have to stop driving and pull off the road, because I might feel that there would be a great wave of drowsiness come over me. I was starting to see, instead of the lights, red light being red light, my brain would register red light as green light and green light as red light. . . . [T]hat had never happened [before]. I had never been overwhelmed while driving, so that I was unable to drive. I had never had lights flashing in front of my eyes. I had never had disorientation to the point that I could not remember the route to a familiar place.

Her doctor then switched her to just Risperdal, with the following results:

> [W]ithin two weeks, I think even less than that, I was hearing voices, some familiar voices, a lot of commanding voices, one in particular that ordered me all over the city, claiming to be God.

3

Faith testified that had never happened before and continued:

> It was as though the [Risperdal] punched a big hole in
> my brain that let all of these spirits or voices into my
> brain. And it didn't get better, sir, it just got worse and
> worse and worse.

Her doctor wouldn't take her off the Risperdal, and Faith knew she needed help. She talked her son into taking her to API. However, API doesn't accept people who want to be there, just people who don't, and they discharged Faith after a few days.

Faith was unable to continue working, was put on disability, and became homeless for a time. Her doctor ended up putting her on Zyprexa. Faith testified she seemed to be okay for a time, but then the problems she'd had on Risperdal were "gradually coming back in full force" on the Zyprexa:

> And not only were they coming back in full force, but
> frighteningly so. The Zyprexa seemed to be a door that
> opened up some very scary effects for me.

Faith had been taking psych drugs voluntarily, but once she decided she needed to get off them, the system took steps to force her to take them. That is where I came in.

Faith was very firm about not wanting to take the drugs and was willing to be locked up in the hospital while we fought it out. A four-month all-out court battle ensued. According to the Alaska statute allowing forced drugging in a non-emergency situation, if the patient is found incompetent to decide whether or not to take a drug, the hospital gets to make them take whatever drugs it wants. Despite Faith's very logical reasons for choosing not to take Zyprexa, the judge found her incompetent. I argued that under the United States and Alaska constitutions, even if a person is found incompetent to decline the drugs, the State cannot drug someone against their will unless it can prove the forced drugging is in the person's best interest and there is no less-intrusive alternative

This is where *Mad in America* and Jackson's Zyprexa Report came in. The FOIA documents provided by Robert Whitaker, which Dr. Jackson reviewed, were not generally known to the medical community. Dr. Jackson's expert, in-depth analysis revealed Zyprexa caused diabetes and other metabolic problems in a large percentage of patients. In addition, Dr. Jackson found the studies conducted by Lilly to obtain FDA approval had been manipulated to exaggerate Zyprexa's benefits and understate its harms. For example, the placebo arm of the studies consisted of people who had been abruptly withdrawn from their current neuroleptic. Abruptly withdrawing from a neuroleptic is known to cause psychosis. This is a drug withdrawal effect, not any underlying "mental illness." These abruptly withdrawn patients in whom psychosis had been deliberately induced were the "control" group. In other words, the research design magnified psychiatric symptoms in the control group and misleadingly compared those people's results with the results from patients given Zyprexa but not abruptly withdrawn from another psychiatric drug. Worse, even though many people develop psychosis when abruptly withdrawn from a neuroleptic, some people get better—but the people who got better were removed from the studies. This made Zyprexa look better by comparison with those left in the study. The researchers called this "placebo washout."

Another example of Zyprexa study manipulation is known as Last Observation Carried Forward. Seventy-three percent of study participants dropped out of one study and 68% out of another, presumably because Zyprexa didn't work or because the negative effects were intolerable, or both. These were, after all, patients who were not court ordered to take the drug, so they could decide to quit. To compensate for this astoundingly high dropout rate, the study's authors assumed that whatever condition the patients were in before they dropped out would not have changed if they had remained in the study to the end. Thus, if someone dropped out at week one, the researchers assumed the person would have been in the same condition at the end of the twelve-week trial. What is the point of doing a twelve-week study if you are going to pretend a person isn't going to be in any different condition at the end of the study than at the beginning? For one thing, many negative effects that could have shown up in twelve weeks will have been missed.

Another misleading aspect of the studies was that the "control" group put on Haldol was given a four to twenty times overdosing of Haldol, which made any comparisons with the lower dose of Zyprexa invalid. The studies didn't include people who had never been put on a neuroleptic in the first place, which would have been the best test.

In ordering Faith be forced to take Zyprexa against her will, the judge found all of this "troubling" but ruled it to be irrelevant because the statute said if she found Faith incompetent to decline Zyprexa, the hospital could force her to take whatever it wanted. We appealed that decision to the Alaska Supreme Court and obtained a stay (delay) of the forced drugging order until the appeal was decided.

Under Alaska law, a person is first committed for up to thirty days. Then the person can be committed for an additional ninety days and after that for successive180-day periods. No jury trial is allowed for the thirty-day commitment, but one is allowed for the ninety- and 180-day commitments. While I disagreed Faith met commitment criteria, I could understand why the judge felt she did, because in the extremely short time frame I hadn't been able to get an expert witness to testify Faith didn't meet commitment criteria. Thinking the judge would follow the law if we presented the evidence that the state was not entitled to have Faith committed, I didn't ask for a jury trial for the ninety-day commitment. At the ninety-day trial, we had a very good expert witness who demonstrated Faith didn't meet either of the commitment criteria of being a danger to self or others or being gravely disabled, but the judge committed her anyway. This made me realize the judge just didn't want to be responsible if something bad happened, and would commit her whether or not Faith met commitment criteria. In other words, the judge was going to do whatever the doctor wanted. This made me decide to recommend a jury trial whenever my client was allowed to have one.

API could not drug Faith because of the stay, so they punished her in various ways. Most fundamental was refusing to free her, even though there was no reason to keep her locked up. They concocted "emergencies" to try to justify giving her Haldol injections. Haldol is the drug used to tranquilize raging lions and tigers that get out of control during "lion-taming" shows, and it has the same effect in people. Once, when Faith got frustrated at staff and dumped crayons on an aide's head, they deemed this to be such an emergency that she needed to be quelled like a wild animal with a Haldol injection. The statute only allows "emergency" drugging if "immediate use of the medication [is required] to preserve the life of, or prevent significant physical harm to, the patient or another person." Dumping crayons on someone's head hardly qualifies. In violation of her rights, they didn't let her go outside and wouldn't even let her go to the cafeteria to eat.

Realizing the judge would commit her regardless of the evidence, at the next trial, which would be for a commitment of up to 180 days, we demanded a jury trial. When I gave my opening statement, the psychiatrist who had filed to commit Faith seemed to be learning for the first time what was legally required. Apparently recognizing Faith did not meet commitment criteria, API dropped the case and let her go. However, our appeal over the original forced drugging order continued.

On June 30, 2006, the Alaska Supreme Court issued its decision in Faith's appeal, agreeing with us that as a constitutional matter, even if someone is found incompetent to decline the medication, the government is not allowed to drug the person against their will unless the state can prove by clear and convincing evidence it is in the person's best interest and no less-intrusive alternative is available. What "available" means in this context was not defined until a later case, but the Alaska Supreme Court ordered the trial courts to consider:

> (A) the patient's diagnosis and prognosis, or their predominant symptoms, with and without the medication;

> (B) information about the proposed medication, its purpose, the method of its administration, the recommended ranges of dosages, possible side effects and benefits, ways to treat side effects, and risks of other conditions, such as Tardive Dyskinesia;

> (C) a review of the patient's history, including medication history and previous side effects from medication;

> (D) an explanation of interactions with other drugs, including over-the-counter drugs, street drugs, and alcohol; and

> (E) information about alternative treatments and their risks, side effects, and benefits, including the risks of nontreatment.

In essence, the Alaska Supreme Court ordered the trial courts to consider the truth about the benefits and harms of a drug when deciding whether to force someone to take it on the grounds it is in their best interest.

Faith had been an advocate for people diagnosed with mental illness before she won her Alaska Supreme Court case and has become quite influential since then. She almost singlehandedly got legislation passed allowing patients to choose the gender of hospital staff providing intimate care. This is important because such a high percentage of people in psychiatric hospitals have been subjected to sexual abuse. Her current mission is trying to obtain legislation to give patients a meaningful right to have their complaints considered.

When Dr. Egilman called me just a few months after Faith's big Alaska Supreme Court win and got around to asking me whether I was interested in obtaining secret documents showing Eli Lilly had been lying about the safety of Zyprexa, you bet I was interested. Such information was central to PsychRights' mission.

Dr. Egilman, an epidemiologist and associate professor at Brown University, is an experienced expert witness, and a physician of conscience. He had been hired by one of the plaintiffs' law firms in the multi-district litigation (MDL) over Eli Lilly not informing doctors about the massive weight gain, diabetes, and other metabolic problems caused by Zyprexa (Zyprexa MDL). The Zyprexa MDL was not a class action lawsuit, where "class representatives" sue on behalf of all the members of the class. Instead, it was the consolidation for settlement and discovery purposes of tens of thousands of separate lawsuits, filed in state and federal courts around the country, into one case in the United States District Court for the Eastern District of New York, in Brooklyn. With so many individual lawsuits, these MDLs are useful to the defendants and to the lawyers for the plaintiffs for litigating and settling a large number of cases. Just as in class actions, they tend to not be very good for the victims, because each victim receives relatively little for the harm they have suffered. Still, as a practical matter, these MDLs and class actions are often the only way victims can get lawyers to pursue their claims.

"Discovery" is the process in which parties are required to produce (give) to the other side documents relevant to the litigation, and to provide pre-trial testimony (depositions) and answer written questions (interrogatories). The reason for consolidating discovery in one MDL is to avoid the duplication and inconsistencies inherent in conducting separate discovery in thousands of separate cases. A large depository of digitized documents was set up for the Zyprexa MDL, with all or virtually all of them marked confidential by Lilly—including newspaper articles and other materials clearly not confidential.

As an expert for some of the plaintiffs, Dr. Egilman was given access to this depository. When he found documents demonstrating Lilly had known from the very beginning that Zyprexa caused massive weight gain, diabetes, and other metabolic problems in a large percentage of patients and not only didn't tell doctors about it, but also actively denied the problems when people started experiencing them, he felt the public had the right to know. He began working with Alex Berenson of *The New York Times* to develop an exposé. The order granting secrecy to the documents produced in discovery (Secrecy Order) had a provision that said if an expert was subpoenaed in an unrelated case, the expert could not produce (hand over) the documents under the subpoena without first giving Lilly notice and a reasonable opportunity to object. This is why they went looking for someone who might subpoena him, and that is where I came in.

When Dr. Egilman called and asked about information I might have on Zyprexa in addition to the Jackson Zyprexa Report, I directed him to the FOIA documents pertaining to Zyprexa's FDA approval. I also directed him to the adverse events database PsychRights had created from the response to a FOIA request Ellen Liversidge had made with respect to six second-generation neuroleptics, of which Zyprexa was one. The FDA sent this information in text files, and I asked a computer wizard friend of mine, Matt Joy, to put the information into database format. Ellen made the FOIA request because her son had been killed by Zyprexa.

Dr. Egilman finally got around to telling me he had access to damning documents in the Zyprexa MDL he wanted me to subpoena and send to *The New York Times*. He told me they were subject to a Secrecy Order but that if someone subpoenaed him for the documents, he simply had to give Eli Lilly notice and a reasonable opportunity to object. I asked Dr. Egilman for a copy of the Secrecy Order, which was titled Case Management Order 3 (CMO-3). Dr. Egilman didn't give me the Secrecy Order, but he did read me the provision related to subpoenaing documents:

14 **Subpoena by other Courts or Agencies**

If another court or an administrative agency subpoenas or otherwise orders production of

Confidential Discovery Materials which a person has
obtained under the terms of the Order, the person to
whom the subpoena or other process is directed shall
promptly notify the designating party [Lilly] in writing
of all of the following: (1) the discovery materials that
are requested for production in the subpoena; (2) the
date on which compliance with the subpoena is
requested; (3) the location at which compliance with the
subpoena is requested; (4) the identity of the party
serving the subpoena; and (5) the case name,
jurisdiction and index, docket, complaint, charge, civil
action or other identification number or other
designation identifying the litigation, administrative
proceeding or other proceeding in which the subpoena
or other process has been issued. In no event shall
confidential documents be produced prior to the
receipt of written notice by the designating party and a
reasonable opportunity to object. Furthermore, the
person receiving the subpoena or other process shall
cooperate with the producing party [Lilly] in any
proceeding related thereto.

Dr. Egilman's refusal to give me the entire Secrecy Order was
suspicious, but I motored right past that red flag.

Dr. Egilman told me he had been working with Alex Berenson on
an exposé because the documents showed Lilly had known about
Zyprexa causing diabetes from the very beginning and hidden this
information from doctors. The Jackson Zyprexa Report had come to
the same conclusion about Zyprexa causing diabetes, so this was not
news to me, but I recognized having *The New York Times* publish an
exposé would make all the difference in the world. So I was very
interested in obtaining the documents. However, I made it clear to Dr.
Egilman he had to comply with the secrecy order.

I told Dr. Egilman that a typical forced drugging case happens
extremely fast, with the hospital often filing the paperwork in the
morning and the trial on it being held that afternoon. This, of course,
doesn't allow time to mount any type of meaningful defense. People
facing these forced drugging petitions are automatically assigned public
defenders, who are there not to provide serious legal representation but
so a box can be checked that the person had an attorney. I told Dr.

Egilman I always insist on a continuance (delay), but I couldn't put off the hearing for long—it would still have to happen very fast. Dr. Egilman said he needed more than a couple of days. I responded that we would just have to see.

While I was willing to subpoena the documents and provide them to *The New York Times*, which was completely consistent with PsychRights' mission, I had my own, independent reasons for wanting the documents. This was for use in PsychRights' strategic litigation and public education efforts. The *Myers* case we had won just five months before had made whether a psychiatric drug was in the person's best interest a central part of whether the state could drug someone against their will. Documents showing Zyprexa to be very harmful would be extremely relevant and very powerful evidence against forcing someone to take it. Being able to demonstrate to the court that the psychiatrist testifying against their patient didn't know about such harm would be good to show the court because it tarnished their reputation as an MDeity.

One concern I had was whether it was permissible for me to have two reasons for subpoenaing the documents: one being the litigation from which the subpoena was issued and the other being to publicize their contents. I wanted the documents so that PsychRights could pursue strategic litigation in Alaska, and I also wanted to make the public aware of the contents of the documents. Based on my research, I concluded that as long as I had a legitimate reason to subpoena the documents, I was free to make any other use of them.

I had a family vacation in Hawaii scheduled from December 22nd until January 15th and told Dr. Egilman I would deal with the subpoena after I got back. Dr. Egilman said I had to do it before I left because another mass settlement was imminent and his access to the documents would be terminated when that happened. Earlier in the Zyprexa MDL, in 2005, Lilly had settled claims of almost 8,000 Zyprexa victims for $700 million, averaging a little under $90,000 per victim. This doesn't seem like a lot for giving someone diabetes, but it is even worse when you consider the lawyers took 40% and then Medicaid or Medicare were reimbursed another 30%. At that point, even the approximately $27,000 individual victims received, on average, put those who were on Medicaid and disability over the asset limit for eligibility. This meant they had to use the money from the settlement to treat their diabetes and otherwise spend it over the course of a year or two to maintain or get back their Medicaid and disability payments.

In any event, I agreed to try and find a case from which to subpoena the documents and have Dr. Egilman send them to me before I left. Getting that case proved to be a bit of an adventure in itself.

Ch. 2. Finding BB

Alaska court rules make involuntary commitment (psychiatric imprisonment) case files secret. The idea is to protect people's reputation because of the great contempt, fear, and loathing that accompany someone being identified as having been psychiatrically hospitalized. This is often referred to as stigma. The secrecy of these cases was a giant obstacle to finding a case quickly. The Alaska Public Defender Agency is automatically appointed to represent people facing involuntary commitment, whether the person has enough money to hire their own lawyer or not. For forced drugging petitions, according to the statute, the public defender is supposed to be appointed only if the person cannot afford an attorney, but this procedure is never followed, and it is just assumed the public defender is going to represent the person in the forced drugging case as well as the involuntary commitment case.

People have the right to choose their own lawyer, but the system is set up so that before PsychRights started doing these cases, the public defenders did virtually all of them. I doubt there had been more than half a dozen cases in the history of the State of Alaska where private lawyers represented psychiatric respondents (patients). Even when PsychRights was doing these cases, the public defenders still did the vast majority of them.

Thursday, November 30th

With the cases secret and the public defenders automatically appointed as everyone's lawyer, I had to figure out some way to find a case. On Thursday, November 30, 2006, I wrote to API, the Alaska Attorney General's Office, the Public Defender Agency, and the Court System, requesting that people currently facing forced drugging petitions be notified of PsychRights' availability. In this letter, I pointed out the Public Defender Agency can only be appointed if the defendant can't afford a lawyer, and since PsychRights was willing to represent them, the court was without authority to appoint the Public Defender Agency unless it determined the person didn't want PsychRights to represent them. I also informed them I would be at API starting at 11:00 the next day, Friday, December 1st, to meet with potential clients for the day's hearing(s) and stay there until the hearings were over. No one responded to the letter.

During late 2006, typically between five and ten commitment hearings were held every Tuesday and Friday, starting at 1:30 and ending by 4:30, by which time all the "trials" would be done, all the respondents would be locked up in the hospital, and the judge, lawyers, and hospital witness(es) would all be home in time for dinner. If there was an accompanying forced drugging petition, the hospital was given a court order allowing it to drug the person against their will.

When PsychRights took a case, it was different. I would put on a real defense. I wouldn't take a case unless the potential client agreed to at least a little delay, because it simply isn't possible to mount any type of real defense in one day. The idea that a single public defender could adequately defend between five and ten cases they had just learned about that morning is ludicrous. That leaves *maybe* fifteen minutes to talk to the client, with no time to investigate and contact, let alone interview, potential witnesses to testify. So the only witnesses were from the hospital, most often just the psychiatrist or other hospital clinician, and maybe the respondent (patient). My view is no matter how good one is at cross-examination (which I am not), one doesn't usually win cases with the other side's witnesses. As for the respondents, anything they say tends to be totally discounted because they are accused of being crazy by a supposed expert. My insistence on having some time to mount a meaningful defense meant they would not be let free that day, but they had a chance of winning a day or few later. If they stayed with a public defender, there was pretty close to a 100% chance they would lose and be subjected to at least a thirty-day court order for commitment, and forced drugging if they didn't agree to take the drugs.

I did things that had never been done in Alaska. I took depositions of the psychiatrists. I filed motions, including to dismiss (throw the case out of court) for failure of the petitions to allege facts legally sufficient to have the person locked up and/or drugged against their will. I would file an "election" (choice) to "have the hearing in a real courtroom" under a statute that provides "the hearing shall be conducted in a physical setting least likely to have a harmful effect on the mental or physical health of the respondent, within practical limits." Having the trial in a real courtroom is actually very important. Trials at the hospital don't have the trappings of a real court trial, resulting in the judges and lawyers not taking the respondents' rights seriously. Just as importantly, the respondents don't feel they got "their day in court" because it does not seem like a real trial.

That same statute allows the respondent "to have the hearing open or closed to the public as the respondent elects." Until I started doing these cases, I don't think any case had ever been open to the public. The respondents simply weren't told of that right. It was way more convenient for the court, the hospital, and the lawyers to have them all closed. Many people don't want anybody to know they are the subject of a petition for involuntary commitment. They have reputations to protect and could lose their jobs, friends, etc. However, other people, such as those whom everyone knows have been in and out of the hospital and have no reputation left to protect, sometimes want the world to know what the hospital is doing to them. While I agree the proceedings should be closed if the person doesn't want them public, the result of having them all closed is the public has no chance to see how unfair the entire process is. In any event, I would always inform my clients of their right to have the hearing open or closed, and I'd discuss the pros and cons in their circumstances. I would advise people to have the hearing closed if I thought an open one might be detrimental to them.

FRIDAY, DECEMBER 1ST

When I arrived at API on Friday, December 1st, I told visitors as they were entering the hospital about my availability. I gave them a handout to let the people they were visiting on the wrong side of the locked door know I was potentially available to represent them. At about 1:00 p.m., I was handed a letter from the hospital's lawyer, Elizabeth Russo (who became my nemesis), informing me there would be no hearings that day. In an attempt to intimidate me, the letter also accused me of violating lawyers' ethics by soliciting clients (i.e., "ambulance chasing"). Since the ethics rules for lawyers specifically allow public-interest law firms such as PsychRights to solicit clients, my actions didn't constitute an ethics violation.

SATURDAY & SUNDAY, DECEMBER 2ND & 3RD

Ignoring the state's threats, over the weekend a couple of volunteers and I handed out flyers at API, trying to get visitors to let people who were locked up and facing a forced drugging hearing know of PsychRights' availability to represent them. We also ran public service announcements, and I contacted people I knew who worked at the hospital and asked them to give the information to patients who were facing forced drugging petitions.

MONDAY, DECEMBER 4TH

API's previous attempt to intimidate me being unsuccessful, on Monday I received an e-mail from Ron Adler, the CEO of API at the time, prohibiting us from distributing the flyers, citing a state facilities management policy he interpreted as allowing him to impose this ban. I e-mailed him back that now, he was violating not just people's constitutional right to counsel but also my right to free speech, and I was inclined to come by and not only hand out the flyers the next morning but post them as well.

TUESDAY, DECEMBER 5TH

Mr. Adler responded by e-mail on December 5th, first directing that I only communicate with his attorneys and then saying, "Of the 1,452 admissions we had last fiscal year, API utilized the Court Ordered Medication process on 57 occasions" and "it doesn't get much better than that!!!" In other words, Adler was saying API forced people to take the drugs against their will only 4% of the time. I responded I wished that were true, but my conclusion was that API, aided and abetted by the Attorney General's Office, "has constructed a legal subterfuge to evade the *Myers* decision of last June." To give an idea of the length to which Mr. Adler pretended API was not all about using force against people locked up there, he referred to them as "guests."

By the end of the day, I had two potential clients who had learned of my availability. One ended up taking too long to decide whether she wanted to get involved in being the vehicle for subpoenaing the documents. The other, William S. (Bill) Bigley, signed on while she was deciding. Once I became Mr. Bigley's attorney, I was obligated to try to achieve his goals in litigation, which I did in that case and in a number of subsequent cases.

While meeting with Mr. Bigley at the hospital that evening, I asked a nurse to give him a Consent for Release of Information form to sign, directing the hospital to provide me with his medical records. Interestingly, the same nurse had been working at API when I was locked up there in 1982. He refused, saying Mr. Bigley had a guardian, and only the guardian could authorize the release of his records to me. When a full guardian has been appointed, as one had in Mr. Bigley's case, the ward (the person who has a guardian) is essentially placed in the legal position of a child, with the guardian given legal authority over virtually all decisions. They are supposed to consult with the ward, but especially when the "Public Guardian" is appointed, which in Alaska is the Office of Public Advocacy (OPA), the guardian can be incredibly indifferent or worse. The Public Guardian is only supposed to be appointed when there is no one else available, and OPA had been appointed Mr. Bigley's guardian.

Now, I think it is fair to say it is extremely rare for me to yell at anyone, but I have to admit that as I argued with the nurse over the hospital refusing to allow Mr. Bigley to give me permission to obtain his records, I ended up raising my voice. That gave me more than the normal twinge about being in a locked ward. Every time I go into a psych hospital and that lock clicks behind me, the thought comes that they might not let me out. In a psych hospital, raising one's voice is labeled a psychiatric symptom, regardless of the provocation.

The refusal to give me my client's records at that time ended up having very serious consequences because I wasn't able to testify a month later in federal court in Brooklyn that Mr. Bigley had been given Zyprexa. In talking with Mr. Bigley, I was pretty sure he had been given Zyprexa, but he had other things on his mind so I couldn't be sure, and I didn't have the records to prove it. Later, when I was able to obtain his medical records, I found, as I thought I would, that he had been given Zyprexa. In fact, he had been forced to take Zyprexa a week or so before he became my client and again a couple of months later. While my powers of persuasion that night were not sufficient to obtain his medical records, at least I had a client for whom I could subpoena Dr. Egilman to produce the documents.

Ch. 3. Lumbering Lilly

Bill Bigley, whom I initially referred to as BB in the Zyprexa MDL, had two potential cases. He had been committed for thirty and then ninety days, with associated forced drugging orders, and the ninety-day commitment was due to expire January 3, 2007. He also had a guardianship case. Since he had already lost his ninety-day commitment case and the hospital had not yet filed a petition to commit him for 180 more days, I decided the commitment case wasn't a great case from which to subpoena Dr. Egilman for the documents. I could have moved to vacate (get rid of) the forced drugging order, but Mr. Bigley really hated the guardianship so it seemed a better vehicle. Another benefit was it didn't have the extremely short deadlines that commitment and forced drugging cases do.

WEDNESDAY, DECEMBER 6TH

The next day, December 6th, I filed paperwork to become Mr. Bigley's lawyer in his guardianship case, along with a petition to:

(1) terminate the guardianship

and, in case the guardianship was not terminated, to:

(2) remove the guardian and appoint a successor of Bill's choice;

(3) amend the powers of the guardian to the least restrictive necessary to meet Bill's essential requirements for physical health and safety as set forth in statute;

(4) review and reverse the guardian's decision to consent to Bill being drugged against his wishes; and

(5) amend the powers of the guardian, eliminating his authority to consent to mental health treatment being administered to Bill.

Items 1–3 were not related to subpoenaing Dr. Egilman for the documents but, instead, to achieving Mr. Bigley's other goals in the guardianship case. The documents were relevant to items 4 and 5 and therefore grounds to subpoena Dr. Egilman for them.

I had subpoenas issued to: (1) Ron Adler, the CEO of API, (2) Steve Young, the person at OPA assigned as Mr. Bigley's guardian, (3) Dr. Grace Jackson, and (4) Dr. Egilman. Mr. Adler's subpoena was for a deposition to be held on December 11th and ordered him to bring Mr. Bigley's medical records as well as all documents related to guardians consenting to psychiatric drugging of their wards. This was to follow up on my suspicion that the guardians were consenting to drugging their wards as a way to bypass the *Myers* decision, which only allowed forced drugging if the court found it to be in the person's best interest and no less-intrusive alternative was available.

Steve Young's subpoena was for a deposition to be held January 24th and ordered him to bring all records pertaining to (1) Mr. Bigley, (2) consenting to the drugging of Mr. Bigley against his will, including the information used in making such decisions, and (3) why he believed he could consent to the drugging of Mr. Bigley in the face of the *Myers* decision. After the subpoena to Mr. Young had been served (delivered by a process server), his boss, Jim Parker, sent me an e-mail saying OPA didn't consent to psych drugs being given to wards against their will. However, just two months later, they did exactly that to Mr. Bigley.

Dr. Jackson's subpoena was for a deposition to be held December 20th. She was ordered to bring with her all documents relating to the effectiveness and safety of psychiatric drugs, as well as to less-restrictive alternatives to involuntary commitment or less-intrusive alternatives to forced drugging.

This was a full-scale assault on the guardianship that had been imposed on Mr. Bigley, including specifically challenging the guardian's authority to consent to forced drugging. The legal theory was that the guardian, not Mr. Bigley, had the right to consent to (or decline) the drugs, and when the guardian consented, such drugging was categorized as voluntary. In such a case, no forced drugging petition needed to be filed. This was how I thought API was getting around the Alaska Supreme Court's decision in *Myers* that they can't drug people against their will without a *judicial* determination that the forced drugging is in the person's best interest and there is no less-intrusive alternative available.

Dr. Egilman was subpoenaed for a telephonic deposition to be held on December 20th, to which he was ordered to bring the Zyprexa documents. He promptly faxed notice to Lilly's general counsel as follows:

I am a consulting witness in the Zyprexa litigation and have access to over 500,000 documents and depositions which Lilly claims are "Confidential Discovery Materials." Lilly defines these as "any information that the producing party in good faith believes properly protected under Federal Rule of Civil Procedure 26(c)(7)."

Lilly has claimed that newspaper articles and press releases fit this definition. I have received a subpoena attached that calls for the production of all these documents and depositions. In compliance with the protective order I am supplying a complete copy of the subpoena which notifies you of all the following:

(1) the discovery materials that are requested for production in the subpoena;

(2) the date on which compliance with the subpoena requested;

(3) the location at which compliance with the subpoena is requested;

(4) the identity of the party serving the subpoena; and

(5) the case name, jurisdiction and index, docket, complaint, charge, civil action or other identification number or other designation identifying the litigation, administrative proceeding or other proceeding in which the subpoena or other process has been issued.

Dr. Egilman sent the notice not to the lawyers handling the Zyprexa MDL but to Lilly's general counsel—the company's top lawyer.

I thought Lilly would be objecting first thing the next morning, at which point I would be arguing to the Alaska Superior Court that Mr. Bigley was entitled to the documents because they were extremely important evidence under the *Myers* decision that the court could not order him to be drugged against his will unless it found by clear and convincing evidence that the drugging was in his best interests. Documents Lilly had hidden, showing Zyprexa caused massive weight gain, diabetes, or other metabolic problems in a large percentage of patients, were clearly relevant to the argument that being forced to take Zyprexa was not in Bill's best interest. Our position would be that Mr.

Bigley was entitled to obtain the documents to defend against forced drugging or, in this case, to make the case that the guardian should not be allowed to consent to him being drugged against his will—at least with Zyprexa. That is what I thought would happen.

In contrast, Dr. Egilman believed Lilly would be slow and he could get the documents to me after a "reasonable opportunity to object" had passed. Dr. Egilman would send me self-destructing e-mails that would disappear after a few days. This was unacceptable to me, and I printed them to permanent computer files before they self-destructed, although I missed some.

FRIDAY, DECEMBER 8TH

On Friday, December 8th, I filed a motion to disqualify John Duggan, the Probate Master (lower-level judge) in Mr. Bigley's guardianship case. The grounds were that Master Duggan, who presided over the vast majority of forced drugging cases, (1) had presumably ordered hundreds, if not thousands of people to be drugged against their will and (2) appeared to be bypassing the Alaska Supreme Court's ruling in the *Myers* case by authorizing temporary guardians to "consent" to the forced drugging of their wards. In addition, I asserted that by refusing the previous week to notify respondents that I was available to represent them he gave at least the appearance of not being impartial.

MONDAY, DECEMBER 11TH

As I thought about the subpoena to Dr. Egilman, I came to realize it had two problems. First, it directed him to bring the documents with him to his deposition, which wasn't going to work since he was going to testify by telephone from Massachusetts. Second, I needed to have the documents ahead of the deposition in order to be able to ask questions about them. Therefore, on December 11th, I had an amended subpoena issued that ordered Dr. Egilman to deliver the material prior to the deposition and in an e-mail asked him to provide them as soon as he could. By this I meant as soon as he had determined he was allowed to give them to me. I told Dr. Egilman he should immediately give Lilly the amended subpoena because the Secrecy Order required Dr. Egilman to tell Lilly "the date on which compliance with the subpoena is requested." Dr. Egilman disagreed, saying he didn't see that it made any difference. I suggested he consult with an attorney about his obligations under the Secrecy Order. He wouldn't change his mind.

In the guardianship case, OPA filed a motion for the appointment of what is called a "court visitor" to conduct an "impartial investigation" and report on whether the court should grant Mr. Bigley's petition to terminate the guardianship or, failing that, remove OPA as guardian or eliminate its right to consent to psych drugs and mental health treatment. The idea of an impartial court visitor sounds good, but the reality is far different. The court visitors are paid by OPA, which constitutes a conflict of interest when OPA is the guardian and the court visitor is supposed to issue a report on whether OPA should be appointed guardian (or removed, in Mr. Bigley's case). It gets worse. In a normal case, OPA is suggested as the guardian, and in addition to a court visitor being appointed to make supposedly impartial recommendations about whether OPA should be appointed guardian, OPA is also appointed to be the lawyer for the person against whom the guardianship is sought! It is a separate section of OPA, but still a huge problem, in my view. My perspective is these guardianship proceedings are normally almost as much of a legal farce as involuntary commitment and forced drugging cases.

Late that afternoon, I received a voicemail message from Brewster Jamieson of the Lane Powell law firm, who identified himself as Lilly's local lawyer and asked me to call him back. I immediately called Dr. Egilman and told him Lilly was closing in. I knew that while Lilly might have been slow off the mark, it would be big and fast once it got going. We talked about whether five days was a "reasonable" time to object. Dr. Egilman said that in another place in the Secrecy Order, Lilly only had to receive three days' notice before documents could be given to someone. Dr. Egilman determined five days was enough time and got ready to upload the files to an FTP server I had set up on an Internet domain I had registered that day, named zyprexadocuments.net. "FTP" stands for file transfer protocol, which was specifically designed to transfer large files and/or large numbers of files.

TUESDAY, DECEMBER 12TH

Not being in a particular rush to talk to Mr. Jamieson, but also not wanting to look like I was avoiding him, I figured I would return the call early the next morning, hopefully before he got in. That is what I did, leaving a message for him around 8:00 a.m. Then, if he called back, I could wait until the next day.

Dr. Egilman began transferring 356 documents that day, December 12th, which took pretty much all day. Once I had them, I called Alex Berenson and gave him the username and password for the FTP server, which were "schizophrenia" and "iatrogenic"—the latter means "caused by treatment." Feeling Lilly's breath on my neck, I wanted to further distribute what at that point became the "Zyprexa Papers." It was dark by that time, and I had rock-and-roll music playing while copying files onto DVDs from my desktop computer, my assistant's computer, and a laptop at the same time, putting them in padded DVD envelopes and addressing the envelopes to various people I wanted to have them. Initially, I sent them to Robert Whitaker, Dr. Peter Breggin, Judi Chamberlin, Dr. Stefan Kruszewski, Laura Ziegler, Dr. David Cohen, and Will Hall.

As mentioned, Robert Whitaker is the author of *Mad in America*, which had inspired me to start PsychRights. I had brought Mr. Whitaker up to Alaska a couple of times to give talks and had gotten to know him fairly well. As he was a journalist in the subject area, I thought he would find the Zyprexa Papers very interesting.

Dr. Breggin, a long-time critic of psychiatric drugs and electroshock, wrote the very important book *Toxic Psychiatry* in 1991, exposing the brain-damaging and other harmful effects of psych drugs and electroshock, euphemistically called electroconvulsive therapy. He has continued to practice humane psychiatry and write many books and articles about the harm caused by psychiatry. Dr. Breggin was a successful and highly sought-after expert witness in cases against psychiatrists who had harmed people.

Judi Chamberlin was one of the founders and an icon of the modern Psychiatric Survivor movement, having written the very influential 1978 book *On Our Own: Patient-Controlled Alternatives to the Mental Health System*, after she had been psychiatrically imprisoned and drugged against her will. I had met Judi many years before I sent her the Zyprexa Papers, when she had come to Alaska to give a talk. I'd had an airplane at the time and flew her around Denali, which was still officially named Mt. McKinley then. I had seen her at a number of annual conferences of the National Association of Rights Protection and Advocacy (NARPA), as well as other conferences and events. Judi was an indefatigable advocate who didn't mince words. She was polite but would never go along to get along. Judi passed away in 2010, courageously blogging about dying of emphysema.

NARPA is a wonderful, unique organization composed mainly of Psychiatric Survivors and mental health rights lawyers. Its primary activity is its annual rights conference. A "Psychiatric Survivor" is someone who identifies as having survived the harm caused to them by the psychiatric system, often as psychiatric inmates forced to endure drugs and/or electroshock they knew to be harmful. Psychiatric Survivors are activists against coercive psychiatry. This is contrasted with "Mental Health Consumers," or simply "Consumers," who are or were psychiatric "treatment" recipients. The term "consumer" came from the idea that "hey, we are the ones receiving the treatments and as 'consumers' should get to say what that treatment should be." Consumers tend to be advocates within the mental health system, while Psychiatric Survivors tend to be outside critics. Another category is "Ex-Patient." Sometimes these three groups are referred together as "C/S/X" or Mental Health **C**onsumer/Psychiatric **S**urvivor/e**X**-patient.

Dr. Stefan Kruszewski is a psychiatrist of conscience. As a fraud investigator for the Commonwealth of Pennsylvania in 2003, Dr. Kruszewski uncovered the abuse, medical mistreatment, and deaths of children diagnosed with mental illness in out-of-state residential treatment centers. He was told to stop looking into this and was fired for refusing to back off. He later won a lawsuit over his firing.

Laura Ziegler is a long-time Psychiatric Survivor activist living in Vermont, whom I also got to know through NARPA, on whose board we both sat for a time. Laura is extremely knowledgeable and is also indefatigable in her advocacy efforts. Despite being delightfully negative about the chance of ever effecting any substantial improvements or real reform, she is an incredible advocate. Laura was locked up and drugged against her will as a mental patient when she was seventeen after she'd been in conflict with her parents. Unusually, Laura was able to get an injunction stopping the drugging, which led to her being let go. It is almost certain Laura had undiagnosed and therefore untreated Lyme disease, which is known to cause psychiatric-like symptoms. It is quite common for people to be diagnosed with mental illness when they actually have Lyme disease; this is true for some other physical illnesses as well. Lyme disease, other medical condition(s), family dynamics, being an independent-minded teenager, or any combination of these could have been why Laura was acting in a way that allowed her parents to get her locked up.

David Cohen, PhD, is a world-renowned expert on psychiatric drugs and effective alternatives to them, whom I got to know through the International Center for the Study of Psychology and Psychiatry (ICSPP), now known as the International Society for Ethical Psychology and Psychiatry (ISEPP). ICSPP was founded by Dr. Breggin as an organization to expose, through research, the truth about psychiatric "treatments." Historically, its main activity is its annual conference, where the latest—and often cutting-edge—research is presented. These conferences also serve as a place where beleaguered mental health professionals of conscience can gather with like-minded professionals and get re-energized in the battle against the psychiatric/pharmaceutical juggernaut.

Will Hall, a Psychiatric Survivor of Native American descent, is a co-founder of the Freedom Center, in Northampton, Massachusetts, which is how I first got to know him. As with most people diagnosed with schizophrenia, he suffered severe trauma as a child. A few years after he graduated from college, he ended up in a psychiatric hospital, where he was hog-tied (euphemistically referred to as "restraint"), put in solitary confinement (euphemistically referred to as "seclusion"), and forced to take mind-crushing psychiatric drugs. He escaped the psychiatric system, got a master's degree, has a counseling, coaching, and therapy practice, and is now also a highly sought-after trainer and speaker around the world.

Dr. Egilman asked me to also send the Zyprexa Papers to Steven Cha, a staff member in the office of Representative Henry Waxman in the U.S. House Committee on Government Reform; Snigdha Prakash, a reporter for National Public Radio; and Emilia DiSanto, the chief investigator for the U.S. Senate Committee on Finance, chaired by Chuck Grassley of Iowa.

Feeling Lilly breathing down my neck, I was quite keen to get the Zyprexa Papers on their way as soon as possible. I called Will Hall and asked whether he knew how to distribute them on the Internet in a way that would be difficult to trace and make it impossible for Lilly to shut down. I told Will I might be ordered to get the files back, and if I asked him to return the files, he should ignore my request. However, I also told him if *he* was ordered by the court to return them, he had to. He asked me not to identify him, and I said I would avoid it to the extent I could, but if I were asked a question during testimony, I would have to answer truthfully. Will courageously still agreed to do it, and to this day, I feel guilty about putting him at such risk. At the same time, the reason was to make the Zyprexa Papers—which showed the massive harm Zyprexa was causing, including killing many thousands of people—available for people to see for themselves. Will granted me permission to identify him in this book, as I want him to receive credit for the important role he played.

Will did know how to get them on the Internet in a way that could not be traced and would protect them from being taken down. It was Tor, which was relatively new at that time. Tor encrypts and then randomly bounces communications through a network of relays run by volunteers around the globe. In this way, people could obtain the documents while remaining untraceable. Many of the servers were located outside of the United States. Will also knew how to use FTP and downloaded the files from the PsychRights website so he didn't have to wait for them to arrive in the mail.

Both Alex Berenson and Dr. Egilman knew I was going to distribute the Zyprexa Papers to other people. I had insisted. One of the people to whom I intended to give them was Lisa Demer of the *Anchorage Daily News*, a journalist who had written about the *Myers* case and with whom I had developed a professional relationship. On December 15th, I e-mailed Lisa that I had some really important material to give her. Mr. Berenson was very upset and told me if I did so, he wouldn't run the series in *The New York Times*. I didn't believe him, because I knew he had been working on the story for weeks, at the very least, and really hard over the last few days. I doubted he would abandon all that work. However, I recognized having the scandal exposed by *The New York Times* was paramount, so I then e-mailed Lisa to say I wouldn't be able to get the documents to her. I don't blame Alex for insisting on the scoop when he had put so much work into it. Apparently, it was okay for me to send them to Ms. Prakash at NPR, as requested by Dr. Egilman. When I asked Dr. Egilman about that, he indicated she wasn't going to do a story. I don't know why he wanted me to send them to her.

It was fairly late that evening by the time I had all the DVDs and envelopes done. I drove out to the main post office at the airport, from where I knew all my little Christmas presents would make it out that night. It amused me to contemplate these DVD bombshells, put into the regular United States mail, getting slowed down by the Christmas rush and showing up in people's mailboxes over the next couple of weeks. Having done what I could to get the Zyprexa Papers out, I relaxed a bit but knew a firestorm would be coming.

When my wife found out what I had been up to, she wanted me to give her a copy. I tried to talk her out of it, telling her it could end up getting her in trouble, but she insisted. There was also an architect in my building, Jerry Winchester, who wanted them too, even after I warned him.

PsychRights had just hired its first (and only) Executive Director, Bruce Whittington, who lived in British Columbia, and he also wanted a copy, which I sent to him. The money to hire Bruce came from attorney fees in the *Myers* case, and one of his tasks was to raise enough money to keep himself employed. Unfortunately, dealing with the firestorm that was soon to be unleashed diverted him from this and the other tasks we had laid out, and PsychRights was only able to keep him for about six months.

After getting the Zyprexa Papers out, it was mostly a waiting game. Dr. Egilman and I would speak on the phone, joking that we didn't think either of us would be buggering targets if we ended up in prison, since we were old and fat. The gallows humor didn't obscure that both of us felt going to prison would be worth exposing the great harm being done by Zyprexa. We were hoping to keep thousands upon thousands more people from being killed by Zyprexa.

Also on December 12th, API filed two motions in the guardianship case: (1) Motion to Quash [void] Subpoenas and Stay [delay] Discovery from the Alaska Psychiatric Institute, and (2) Motion for More Definite Statement. API asserted in its Motion to Quash: "This is not a routine petition for review of a guardianship, rather it is a thinly disguised suit challenging the validity of [statutes pertaining to guardianships] and whether guardians may consent to psychotropic medication on behalf of their wards." I don't think it was disguised at all, thinly or otherwise. The state wanted to put all of the depositions on hold until a status conference with the judge could be held. API also moved for expedited consideration of the Motion to Quash because the normal times for handling a motion wouldn't be fast enough, since depositions had been scheduled for the next couple of weeks.

In the Motion for More Definite Statement, API asked the court to order us to provide more facts about why the guardianship should be terminated or a new guardian appointed. In my view, API was not a party to the guardianship—basically because it was not a family member or someone similar—and thus had no right to file motions in the case even though it had filed the original petition for guardianship four years earlier.

WEDNESDAY, DECEMBER 13TH

On Wednesday, December 13th, OPA joined API's Motion to Quash, meaning it was making the same motion, and filed non-oppositions to expedited consideration of the Motion to Quash and the Motion for More Definite Statement, meaning they agreed with API.

THURSDAY, DECEMBER 14TH

On December 14th, Vera Sharav called and asked whether I had secret documents about Zyprexa. She had heard about them and wanted them. Vera, a Holocaust survivor and a librarian by training, had become the pre-eminent advocate in the country—perhaps the world—for the ethical treatment of medical human research subjects, having founded the very well-regarded organization Alliance for Human Research Protection (AHRP). Her son had been killed by the first of the second-generation drugs, Clozapine, when it caused neuroleptic malignant syndrome, and the harms of psychiatric drugs were another focus of her work.

AHRP is a group of professionals and lay people whose mission is to protect the rights of human subjects in medical research and to inform the public about concealed adverse drug events. Vera has testified at various government agencies, including the FDA and the Institute of Medicine, and has presented at the National Academy of Sciences. AHRP had an extensive e-mail list and would send out information on the evils of psychiatric drugs as well as abuses in human medical research. I gave her the information for downloading the Zyprexa Papers through FTP, but she called me back to say she couldn't access them and to ask that I please send her *two* DVDs. I did.

In the guardianship case, Judge Morgan Christen, who had presided over Faith Myers' case, issued an order requiring any opposition to API's and OPA's Motion to Quash be filed in chambers (at her office) by noon on the following Monday, December 18.

Brewster Jamieson never called me back, but a little after 6:00 p.m. Alaska Time on December 14th, he faxed Dr. Egilman and me a letter, which I didn't see until a little after midnight. The letter purported to object on behalf of Lilly to the production of the documents, under Rule 45(d)(1) of the Alaska Rules of Civil Procedure, which are modeled after the Federal Rules. This rule provides that if a party who has been served with a subpoena to produce documents objects, the party seeking the documents can't get them without the court's approval. I say "purported to object" because Lilly wasn't served with the subpoena—Dr. Egilman was. Thus, only Dr. Egilman could object to the subpoena. Under the Secrecy Order, Dr. Egilman was required to cooperate with Lilly, so what Lilly should have done was direct Dr. Egilman to object, which he was required to do under the Secrecy Order. Mr. Jamieson's letter also asked Dr. Egilman to refrain from producing the documents and asked me to refrain from further seeking production without a court order authorizing production. This was the procedure I had expected to follow, on the assumption Lilly would object in time. Unfortunately for Lilly, they were too late.

FRIDAY, DECEMBER 15TH

I responded in a letter to Mr. Jamieson the next morning that I was skeptical Lilly had properly invoked the rule, but I was open to Lilly providing me with some legal basis for the claim. I also informed Mr. Jamieson that certain material had already been produced. I wrote that in an abundance of caution, though, I would temporarily act as if Civil Rule 45(d)(1) had been properly invoked. In other words, I would not try to enforce the subpoena until the court had ruled. Unsurprisingly, this gave them no comfort. This was no concession on my part because I had already received the documents. I wasn't giving up anything. I also pointed out that while I hadn't had a chance to review the materials in any detail, everything I had seen was, in my opinion, discoverable in the guardianship case, and it was hard to see how at least some of it was confidential.

Around noon-thirty, I received a faxed copy of a letter that Richard Meadow of the Lanier law firm (which had employed Dr. Egilman as an expert witness) wrote to Andrew (Andy) Rogoff of the Pepper Hamilton law firm, which represented Lilly in the Zyprexa MDL. In that letter, Mr. Meadow demanded on behalf of Lilly that I not give the documents to anyone until the court handling the Zyprexa MDL had a chance to decide whether I was allowed to. Of course, it was too late.

A few minutes after Meadow's letter came through, I received a faxed letter from Andy Rogoff, stating they had been told I gave the Zyprexa Papers to *The New York Times*. He demanded that I return the papers and refrain from further publishing or publicizing them, and insisted that I request the return of the materials from anyone I'd sent them to and identify such people. He also threatened to go after my law license and have me punished by the Zyprexa MDL court, ending with: "We request your cooperation in this regard," which I thought was humorous after his threats.

I think it was about an hour and a half later, around 6:00 p.m. New York time, 2:00 p.m. Alaska time, that Special Discovery Master Peter Woodin, who had been appointed to manage discovery in the Zyprexa MDL, left me a voicemail message that I should call him about my receipt of the Zyprexa Papers. I understood him to say I could call him anytime over the weekend. However, another of Lilly's lawyers, Sean Fahey, wrote half an hour later that the Special Discovery Master had ordered me to return the documents. I do not recall that, and I don't think he had done so. Lilly's lawyers later proved to have a habit of mischaracterizing (lying about) such things. I don't see how Sean Fahey could have known what was in that voicemail unless he was listening to Special Master Woodin leaving it or Master Woodin told him that was what he had said. I think Fahey just made it up.

In his letter, after asserting I had been instructed to return the documents immediately, Fahey also threatened to go after my law license and seek punishment by the Zyprexa MDL court:

> If you do not confirm in writing that you will immediately return these documents, by the close of business today, I will be left with no choice but to file a complaint with the Alaska attorney discipline board, and seek sanctions against you in the Zyprexa MDL, for your willful violation of a Federal order.

Just before 9:00 p.m. in Anchorage, which was almost 1:00 a.m. in New York, I received an e-mail from the Special Discovery Master, stating that "in the exercise of my authority as Special Discovery Master," since I had not responded to his voicemail yet, he had issued an order against me, which he helpfully attached. The order required me to return to him all copies of the Zyprexa Papers I had in my possession.

SATURDAY, DECEMBER 16TH

I immediately started working on a written response to the Special Discovery Master, but it was taking too long so I sent him a preliminary e-mail the next day, Saturday, December 16th, at 7:00 p.m. Alaska time. I first noted I'd understood from his voicemail that I could return his call anytime during the weekend. I reassured him I had voluntarily ceased further dissemination of any of the Zyprexa Papers after receiving Mr. Jamieson's fax on December 15th, and wouldn't further disseminate them without at least reasonable notice. I said I thought it irregular for him to issue an order "based on the facts described by Eli Lilly and the Plaintiffs' Steering Committee" without giving me an opportunity to respond to those alleged facts.

The most basic tenets of United States law are (1) meaningful notice of what you are charged with and (2) a meaningful opportunity to respond before any court action can be taken against you. It is called "due process of law" or simply "Due Process." There are exceptions, where "exigencies" exist, the easiest of which to understand is perhaps the search warrant situation where if the person against whom the search warrant is sought were given advance notice, the evidence being sought would likely disappear. I will say that based on how things looked to them, there was a pretty good argument for denying me notice and an opportunity to be heard before ordering me not to further distribute the Zyprexa Papers.

I also questioned whether the Special Discovery Master had authority to order me about, and I asked him to provide me with a copy of the document granting him such authority. I suggested he didn't have jurisdiction over me, and said I would maintain the status quo, meaning I would not further distribute the documents. I wrote that this eliminated any urgency (to the extent they believed me, which they didn't). Court jurisdiction is about what people or things and issues a court has power over. A court cannot just order people anywhere in the world to take or not take actions. I wasn't a party or lawyer in the Zyprexa MDL, and I wasn't a party to the Secrecy Order.

I was in Alaska. How was it the Special Discovery Master in a New York case, albeit a federal one, had the authority to order me to do anything?

SUNDAY, DECEMBER 17TH

The next day at around 7:30 p.m., I sent the Special Discovery Master a draft response to his order. It described PsychRights' mission, how I had come to obtain the Zyprexa Papers, that I believed I had not violated the Secrecy Order, and that the Zyprexa Papers had lost their secrecy protection once I received them pursuant to the subpoena. This is a general legal principle regarding confidentiality: once a document has lost confidentiality, that confidentiality is permanently gone. I also wrote that while one normally has to follow a court order even if one thinks it was not properly issued, this is not true if the court doesn't have jurisdiction, and since the Special Discovery Master did not have jurisdiction over me, I was not going to follow it.

But by then, the first of *The New York Times* front-page articles exposing Lilly's outrageous conduct had been published.

Ch. 4. Fifteen Minutes of Fame

On December 17, 2006, *The New York Times* published Alex Berenson's story "Eli Lilly Said to Play Down Risk of Top Pill" on the front page. The article opened with:

> The drug maker Eli Lilly has engaged in a decade-long effort to play down the health risks of Zyprexa, its best-selling medication for schizophrenia, according to hundreds of internal Lilly documents and e-mail messages among top company managers.

> The documents, given to *The Times* by a lawyer representing mentally ill patients, show that Lilly executives kept important information from doctors about Zyprexa's links to obesity and its tendency to raise blood sugar — both known risk factors for diabetes.

> Lilly's own published data, which it told its sales representatives to play down in conversations with doctors, has shown that 30 percent of patients taking Zyprexa gain 22 pounds or more after a year on the drug, and some patients have reported gaining 100 pounds or more. But Lilly was concerned that Zyprexa's sales would be hurt if the company was more forthright about the fact that the drug might cause unmanageable weight gain or diabetes, according to the documents, which cover the period 1995 to 2004.

> Zyprexa has become by far Lilly's best-selling product, with sales of $4.2 billion last year, when about two million people worldwide took the drug.

The article went on to note Lilly continued to deny Zyprexa causes diabetes, in spite of the Zyprexa Papers revealing (1) a 1999 e-mail from Zyprexa's chief scientist stating Zyprexa-associated weight gain was a major threat to the long-term success of Zyprexa; and (2) a 2000 letter from a group of diabetes doctors Lilly had hired, stating, "unless we come clean on this it could get much more serious than we might anticipate."

Mr. Berenson also reported on a California doctor who stated eight of his thirty-five patients on Zyprexa had developed high blood sugar, two of whom had to be hospitalized. The Zyprexa Papers showed Lilly encouraged its sales representatives to play down these effects when talking to doctors. To reassure doctors, Lilly also publicly said that when it followed up with patients who had taken Zyprexa in a clinical trial for three years, it found that weight gain appeared to plateau after about nine months. But the company did not disclose its early 1999 finding, revealed by the Zyprexa Papers, that blood sugar levels in the patients had increased steadily for those three years.

In a letter to the editor regarding the story, Joanne Doroshow, the Executive Director of the Center for Justice and Democracy, wrote:

> The article also illustrates the problems caused when companies settle cases and force the injured to sign confidentiality agreements, as was apparently done in this case. In such cases, wrongdoers can prolong misconduct and suppress information for years.

MONDAY, DECEMBER 18TH

I received many communications from Zyprexa victims as a result of *The New York Times'* story, including the following e-mail, which arrived the next day, December 18th:

> On February 22, 2005 my brother was found dead on the floor of the board and care home where he was living. I had spoken with him the night before and he seemed fine. I asked the coroner to order a toxicology. Sure enough, he was found to have 430mg/mL of olanzapine in his blood. I found out that the toxic level for olanzapine is 250mg/mL. The autopsy showed nothing wrong. In fact they stated that he had a normal body of a healthy adult male.

That day, in another front-page story titled "Drug Files Show Maker Promoted Unapproved Use," Berenson reported Lilly encouraged family doctors to prescribe Zyprexa for people not diagnosed with schizophrenia or bipolar disorder, formerly known as manic-depressive disorder—the only two conditions for which the FDA had approved its use. This is important because under United States law, drug companies are not allowed to market drugs for any unapproved use, known as "off-label" prescribing. Doctors can prescribe drugs for any condition, but drug companies are not allowed to promote or market them for off-label use.

Berenson wrote that Lilly told its sales representatives to suggest doctors prescribe Zyprexa to older patients with symptoms of dementia, even though this was an unapproved use. I have learned that staff at nursing homes like prescribing Zyprexa and other neuroleptics to their patients because it disables them so much they aren't any trouble; in many cases, they can't even get out of bed anymore. Worse, Zyprexa doubles the death rate for the elderly. As Mr. Berenson reported, Zyprexa carries a prominent ("black box") warning that it increases the risk of death in the elderly. People tell me that when their parents die after being given a neuroleptic such as Zyprexa, the doctor says something along the lines of, "Well, your mother was old." I have also heard stories from people who tell me their parent dramatically improved once they were taken off Zyprexa or other neuroleptics. The December 18th article reveals how successful these illegal marketing practices were, with one campaign leading to 49,000 new prescriptions in three months and the overall doubling of Zyprexa sales from $1.5 billion in 1999 to $3 billion in 2002.

As reported by Mr. Berenson, at a 2001 meeting with Zyprexa sales representatives, Lilly praised sixteen sales reps by name for the number of prescriptions they had convinced doctors to write using a prepared script, and noted, "more than 100 other sales representatives had convinced doctors to write at least 16 extra prescriptions and thus 'maxed out on a pretty sweet incentive.'"

Mr. Berenson had interviewed me the day after the first story came out, and I had emphasized information about the drug's harms as revealed by the Zyprexa Papers should be available to people resisting forced drugging orders:

> Mr. Gottstein said yesterday that the information in the documents should be available to patients and doctors, as well as judges who oversee the hearings that are required before people can be forced to take psychiatric drugs.
>
> "The courts should have this information before they order this stuff injected into people's unwilling bodies," Mr. Gottstein said.

Meanwhile, in the guardianship case, I filed an agreement PsychRights, API, and OPA had negotiated that all of the depositions would be rescheduled for some time after February 1st. The Motion to Quash was therefore withdrawn. That same day, API filed its opposition to disqualifying Master Duggan. Lilly also filed a motion to intervene in the guardianship case and quash (void) my subpoena to Dr. Egilman. Frankly, this was more than a little humorous to me, as it was closing the barn door after the cows had escaped.

TUESDAY, DECEMBER 19TH

The following day, *The New York Times* ran an editorial titled "Playing Down the Risks of a Drug," citing Alex Berenson's front-page articles of the past two days. The editorial started out:

> It was bad enough when studies showed that the newest and most heavily promoted drugs for treating schizophrenia weren't worth their high cost. Now the disturbing tale of their excessive use has taken a tawdry turn with revelations that Eli Lilly, a pharmaceutical giant, has consistently played down the risks of its best-selling antipsychotic drug, Zyprexa, and has promoted it for unapproved uses.

The author called for a Congressional investigation.

The day this editorial was published, Catherine Penney wrote me:

> As an RN working in a county mental health outpatient clinic I have seen a lot of clients who have developed diabetes after they were started on Zyprexa, and many more who have become obese. Also, I have seen clients develop cardiac problems while on some of the new generation antipsychotic medications. Most of these clients were not adequately informed of these potential risks. The Eli Lilly reps have often come to our clinic and played down the diabetes and weight gain risks.

Cathy is an absolutely amazing psychiatric survivor who lucked into a wonderful psychiatrist, Daniel Dorman. Dr. Dorman got her off the drugs and used talk therapy to bring her out of an extended period of what was diagnosed as catatonia. Dr. Dorman wrote a spellbinding book about his work with Cathy, *Dante's Cure: A Journey Out of Madness*, which I highly recommend. Cathy ultimately obtained a degree and license in nursing and became a psychiatric nurse, so she had seen first-hand what Berenson wrote about.

Also, starting December 19th, the intrepid, independent investigative reporter Evelyn Pringle published a series of terrific articles, mostly on OpEdNews, describing what the Zyprexa Papers revealed and Lilly's misinformation campaign to deal with the scandal. These went beyond *The New York Times'* articles.

MONDAY, DECEMBER 20TH

On December 20th, after I had responded to his congratulations with, "I am dealing with Evil Lilly's wrath right now," Dr. David Antonuccio wrote back: "think of them as the evil empire from Star Wars. I'm sure they have a Darth Vader like lawyer you will have to deal with." That proved so true.

THURSDAY, DECEMBER 21ST

On December 21, 2006, on the front page of the business section, *The New York Times* ran another article by Berenson, titled, "Disparity Emerges in Lilly Data on Schizophrenia Drug," exposing Lilly's lies to doctors. It began:

> For at least a year, Eli Lilly provided information to doctors about the blood-sugar risks of its drug Zyprexa that did not match data that the company circulated internally when it first reviewed its clinical trial results, according to company documents.

> The original results showed that patients on Zyprexa, Lilly's pill for schizophrenia, were 3.5 times as likely to experience high blood sugar levels as those taking a placebo, according to a February 2000 memo sent to top Lilly scientists. . . .

> But the results that Lilly eventually provided to doctors until at least late 2001 were very different. Those results indicated that patients taking Zyprexa were only slightly more likely to suffer high blood sugar [than] those taking a placebo, or an inactive pill.

> Another Lilly report, from November 1999, shows that Lilly found after examining 70 clinical trials that 16

percent of patients taking Zyprexa for a year gained more than 66 pounds.

The company did not publicly disclose that figure, instead focusing on data from a smaller group of clinical trials that showed about 30 percent of patients gained 22 pounds.

Mr. Berenson went on to note that Zyprexa was by far Lilly's best-selling drug, with $4.2 billion in 2005 sales. This article also reports on Lilly's misrepresentation of clinical trial data to doctors:

Lilly had reviewed data from its clinical trials and found that "the incidence of treatment-emergent hyperglycemia in olanzapine group (3.6%) was higher than that in the placebo group (1.05%)." Olanzapine is the generic name for Zyprexa.

But when Lilly subsequently discussed the clinical trial results with doctors, it used a different comparison. Lilly told doctors that Zyprexa had caused 3.1 percent of patients — not 3.6 percent — to have high-blood sugar. And it said that 2.5 percent of patients on the placebo — not 1.05 percent — had high-blood sugar. As a result, the rates of high blood sugar in the two groups seemed almost identical in the revised data.

In the meantime, Lilly had spurred the United States District Court for the Eastern District of New York into action to prevent the public from gaining access to these documents that proved Lilly had sacrificed its customers' lives on the altar of corporate profit.

Ch. 5. Here Come the Judges

MONDAY, DECEMBER 18TH

Backing up a few days, in the morning of Monday, December 18th—the day after the first *Times* front-page story ran, I received a call from Magistrate Judge Roanne Mann, demanding I participate right then in a telephonic hearing. Sean Fahey presented Lilly's side, and I presented most of my point of view. There was what I find to be a rather humorous exchange where the judge asked me whether I wanted to add anything, yet when I said yes, she didn't let me speak. Instead, she expressed her view that what I had done was improper, but that as a magistrate judge,

> I personally am not in a position to order you to return the documents. *I can't make you return them but I can make you wish you had* because I think this is highly improper not only to have obtained the documents on short notice without Lilly being advised of the amendment but then to disseminate them publicly before it could be litigated. It certainly smacks of bad faith. [italics mine]

She then suggested that Lilly and the plaintiffs' lawyers get District Court Judge Cogan to issue an order against me.

Finally, I got a chance to speak:

MR. GOTTSTEIN: . . . I do want to say that I did advise Dr. Egilman to give the amended subpoena to Lilly and he didn't seem to think it made any difference.

THE COURT: Well, don't you think that you should have done that directly? You were aware of the fact that these documents were subject to a confidentiality order and you chose to go through the expert who had them solely for purposes of this litigation rather than subpoena Lilly directly. So don't you think that you had an obligation to inform Lilly?

MR. GOTTSTEIN: No.

I did say I would not further disseminate the Zyprexa Papers. Of course, agreeing to not further disseminate the Zyprexa Papers wasn't much of a sacrifice on my part since I had already gotten them out to the people I wanted to receive them. It was also not of much comfort to Judge Mann, who felt I had blatantly violated the Secrecy Order. Presumably, she did not trust me.

I also said in the Mann hearing that I would try to obtain a lawyer, so I called John McKay to see whether he would represent me. John is hands down the preeminent media and First Amendment (free speech) lawyer in Alaska and is well known around the country as well. He is meticulous in analyzing and discussing issues at length from every angle imaginable. One of the benefits of the whole Zyprexa Papers affair for me was getting to know John better.

A couple of hours after the hearing with Magistrate Judge Mann ended, Lilly got United States District Judge Cogan on the phone for another hearing. The judge assigned to the case, the legendary Jack Weinstein, was on a trip to Antarctica and not due back until after Christmas. While I was trying to get John McKay on the phone, I put the court and attorneys on hold. My hold music at the time was Bob Dylan and this occasioned a disgruntled comment by Judge Cogan. I was able to get John on the phone, but the connections were bad, so people had a hard time hearing each other.

Citing Magistrate Judge Mann's Report, Judge Cogan stated I "undertook procedures to help [Dr. Egilman] try to circumvent the restrictions that were on him" and had "deliberately aided and abetted Dr. Egilman in getting these documents released from the [Secrecy] Order's restrictions." Simply as a matter of logic, this doesn't make sense. Dr. Egilman didn't need any help to "circumvent" the Secrecy Order's restriction. He could have simply given them to *The New York Times* and not have his name disclosed. He wanted to follow the Secrecy Order's procedures, not circumvent them. Also, I felt there had been nothing wrong in subpoenaing Dr. Egilman to get the Zyprexa Papers released from the Secrecy Order's restrictions. The idea was to follow the Secrecy Order's rules to get the Zyprexa Papers released from its restrictions, not violate it.

At the hearing before Judge Cogan, John pointed out he hadn't received any motion to which he could respond, so he didn't know what relief Lilly was seeking (what Lilly wanted from the court). Lilly responded that the court had inherent jurisdiction to enforce its orders and it was seeking criminal contempt against me. Judge Cogan said it had been an oral application. Frankly, this was outrageous from a legal process perspective. I was entitled to know what Lilly and the

Plaintiffs' Steering Committee were seeking, so I would have a chance to oppose it. Judge Cogan bladed over my lawyer's objections and orally ordered

> [t]hat as of this moment, [Mr. Gottstein] is under a mandatory injunction to return those documents to Mr. Woodin [the Special Discovery Master], to take them down from any websites that he may have posted them on, and to take any reasonable effort to recover them from any sites or persons to which he has delivered them.

This was the first we knew exactly what Lilly had sought from the court, although I can't say any of it was a surprise. Judge Cogan told Lilly to fax him the form of order it would like him to sign. This was not out of the ordinary.

Later that day, Judge Cogan, writing that I had deliberately and knowingly aided and abetted Dr. Egilman to violate the Secrecy Order—an assertion I disputed—ordered me to, within twenty-four hours:

1. Return all copies of the Zyprexa Papers to Special Discovery Master Woodin;

2. Identify everyone to whom I sent the Zyprexa Papers;

3. Identify the specific documents for all of the Zyprexa Papers by the "Bates Stamp" numbers on the documents. Bates stamps sequentially put a unique number on each document in a set of documents, which makes it easier to locate the document to which reference is made;

4. Take steps to retrieve the Zyprexa Papers and return them to the Special Discovery Master; and

5. Preserve all documents, voice mails, e-mails, material and information relating to Dr. Egilman or any other efforts to obtain documents produced by Lilly.

Even before the written order came out, I started sending e-mails to the people I had given the Zyprexa Papers, saying:

> I mailed you a DVD with some documents on them pertaining to Zyprexa and have been orally ordered to

have them returned to [Special Discovery Master Woodin].

A copy of the proposed written order is posted at http://psychrights.org/States/Alaska/CaseXX/Eillilly/ProposedOrder.pdf with a comment about certain language which I strenuously disagree with and we are trying to get eliminated from the signed order. Regardless, please return the DVD, hard copies and any other copies to Special Master Woodin immediately. If you have not yet received it, please return it to Special Master Woodin when you do receive it. In addition, please ensure that no copies exist on your computer or any other computer equipment, or in any other format, website(s) or FTP site(s), or otherwise on the Internet.

There is a question in my mind that the court actually has jurisdiction over me to issue the order. I believe I came into the documents completely legally, but the consequences to me if I am wrong about the jurisdiction issue are severe, so I will very much appreciate your compliance with this request.

To say I went to work to comply is an understatement, but one big problem was that to make a list of the Bates Stamp numbers would take a long time and meant I had to retain a copy while I was making the list. I was scheduled to go to Hawaii for a family vacation with my family on December 22nd, and it wasn't looking good for me to go.

WEDNESDAY, DECEMBER 20TH

On December 20th, *The New York Times* published an article titled "Court Orders Lawyer to Return Documents About an Eli Lilly Drug," this time by Julie Creswell instead of Alex Berenson. In that article, Michael J. Harrington, Lilly's deputy general counsel, is quoted as saying:

Lilly is concerned that this deliberate violation of a court order and the selective disclosure of incomplete information may cause unwarranted concern among patients that could cause them to stop taking their medication without consulting their physician.

It was a crock for Lilly to say disclosure of incomplete information might cause unwarranted concern. Lilly had produced over eleven million pages, all of which had been designated confidential, including newspaper articles—and of course, someone needed to go through it and find the important documents. If Lilly had documents that rebutted what the Zyprexa Papers revealed, they could cite these other documents. Instead, Lilly said the Secrecy Order prohibited them from doing so. That was a double crock. Lilly could de-designate anything it wanted to no longer be secret. The truth is Lilly had been caught lying to doctors and the public, and it wanted the evidence of those lies to be re-suppressed.

Ms. Creswell also reported I had asked Mr. Berenson by e-mail and phone to return the Zyprexa Papers, and George Freeman, a *Times* lawyer, had "declined to comment on the court order, other than to say, 'Our customary practice is to retain documents which we legitimately [acquired] during our news gathering process and which are likely to be relevant to future reporting.' "

When I hadn't been able to accomplish everything required in the December 18th order within twenty-four hours, at 7:35 in the morning in Alaska on December 20th, the Special Discovery Master e-mailed my lawyer, John McKay, asking where was the list of persons to whom I had given the Zyprexa Papers. Twenty-five minutes later, he sent another e-mail asking why I hadn't yet returned the documents. At 9:37 a.m., Lilly lawyer Sean Fahey left John a voicemail message saying he had not yet received confirmation that all copies had been returned, and since it was after 1:30 p.m. his time, he was going to have Judge Cogan hold another hearing that afternoon. Two minutes later, he e-mailed John, asking him to confirm I had already returned the Zyprexa Papers to the Special Discovery Master. Three minutes after that, Fahey e-mailed John that there would be a hearing at 4:00 p.m. New York time, noon in Alaska. John is a prominent attorney and was attending to other pressing matters. In any case, expecting him to respond to Fahey's first e-mail within three minutes was hardly reasonable.

For that hearing, John and I decided it was best for me not to be there. The Special Discovery Master started out the hearing in front of Judge Cogan by saying he hadn't gotten the list of people to whom I had given the Zyprexa Papers, nor had he received any of the papers back. He didn't mention I had copied him on my e-mails to the people to whom I had given the Zyprexa Papers, asking them to send the copies to him.

John continued to question whether the court had jurisdiction over me, noting that despite this doubt about jurisdiction, I would cooperate. He also indicated there were some problems with the proposed order that had been circulated, but when he had tried to raise them with Lilly's lawyers, John said, "no one was interested in comment from me." He told the court that even before the written order had been issued, I had e-mailed the people to whom I had sent the Zyprexa Papers and asked them to send them to the Special Discovery Master. He also informed Judge Cogan that the Special Discovery Master had been copied on all of those e-mails, as had Lilly's lawyers. He mentioned I was working on the list as well as the other requirements, but he pointed out the order was contradictory in requiring me to return all the documents and also identify them by Bates Stamp numbers, because it meant I had to retain the documents to make the list. Instead, we had proposed to just give them the files, which identified the documents. John also informed the court that after the hearing two days previously, the lawyers had stayed on the phone and agreed I would give the Zyprexa Papers to Lilly's local lawyer, which I had done shortly before the hearing.

Only after Judge Cogan asked John, "So your position is that Mr. Woodin [the Special Discovery Master], in fact, has the names of those people?" did Mr. Woodin acknowledge he had received copies of the relevant e-mails.

Lilly complained they couldn't identify some of the people from the e-mail addresses and the e-mail I had sent out expressed concern about whether the order was binding on me. He said when I wrote "it seems inevitable we will be taking steps to challenge the order's validity but in the meantime it should be complied with," I was sending a mixed message. This was a classic Lilly lawyer lie, or at the very least misleading. I used that language in e-mails to only two people, I think; for all the others, I sent the e-mail I've quoted above, which while preserving my position that the court didn't have jurisdiction, was very clear I would appreciate it if the Zyprexa Papers were returned.

One of the two that had the language cited by Lilly was to my computer network consultant, Matt Joy, about making sure there were no copies of the Zyprexa Papers in any backups. I hadn't sent him the

Zyprexa Papers at all. The order (drafted by Lilly's lawyers) requiring me to return the Zyprexa Papers didn't even deal with backups. In order to comply with the spirit of the order, I was going beyond what it specified.

The second was to Stephen Cha, MD, who was a member of the minority's staff of the United States House of Representatives Committee on Government Reform. I had forgotten Dr. Cha had them. Special Discovery Master Woodin didn't correct Lilly's misquoting of the e-mails I had sent to all but one of the people to whom I had given the Zyprexa Papers.

A little before 10 p.m. New York time, Lilly lawyer Fahey e-mailed John, saying they still hadn't received certification that I had deleted all of the Zyprexa Papers from my computers. In his response, John remarked, "Good to know lawyers are hard at work on the East Coast as 10:00 p.m. approaches," and assured Fahey I had been working diligently on various aspects of complying fully with the court's order. Mr. Fahey responded:

> It appears that Mr. Gottstein is able to update his website, to include such recent developments as Mr. Brewster's letter to Mr. Woodin, so I would ask that you both focus your efforts on complying with Judge Cogan's order and certify the deletion of the documents this evening.

There was a lot to do to comply with the order, but the delay was mainly because John wanted to draft what we ended up calling the Compliance Certificate to try to preserve my rights and protect me. Updating the website did not delay compliance.

Earlier that day, I had filed an entry of appearance to also formally be Mr. Bigley's attorney if API filed petitions for a 180-day commitment and forced drugging.

THURSDAY, DECEMBER 21ST

On December 21st, Congressman Waxman wrote to the Special Discovery Master, saying that while under the Constitution, Congress had the right to keep the Zyprexa Papers, out of deference to my wishes (drat) and respect for the judicial branch, he was returning them and had had them all deleted from his committee's computers.

I digitally signed the Compliance Certificate around 5:30 in the afternoon on December 21st and sent it along to John, who forwarded it to the Special Discovery Master, with copies to Lilly's lawyers, around 10:30 that evening, which was 2:30 in the morning in New York. A half an hour later, which was 3:01 in the morning on the East Coast, Fahey e-mailed John:

> Thank you for your letter. Although I have not reviewed the letter in detail, I note that you have not provided the date(s) on which these documents were disseminated to each individual, as required by Judge Cogan's rulings. In addition, in paragraph 3 of your letter, you say that documents have been retrieved from certain individuals (listed in paragraph 7a), but do not identify whether you have retrieved materials from any of the individuals identified in paragraph 7b. Please provide this information, consistent with Judge Cogan's rulings.

A little bit later, John e-mailed the Special Discovery Master, with copies to Lilly's lawyers, as follows:

> Not having heard back from you yet, I decided that before turning to other matters I should check the copy I sent to myself of my transmission to Master Woodin and counsel, to make sure it came through OK. In doing so, I noticed that the last page of the Certification, which I received from Mr. Gottstein and forwarded to the Master and counsel, seems to have lost Mr. Gottstein's digital signature in the forwarding process. To avoid having anyone lose sleep wondering if the document had in fact been signed, or worse yet, waste time in your morning hours while we are still asleep in Alaska preparing a motion to compel a signature, I have gone back to the original, taken a screen capture shot of the signature block, and inserted it in this e-mail.

Promptly at 8:04 the next morning, Fahey responded:

> Mr. McKay, I understand that you and your client may not appreciate the seriousness of this issue, but Special Master Woodin, Magistrate Judge Mann, and Judge

Cogan all did. Your sarcasm relating to our efforts to simply ensure compliance with a Federal Order is disappointing.

Then at 1:20 p.m. Anchorage time, Fahey e-mailed John:

Mr. McKay do you plan to respond to the issues raised [in my 3:01 a.m. e-mail], or should we assume that you are not going to provide this information required by Judge Cogan?

John informed Fahey he would be responding to the Special Discovery Master shortly and did so a couple of hours later.

And what was I doing? Heading to Maui with my family for a not-so-restful vacation.

Ch. 6. Psychiatric Survivors Spring Into Action

SATURDAY, DECEMBER 23RD

On December 23rd, psychiatric survivor Eric Whalen e-mailed a listserv (e-mail list) of psychiatric survivor activists called Actmad, writing, "Looks like someone put copies of Zyprexa product liability documents online here – http://zyprexakills.pbwiki.com" and indicating he had put a copy on his website. The copy Will Hall downloaded had made it to the Web.

Zyprexakills.pbwiki.com states:

Press Release - Memos released!

. . . Eli Lilly's motion to suppress the evidence has been denied by an inter-galactic court of appeals. Justice will be served over HTTP [World Wide Web language].

As we speak, the slick marketing plans drawn up by the smartest boys in the drug dealing business are propagating across the Internet. Bittorrents have been internationally seeded; p2p [peer-to-peer] networks like morpheus, kaaza, gnutella, and limewire are already trading vigorously; photos laced with the data have been posted to public photo sharing sites like flickr; movies containing slideshows are circulating on video sharing sites like YouTube; Usenet isn't obsolete yet, and yes, backups have been uploaded to freenet (freenetproject.org), the virtual data haven;

Information wants to be free. Look for a file named ZyprexaKills, or any of its l33t variants.

For those of you without easy access to these services we have temporarily posted these files in this convenient location:

http://files-upload.com/files/34036/ZyprexaKills.tar.gz.html

Please be careful when obtaining them - we are up against some of the most greedy and powerful elites in the world. You may want to consider using the tor program (tor.eff.org) to preserve your anonymity. If it's

difficult for you to install this program, try
www.torify.com, a web based surfing solution.

Send this message to as many friends and mailing lists
that you can think of.

Please tag all netroots activity relating to this campaign
with the tag 'zyprexakills'.

This message is also available at:

zyprexakills.wordpress.org
zyprexakills.pbwiki.com

Agent Fred
Chief of Security
Bonkers Institute for Nearly Genuine Research
www.bonkersinstitute.org

SUNDAY, DECEMBER 24TH

On December 24th, Ben Hansen, who ran the Bonkers Institute, e-mailed the following to a number of people, including me:

> It has come to my attention that there's an item
> circulating on the internet (see this site:
> http://zyprexakills.pbwiki.com/) which is signed:
> "Agent Fred, Chief of Security, Bonkers Institute for
> Nearly Genuine Research."

> I wish to make it clear that this posting was NOT
> authorized by the Bonkers Institute, and I do NOT
> know the identity of the person claiming to be "Agent
> Fred." Therefore, I cannot verify whether this posting is
> well-intentioned, or if it is malicious, unless and until I
> communicate with the person or persons behind it. If
> anyone knows the true identity of "Agent Fred," please
> ask them to contact me immediately. In the meantime, I
> would exercise caution whenever receiving, forwarding,
> or downloading material of this kind.

> In solidarity,

> Ben Hansen
> aka Dr. M.I. Bonkers

I don't know whether Ben was the creator of zyprexakills.pbwiki.com or not, because Ben died at age 60 in 2010, so I wasn't able to ask him before writing this book. It does sound like him.

Ben was wonderful, and the Bonkers Institute, well worth a visit, is still on the Internet as of this writing. Ben was interviewed in July of 2007 and had this to say about why he got interested in psychiatry's abuses:

> In 1999, following the death of my father and the suicide of a friend on the same day, I suffered a breakdown and soon found myself on the receiving end of our mental health system—a system that offered nothing but drugs, drugs, drugs. The experience radicalized me and opened my eyes in many ways. I agree with author Leonard Roy Frank: "Psychiatry is to medicine what astrology is to astronomy." That's why I founded bonkersinstitute.org—to expose psychiatry as fraudulent pseudoscience, and to expose psychiatrists as incompetent pill-pushing quacks.

That same day, December 24th, an independent listserv at Johns Hopkins University was created, called Zyprexa-discuss. It stated, "This list is for discussing the drug's safety and how we can learn more about it," but it actually was focused on disseminating and publicizing the Zyprexa Papers on the Internet. I didn't know much about it until starting work on this book, and it seems to have disappeared since then. The first post noted that Lilly had already registered domains using zyprexakills in order to prevent other people from using them. However, Lilly had not registered zyprexakills.us, so someone in this group had.

MONDAY, DECEMBER 25TH

The nongovernmental organization (non-profit) MindFreedom International, founded by David Oaks, which had been sending news alerts to its 8,000 or so members about the *Times* articles, then began to publicize the availability of the Zyprexa Papers:

> MindFreedom News - 25 December 2006
>
> http://www.mindfreedom.org - please forward
>
> "We are all Jim!" - Eli Lilly secrets on Zyprexa exposed

How *you* may be able to keep a spotlight on Zyprexa

Grassroots campaign keeps exposed documents exposed

A grassroots Internet campaign today is outflanking well-heeled attorneys from the huge drug company Eli Lilly who are still trying to suppress internal documents about their psychiatric drug Zyprexa.

And you may participate, including by downloading the secret documents yourself, if you so choose:

http://www.mindfreedom.org/know/psych-drug-corp/eli-lilly-secrets/

The anonymous individuals distributing this unusual "Christmas gift" of hundreds of Zyprexa documents are apparently counting on the fact that many courts are closed today.

Background:

The NY Times ran three pieces this past week based on revelations from courageous attorney Jim Gottstein who exposed court materials showing that Eli Lilly covered up hazards about Zyprexa, and marketed to unapproved populations.

Even though the Eli Lilly materials are now exposed, Eli Lilly attorneys have still been attempting to suppress these in-house documents and keep them from being disseminated, including filing in court against Jim Gottstein and his law firm.

"The genie is out of the bottle. But Eli Lilly is still paying their hard-hitting attorneys to try to cover-up evidence of their fraud," said David Oaks, director of MindFreedom International. "This is reminiscent of the way the Nixon administration tried to keep the Pentagon Papers secret even after the materials were in the hands of the NY Times."

Enter the Internet. Unknown individuals have placed a digital folder of several hundred megs of Eli Lilly documents into areas of the Internet where anyone may download the materials. Apparently, these individuals don't expect any court orders over Christmas.

In the public interest, MindFreedom is forwarding the anonymous alert. To view the forwarded alert go to:

http://www.mindfreedom.org/know/psych-drug-corp/eli-lilly-secrets/

or http://tinyurl.com/yx6k9x

or see this wiki edited by anonymous individuals:

http://zyprexa.pbwiki.com

Disclaimers: MFI did not originate these alerts, MFI is not advising or encouraging any illegal activity, MFI does not vouch for authenticity or accuracy of alerts, that's all the information we have, MFI is not providing advice about the legality of downloading the materials.

As background, you may read the text of the three recent pieces in the NY Times about Zyprexa here:

http://www.mindfreedom.org/aff-spon/act/usa/psychrights/nytimes- gottstein-vs-eli-lilly

or http://tinyurl.com/ycsgcv

"Even though Jim legally revealed Zyprexa materials to the NY Times to alert the public," said Oaks, "Eli Lilly lawyers are still going after him to try to put their horses back in the barn. Today everyone on the Internet 'can be Jim' if they choose to download secret Eli Lilly documents themselves. By the way, Jim Gottstein or his group PsychRights have nothing to do with these alerts. He's on vacation."

Please forward.

David Oaks is, I would say, one of the two or maybe three icons of the psychiatric survivor movement, along with Judi Chamberlin and Rae Unzicker. David grew up in a working-class family in Chicago and was awarded a scholarship to Harvard University. The Harvard world, with its rich, privileged kids, was so alien to him he had a hard time adjusting and fitting in. He had a mental breakdown, then was diagnosed with schizophrenia, drugged against his will, and placed in solitary confinement. He got through Harvard, and the experience of losing all of his rights and being psychiatrically abused led him to his lifelong calling of advocacy against psychiatric force. He founded what is now called MindFreedom International about thirty years ago and ran it until a tragic accident in late 2012 left him paralyzed. The accident forced him to resign from MindFreedom and regroup, but since then he has resumed his larger advocacy about the environment and global warming from his wheelchair and continues to consult for MindFreedom.

With the possible exception of Judi Chamberlin, David is probably the most known psychiatric survivor in the world. He inspired Robert Whitaker to write *Mad in America* when he challenged Whitaker to look at the scientific literature. David calls for a peaceful revolution in the mental health system to transform it into one that is helpful and non-coercive. When I refer to MindFreedom doing this or doing that, it was mostly David.

TUESDAY, DECEMBER 26TH

On December 26th, Lilly wrote to Judge Weinstein, "We intend to file a motion for contempt against Dr. Egilman"; they also asked for an order requiring Dr. Egilman to submit to a deposition and turn over all "documents" pertaining to his producing the Zyprexa Papers to me, and to turn over any computer(s) and other electronic media that might hold such information. In my experience, such requests normally have to be filed as a formal motion, but it certainly appeared to be the practice in the Zyprexa MDL to just write the judge letters. Back from his Antarctica sojourn, unbeknownst to us, Judge Weinstein in a December 26th order that didn't show up on the court's docket sheet until January 3rd ordered Dr. Egilman to "show cause" (tell the court) at a hearing set for December 28th why he shouldn't be ordered to give testimony at a deposition within five days and turn over his computer(s) and hard drives to Lilly, as well as everything else he had pertaining to sending me the Zyprexa Papers.

Since I was scheduled to be out of state until January 15th, Anchorage attorney Steven Priddle, whom I like very much, at my request got into the guardianship case and filed a non-opposed motion to extend the deadline to respond to all pending motions until February 2nd. I had also arranged for Mr. Priddle to file "elections" in Mr.

Bigley's involuntary commitment and forced drugging case for a jury trial, to have the trial in a real courtroom, and for Mr. Bigley to be free of the effects of medication, as also provided in statute, in the event API filed 180-day petitions for involuntary commitment and forced drugging.

THURSDAY, DECEMBER 28TH

Before the hearing on December 28th, Alexander Reinert with the Yonkers law firm of Koob & Magoolaghan wrote a letter to Judge Weinstein on behalf of Dr. Egilman, objecting to being forced to provide evidence for Lilly to use in contempt proceedings against him. Mr. Reinert pointed out, citing relevant precedent, that before it could take Dr. Egilman's deposition, Lilly was obligated to initiate a contempt proceeding, specifying the grounds and identifying whether Lilly was seeking civil or criminal contempt. Whether it was civil or criminal mattered because if criminal, the Fifth Amendment applies (with its privilege against self-incrimination), as well as the presumption of innocence, and the requirement of proof beyond a reasonable doubt.

Mr. Reinert also pointed out a number of lies in Lilly's letter, such as that the Secrecy Order "clearly and unambiguously" required Dr. Egilman to notify the outside law firm of Pepper Hamilton, which Lilly had hired to defend it in the Zyprexa MDL. The Secrecy Order required Dr. Egilman to "notify the designating party," which was Lilly. That is what Dr. Egilman had done. Even though the Secrecy Order did not specify Pepper Hamilton, in litigation, notifying a party normally means notifying the party's lawyer in the case, so Lilly did have a point. It was not clear and unambiguous, though. Mr. Reinert also argued Lilly had not told the court anything about why "Lilly had waited more than a week to send Dr. Egilman a letter, *by regular mail,* from *Alaska* asking him not to comply with the subpoena" (emphasis in original).

Mr. Reinert asked that the court postpone forcing Dr. Egilman to attend the deposition and produce documents until after Lilly actually made a formal request for a finding of contempt, and identified both the grounds and specified whether it was seeking civil or criminal contempt—or at least until after the issues could be fully briefed. Lilly didn't bother to respond in writing, and at the hearing held on December 28th didn't address Dr. Egilman's point that it was improper to hold a deposition before any contempt motion had even been filed.

At that hearing, Judge Weinstein politely listened to Dr. Egilman's lawyer, then granted Lilly's motion without addressing Dr. Egilman's point about it being improper to do so without any motion for contempt even having been filed. Judge Weinstein ordered Dr. Egilman to turn over his computers, hard drives, and all other relevant materials by the time of his deposition, to be held on January 4th, which would be supervised by Special Discovery Master Woodin. The written order didn't show up on the court's docket sheet until January 9th, and I didn't know what had happened at that hearing until I ordered the transcript as part of my research for writing this book.

FRIDAY, DECEMBER 29TH

Even though Judge Weinstein was already back, on Friday, December 29th at 4:00 p.m. Judge Cogan issued an Order for a Temporary Mandatory Injunction. This order not only enjoined me and most, but not all, of the people to whom I had given the Zyprexa Papers "from further dissemination" but also required any website that had posted them to remove them. The people to whom I had given the Zyprexa Papers who were not enjoined from further dissemination were Alex Berenson of *The New York Times*, Snigdha Prakash of National Public Radio, and Dr. Cha of Congressman Waxman's committee staff.

I don't think we had seen or been informed that an injunction against all websites had been requested, which prevented my lawyer, John McKay, from having a chance to argue to the court why such an injunction was improper. This was again a violation of fundamental Due Process. On the other hand, I suspect the court would not have been inclined to hear from the lawyer of the guy who got the Zyprexa Papers out—in what it considered a flagrant violation of its Secrecy Order—why website recipients of such documents should not be enjoined. The temporary mandatory injunction was to remain in force and effect until a hearing set for January 3, 2007, at which Judge Weinstein would preside. I notified people of the temporary mandatory injunction through PsychRights' e-mail list, as did MindFreedom.

SATURDAY, DECEMBER 30TH

First thing the next morning, December 30th, Lilly lawyer Fahey e-mailed Eric Whalen to tell him he was facilitating the violation of a federal court order by linking to the ZyprexaKills.tar.gz and told him to remove the link immediately, "or we will take further legal action against your website." Mr. Whalen is a psychiatric survivor and e-mailed back:

> The documents linked to on my website were
> downloaded from an anonymous source. As far as I
> know I'm not under any court order. Dissemination of
> the contents of the documents is clearly in the public
> interest. Is there a legal basis for your request?

Fahey responded at 10:46 a.m. that Mr. Whalen was subject to the order, and if he didn't take the link down immediately, they would take further action to shut down his website and "seek all available remedies." At 12:02 p.m., Fahey e-mailed Mr. Whalen: "I need to know your intentions promptly, sir."

At 2:16 p.m., Fahey e-mailed Mr. Whalen:

> Attached is the order referenced below. As your own
> website indicates and as our independent research
> confirms, the documents available for download on
> your website are the documents improperly obtained by
> James Gottstein. These documents are subject to a
> Federal Court protective order, and the further
> dissemination of these documents is enjoined until at
> least January 3, 2007, at which time the arguments you
> raise below may fully be heard. If you have any doubts
> about the import of this Order, please state so
> immediately and we will seek further guidance from the
> Court today [a Saturday]. You have been on notice now
> for several hours that you are operating in violation of a
> Federal Court Order, and you have thus far, refused to
> assure your compliance. Please shut down the link
> immediately, remove any cached materials immediately,
> and confirm that you will comply with the attached
> order.

By 5:00 p.m. East Coast Time, MindFreedom was reporting in its Public Alert 10 that it was not aware of any remaining functional links making the Zyprexa Papers available. MindFreedom sent out an e-mail to one of its e-mail lists shortly after that with a link to the e-mail exchange with Eric, saying:

> Eli Lilly is threatening a second MindFreedom member with legal action. . . . This one is member Eric Whalen who apparently made copies of Zyprexa materials available on his blog for free public download.

Mr. Whalen had removed the link. He had also been copied on an e-mail from me in which I'd indicated that due to the previous order, I too was asking that the Zyprexa Papers be taken down. Within a couple of hours, though, MindFreedom reported they were available through Tor, which was not so easy to use. MindFreedom also noted:

> For the last six last days, a grassroots campaign appears to have successfully made hundreds of secret documents from Eli Lilly available using multiple web sites to hundreds of individuals who have downloaded the suppressed materials.

Responding to MindFreedom's alert about Lilly threatening Eric, Ted Chabasinski wrote to the MindFreedom USA listserv:

> I'm an attorney, and I think the reason Lilly is panicking is that these documents literally show a conspiracy to commit murder.

> People talk about how these documents show that Lilly committed fraud. They do, but more importantly, if someone deliberately does something that they know will cause the death of another person, they have committed a homicide (murder). Lying about the effects of Zyprexa has led to the deaths of many people.

> I hope whatever lawyer is dealing with the apparent TRO [a short-term injunction] that Lilly obtained, raises this point. The court should not be protecting Lilly's executives from criminal prosecution.

> Since Lilly does business in almost all states, and since people died as a result of Lilly's behavior as evidenced by these documents, if there were a courageous prosecutor somewhere who saw these documents, conceivably Lilly's executives could go to jail.

I think we should be raising this point everywhere we can.

Ted Chabasinski, J.D.

In another e-mail, Ted suggested people contact the attorney general in their state to advocate for murder charges against Lilly executives. All of these e-mails were admitted into evidence by Lilly at the trial held January 17th.

Ted has fought against psychiatric oppression for almost fifty years. He was born in 1937 to a poor, unmarried, immigrant mother named Anastasia who worked in a garment factory in New York City. In the year before Ted was born, Anastasia had an emotional breakdown, was diagnosed with schizophrenia, and was locked up in Brooklyn State Hospital (a psychiatric institution). She was locked up again after Ted was born, and spent thirty-five years in locked wards, being drugged and electroshocked into oblivion. When he was six, because he was the son of someone diagnosed with schizophrenia, Ted was taken from his foster parents—despite their objections—and locked up in infamous Bellevue hospital. There, he was diagnosed by Lauretta Bender with childhood schizophrenia, which was a crock. Bender was starting to conduct a study on electroshocking little children, and she needed guinea pigs. So during the early part of being psychiatrically imprisoned as a little boy, he was repeatedly electroshocked—again, despite his foster parents' objections—becoming one of the first children ever to be electroshocked.

Ted has described the experience in the following way:

> It made me want to die . . . I remember that they would stick a rag in my mouth so I wouldn't bite through my tongue and that it took three attendants to hold me down. I knew that in the mornings that I didn't get any breakfast that I was going to get shock treatment.

> I wanted to die but I didn't really know what death was. I knew that it was something terrible. Maybe I'll be so tired after the next shock treatment I won't get up, I won't ever get up, and I'll be dead. But I always got up. Something in me beyond my wishes made me put myself together again. I memorized my name, I taught myself to say my name. Teddy, Teddy, I'm Teddy . . .

I'm here, I'm here, in this room, in this hospital. And my mommy's gone . . . I would cry and realize how dizzy I was. The world was spinning around me and coming back to it hurt too much. I want to go down, I want to go where the shock treatment is sending me. I want to stop fighting and die . . . and something made me live, and go on living.

They no longer use rags to keep people from biting through their tongues (or breaking bones from the strength of the convulsions induced by the electroshock) because they now give people a muscle relaxant to avoid the muscle convulsions, and a short-acting anesthetic to prevent patients from experiencing the terrifying feeling of suffocation that can accompany muscle relaxants. Psychiatry says this is an improvement, but it means they need to send more electricity through the person's brain to get the convulsions in the brain they falsely claim to be therapeutic.

Ted was then sent to Rockland State Hospital, where he spent his entire childhood until release at seventeen. Then, as he says, "being the unmedicated schizophrenic that I was, I worked my way through college and law school." He has been active in the psychiatric survivor movement since 1971, including successfully spearheading a ban on electroshock in Berkeley, through a voter's initiative. It won by 62% to 38%, but the American Psychiatric Association challenged it in court and was able to get the courts to overturn the people's vote.

SUNDAY, DECEMBER 31ST

The next morning, December 31, 2006, in what is my favorite response to Lilly's bullying, long-time psychiatric survivor and activist Pat Risser e-mailed Lilly's lawyer Sean Fahey:

Gosh, what a mess. I'm sorry but I wasn't aware of any court order at the time I downloaded the "secret zyprexa documents" so, I not only downloaded them but I made several copies (burned them to CDs) and distributed them. I mailed them to some family and friends as well as several newspapers (in Ohio and Oregon). Since I had some extra copies (about 40 or so) I also passed them out to folks who seemed interested as I stood outside of a shopping center store. I have no idea who these strangers were so I can't possibly get

these CDs returned. I'm so sorry. I figured since you're
making such a fuss over the thousands of copies that
went over the internet, I'd better let you know that this
"secret" has spread and I really can't help stop the
spread at this point. Sorry.

Pat, who passed away in 2016 at 63, was an incredible psych survivor
advocate. A victim of childhood sexual abuse, he had been hospitalized
more than twenty times when he told mental health professionals he
felt suicidal, "[e]very time I'd tell a psychiatrist or therapist that I was
suicidal, I'd get locked up, forcibly drugged, secluded and restrained."
Pat was a good mental patient, taking all of the drugs and doing what
he was told. However, he came to realize they were not the answer,
quit telling mental health professionals when he felt suicidal, quit taking
the drugs, never looked back, and embarked on what would become a
twenty-five-plus-year career in peer support and advocacy. He wrote
the following about an incident that had occurred when he worked in a
psych ward:

> One of the large men on the unit had raised a chair
> over his head and was threatening one of the nurses.
> The chair was one of those sort that are designed to be
> so heavy that the patients aren't supposed to be able to
> lift them. The other staff were in position to do a "take
> down" and had the Thorazine injection ready. I
> approached the guy and while maintaining good eye
> contact, I said, "Do you want something to eat? Would
> you like a sandwich or a donut?" He looked amazingly
> startled and then he set the chair down and said, "yes."
> I unlocked the doors of the unit and walked with him
> across the street where I bought him a cup of coffee
> and a sandwich. While he was eating, I said, "You
> looked angry back there. Want to talk about what was
> going on?" Well, we had a good talk and he was
> considerably calmed down by the time we returned to
> the unit. From then on, I was teased by the other staff
> about practicing "sandwich therapy."

I told Pat I loved that story, and he told me the person said he
would grab the chair when he felt he was about to lose control and
hurt someone, knowing staff would "take him down," which would
keep him from hurting anyone. Being a psychiatric survivor, Pat could

relate to psychiatric patients in ways staff without such personal experience from the wrong side of the locked door could not. To say Pat is dearly missed is an understatement. Everyone loved Pat.

JANUARY 2ND

On January 2nd, Lilly's head lawyer in the Zyprexa MDL, Nina Gussack, wrote Judge Weinstein, asking him to order me to submit to a deposition in New York City within five days of when the order might be signed, and to produce all relevant documents, *as well as all computers and hard drives* that had information on the Zyprexa Papers.

On January 2, Ted Chabasinski wrote Judge Weinstein to inform him that he was representing MindFreedom and Judi Chamberlin and that Judge Weinstein should dissolve the temporary mandatory injunction:

> This carelessly-drawn injunction, obtained at the court's close of business just before a five-day recess, is an abuse of process.
>
> As everyone is aware at this point there are thousands of copies of the documents in question circulating on the Internet and in the hands of innumerable people. The defendants' lawyers know full well that any injunction intended to recover the documents is a futile gesture. There is no way to keep these documents secret any longer. While the injunction purports to be an attempt to recover the documents, it is clear that its real purpose is to intimidate Lilly's critics, and the court should refuse to cooperate with this.
>
> While the underlying case is civil, what these documents show is **CRIMINAL** behavior on the part of Lilly's executives. They have chosen a course of action, lying about and hiding the real effects of Zyprexa, that they knew would lead to the injury and death of literally thousands of people. If this isn't criminal, I don't know what is.
>
> My clients, and many other people involved in the issue of protecting psychiatric patients' rights, are calling for the criminal prosecution of the people responsible for this situation. . . .

> Furthermore, the defendants have created a massive
> public health problem by dishonestly inducing mental
> health authorities to administer this drug, often forcibly,
> to many thousands of people, whose drug-caused
> disabilities will now be a drain on the public health
> system for many years.
>
> It is not in the public interest to keep documents secret
> when it will have the effect of making it much more
> difficult to prevent the disability of thousands of
> people.
>
> Nor is it legitimate for the defendants to be allowed to
> frighten citizens from petitioning the government for
> redress of grievances, which is the real purpose of this
> injunction. . . .
>
> I urge the court to dissolve the present injunction and
> to issue no further injunctions of the same kind, both
> because it would be a futile gesture and because such a
> further injunction would clearly be against the public
> interest.

In the guardianship case, Judge Christen issued an order extending
the time to respond to all pending motions until February 2nd and set a
scheduling conference for February 21st. This meant I didn't have to
deal with the guardianship case in Alaska and the Zyprexa MDL in
New York at the same time.

JANUARY 3RD, 2007

At the January 3rd hearing in the Zyprexa MDL, Lilly lawyer Fahey
told the court:

> There has been discussion about whether these have
> been widely disseminated or not. The Internet is a very
> large place, your Honor, but we can tell you that we see
> no evidence of widespread dissemination. The fact is
> that as soon as we learned of Websites that attempted
> to disseminate this information, we have had them shut
> down.

Fahey then quoted David Oaks' December 30th statement that he
knew of no source for anyone to download these documents at this

time. He did not tell the court David had e-mailed a couple of hours later to say they were still available through Tor.

At the end of this hearing, Judge Weinstein set January 16th to hold a hearing on whether the Secrecy Order had been violated and, if so, what to do about it. He also set the same time to hear whether I should be compelled to give Lilly my computer equipment and Zyprexa-related documents and testify at a deposition. He not only extended the temporary mandatory injunction until January 16th but also extended it to parties and websites identified by Lilly. This was put in a written order signed on January 4th. These included Eric Whalen and his website, MindFreedom, which had never posted the documents, and AHRP.org. The extended temporary injunction further required the removal of Zyprexa Papers "posted at any website" and prohibited all of the persons named in the injunction from posting information to websites to facilitate dissemination of the Zyprexa Papers, which meant it prohibited links to the Zyprexa Papers.

As to Mr. Bigley's psychiatric imprisonment and forced drugging case, apparently not wanting to go through a real trial, API did not file a petition to commit Mr. Bigley for 180 more days, letting him go on the last day of his commitment, January 3rd, 2007.

FRIDAY, JANUARY 5TH

On Friday, January 5th, Judge Weinstein set a hearing for Monday, January 8th to address MindFreedom's and Judi Chamberlin's request to reargue the extension and modification of the December 29th temporary injunction.

MONDAY, JANUARY 8TH

In advance of the January 8th hearing, early in the morning, "John Doe," represented by Fred Von Lohmann of the Electronic Frontier Foundation, submitted a motion for the injunction to be reconsidered or at least stayed (delayed) so that John Doe could file an appeal. John Doe had "personal experience with psychiatric misdiagnosis" and was one of the people who contributed to Zyprexa.pbwiki.com, which had been helping to distribute the Zyprexa Papers. Zyprexa.pbwiki.com was specifically enjoined from posting the Zyprexa Papers in the January 4th extension and modification of the temporary injunction.

John Doe argued that since he was not a party to the Zyprexa MDL, the court had no power to order him to do or not do anything.

This comes from the legal principle, enunciated by a famous early twentieth-century judge named Learned Hand, that "a court cannot lawfully enjoin the world at large." Recognizing this principle, Civil Rule 65(d), the rule pertaining to injunctions, provides:

> Every order granting an injunction and every restraining order . . . is binding only upon the parties to the action, their officers, agents, servants, employees, and attorneys, and upon those persons in active concert or participation with them who receive actual notice of the order by personal service or otherwise.

John Doe was right.

He also argued the injunction against zyprexa.pbwiki.com and against him as one of its contributors was an unconstitutional "prior restraint" on speech:

> The Court's January 4 Order is additionally improper because, as drafted and as applied to Doe, it is a prior restraint on speech in violation of the First Amendment. "[P]rior restraints on speech and publication are the most serious and the least tolerable infringement on First Amendment rights." Accordingly, any prior restraint "bears a heavy presumption against its constitutional validity." Furthermore, "[a] prior restraint is not constitutionally inoffensive merely because it is temporary." [citations omitted]

John Doe was right about this, too.

At the hearing, Fred Von Lohmann went over these principles, and Ted Chabasinski—representing MindFreedom, Judi Chamberlin, and Robert Whitaker—as well as Alan Milstein, representing Vera Sharav, agreed with him. Fahey repeated David Oaks' statement that "I know of no place on the Internet where these documents can be located" and again omitted that a couple of hours later, David had reported that they were still available through Tor.

During the hearing, Judge Weinstein said that all of the issues would be heard and considered at the January 16th hearing.

TUESDAY, JANUARY 9TH

On January 9th, through Alan Milstein, their attorney, Vera Sharav and Dr. David Cohen formally moved to vacate (get rid of) the Secrecy Order or dissolve the injunction, partly on the grounds that the public had the right to know information critical to making an informed decision as to whether to take Zyprexa. As a public advocate for human rights in medicine, Ms. Sharav wished to publish and publicize the Zyprexa Papers to inform the public. Dr. Cohen is an internationally recognized expert in psychiatric drugs, with many published articles and books, who stated the Zyprexa Papers included invaluable information on how neuroleptics are marketed to doctors, and the public should have access to them. Dr. Cohen stated:

> I wish to undertake analysis and dissemination of some information contained in the Documents, in the form of articles and other publications destined for professional or popular audiences, in accordance with the research and scholarly interests I have pursued as a university professor for nearly two decades.

Through Mr. Milstein, Ms. Sharav and Dr. Cohen pointed out the plaintiffs' lawyers agreed to keep documents secret from the public in order to benefit their individual clients. Milstein's brief argued the injunction was improper for three reasons:

- The Injunction is not in the public interest, as any injunction must be. The important data in the Documents and the long history of cover-ups by "Big Pharma" made this clear.

- Lilly cannot show that the balance of hardships tips in its favor, as any party must do in order to be entitled to an injunction. The Documents were generated by Lilly itself and, if their disclosure is damaging, it is because the Documents reveal the Company's admissions about the risks of Zyprexa. On the other hand, the harm to the public in not having material information about the dangers of a particular drug is manifest.

- Finally, Lilly cannot show that it will be irreparably harmed in the absence of an injunction, as it is required to. *The Times* articles let the cat out of the bag, particularly in the Internet-dominated universe we inhabit today; no further "harm" will come to Lilly. In addition, *The Times* still has the documents and Lilly has not asked this or any court to order the *Times* either to return them or to not publish them. They are, therefore, in the public domain.

This is "Black Letter Law," meaning these legal principles are well established and no longer subject to reasonable dispute.

In arguing why the Secrecy Order should be modified to allow public access to the Zyprexa Papers, Sharav's and Cohen's motion cited a trial court decision explaining the courts' role in making sure secrecy (protective) orders do not harm the public:

> While parties to litigation can agree among themselves what information, if any, they will not release to the public, the Court has the power to decide what material will ultimately be unavailable to the public. The reasons for this are clear. The inherent pressures of litigation will often provoke parties to consent to protective orders during discovery. Frequently, a party will agree to the opposing party's request for a protective order so as to expedite the discovery process and reduce the cost of litigation. There are plainly many incentives for parties to agree to a protective order, while there are few incentives for parties to oppose one. Moreover, a party consenting to a protective order will rarely, if ever, take into consideration the public's interest in such matters. In such cases, the good cause requirement [of Federal Rule of Civil Procedure 26(c)] acts as a guardian of the public's right of access to discovery documents by requiring parties to make a threshold showing before documents will be withheld from public view.

That case involved whether videotaped depositions of rappers Dr. Dre and Eminem should be confidential. The court ruled the public interest was not served by keeping the depositions secret. To me, access to deposition videos of Dr. Dre and Eminem was far less important to the public interest than allowing access to the Zyprexa Papers. Vera's lawyer also cited an appellate opinion, which noted that "disturbingly, some courts routinely sign orders which contain confidentiality clauses without considering the propriety of such orders, or the countervailing public concerns which are sacrificed by such orders."

Most interestingly, Mr. Milstein cited an article by Judge Weinstein himself, in which he wrote:

> Protective orders may have a legitimate role when there is no public impact or when true trade secrets are involved. But we can strike a fairer balance between privacy interests of corporations and the health and safety of the public. *A publicly maintained legal system ought not protect those who engage in misconduct, conceal the cause of injury from the victims, or render potential victims vulnerable.* Moreover, such secrecy defeats the deterrent function of the justice system. [emphasis added]

Lilly was complaining the Zyprexa Papers were just a few of the millions of pages produced under the Secrecy Order and did not give a balanced view of Zyprexa. In addition to noting there was nothing to prevent Lilly from bringing forth documents to make that case, Mr. Milstein pointed out:

> Lilly has settled many of the cases brought by victims of Zyprexa for hundreds of millions of dollars, yet the company continues to take the public stance that the drug does not cause excessive weight gain or diabetes. The Documents prove otherwise.

FRIDAY, JANUARY 12TH

In a supplemental brief dated January 12th but not docketed until January 19th, which was after the trial set for January 16–17th, John Doe submitted evidence that, contrary to what Lilly had informed the court, the Zyprexa Papers were still available on the Internet. One of the exhibits was from a January 8th post by Bill Childs, published on the TortsProf Blog, in which he reported he was able to find the Zyprexa Papers on the Internet in nineteen minutes. This was the same day Lilly told the court the Zyprexa Papers could no longer be found on the Internet. Professor Childs later reported that when he thought of a better way to look, he found them within thirty seconds.

The other exhibit was a declaration (affidavit) from Laura Mason, a law student intern at the Electronic Frontier Foundation, who stated she had successfully downloaded the Zyprexa Papers from two separate locations on the Internet, using Tor for one of them and BitTorrent for the other. Ms. Mason reported that one of the sites appeared to be located on Christmas Island, a territory of Australia.

So once again, Lilly had been exposed as lying to the court. It didn't matter.

Also on Friday, January 12th, Lilly wrote to Judge Weinstein that it intended to seek sanctions against Dr. Egilman and me at the January 16th hearing, stating Dr. Egilman had deleted and destroyed information. Knowing Lilly's pattern of lying, I think it is probable Lilly was referring to Dr. Egilman's self-destructing e-mails, which had occurred prior to the December 28th order requiring Dr. Egilman to preserve evidence. Lilly had obtained access to Dr. Egilman's computers and had used a computer expert to recover deleted files. Dr. Egilman's deposition still hadn't taken place, despite Judge Weinstein ordering it to take place within five days of December 29th, because Lilly was still trying to get more material from Dr. Egilman, including computer files.

Lilly also proposed that Vera Sharav's and Dr. Cohen's motion to declassify the Zyprexa Papers—i.e., remove their confidential status— be referred to the Special Discovery Master, which would basically consign it to a black hole from which it would never emerge. Lilly also wanted to extend the injunction.

Of most concern to me was Lilly wanted to get an order requiring me to give them:

> copies of any and all documents and information including, but not limited to, all computers, hard-drives, other electronic storage media, hardcopy documents, emails, e-documents, text messaging, instant messaging, phone records and voice mails, that refer or relate to Zyprexa.

It was the computers, hard drives, and other electronic storage media that concerned me the most, because as a lawyer, I have an obligation to keep client communications and other confidential material secret. Lilly also wrote, "Once Mr. Gottstein's deposition is completed, Lilly will promptly file its motions for sanctions against Mr. Gottstein." I wanted to avoid a deposition by just testifying in front of Judge

Weinstein on January 16th and 17th and bringing everything relevant with me to Brooklyn.

SATURDAY, JANUARY 13TH

On Saturday, January 13th, John McKay, my attorney, wrote Lilly and Judge Weinstein to say I was going to come to Brooklyn to testify for the January 16th hearing, "as necessary, concerning the matters before the court Tuesday." These matters included whether to continue the injunction and whether I was to be subjected to a deposition.

SUNDAY, JANUARY 14TH

I cut my vacation short and flew back to Anchorage to pull things together to take to Brooklyn. John and I flew through Chicago on a red-eye, leaving Sunday, January 14th at 10:00 p.m., flying all night and half the day (losing four hours to time zone changes), and arriving at New York's La Guardia airport a little after noon on January 15th. The hearing was the next afternoon at 2:00 p.m., which was 10:00 a.m. Alaska time.

As I mentioned in Chapter 1, I am not someone who tolerates sleep deprivation well, having ended up in the psych hospital twice in the 1980s when I got too sleep deprived. In fact, most people who experiences psychosis are sleep deprived. For me, it is almost always work related. If I am working on a project that has a looming deadline I am not on top of, I can't stop thinking about it and don't sleep. To prevent this, I usually make sure I can file things the day before they are due. On the rare occasions when I get into trouble, I will take the much-maligned benzodiazepine Halcion (triazolam). It is much maligned because a number of people committed murder on it, especially in Britain. When I asked my psychiatrist at the time about it, he said those people had been given much higher doses than I took. I often go a year or more without it. Benzodiazepines, also known as "benzos," are highly addictive, so it is good to take them as infrequently as possible. Unlike me, John seems to do fine with little sleep and pulls all-nighters with some frequency, from my observation, grabbing snippets of sleep. That said, he once fell asleep in the middle of composing an e-mail to me.

MONDAY, JANUARY 15TH

On Monday, January 15th, Lilly wrote John it did not expect I would be testifying regarding whether I would be ordered to turn over materials and subjected to a deposition. In that letter, Lilly also noted the BB guardianship case was sealed and therefore they didn't have a copy of the petition I had filed on BB's behalf, which they wanted to use in my deposition. I have to admit to some amusement over this. By Alaska statute, guardianship cases, except for orders for guardianships, are confidential. This is to protect the privacy and reputation of the person against whom these cases are filed, including from embarrassment by what the court files might contain. From my perspective, however, this confidentiality most often operates to hide from public view the great abuses that occur in these cases, rather than to protect the person; basically, people tend to be railroaded. Here, however, I felt turnabout was fair play since Lilly had designated as secret hundreds of thousands of documents for which there was no legitimate basis for confidentiality.

In any event, the trip to Brooklyn to testify in front of Judge Weinstein the day after I had flown all night to get to New York was not good in terms of getting sleep. The late start on January 16th offered me the potential of getting a reasonable amount of sleep, but things did not work out that way.

Ch. 7. The Heroine

TUESDAY, JANUARY 16TH – DAY ONE OF THE TRIAL

Tuesday, January 16th was the deadline to file our opposition to Lilly being able to seize my computer equipment and depose me. The filing theoretically was not due until the end of the day, but we wanted the judge to accept my testimony at the hearing in lieu of me being required to testify at a deposition and have my computer equipment pawed over by Lilly's computer people. This meant we needed to file it as early as we could before the 2:00 p.m. hearing. John kept calling me, all night and into the early morning, asking questions so he could finish his brief and my accompanying declaration (affidavit). As a result, I was fairly sleep deprived when called to the witness stand that afternoon.

The brief we filed asserted neither I nor Dr. Egilman had violated the Secrecy Order, and even if Dr. Egilman had, I hadn't aided and abetted in such a violation because I'd told Dr. Egilman he had to comply with the Secrecy Order, and I had my own, separate reasons for wanting the Zyprexa Papers. From this it followed that I couldn't be prosecuted for contempt, so there was no reason to seize my computer equipment and depose me. Also flowing from this was that there should be no injunction, because I had received the Zyprexa Papers legally and they had lost confidentiality.

In the brief, John pointed out that under applicable precedent, in order to establish contempt, Lilly would have to prove:

1. the Secrecy Order was clear and unambiguous,

2. the proof of violation was clear and convincing, which meant highly probable, and

3. I had not diligently attempted to comply in a reasonable manner.

John pointed out that the meaning of a "reasonable opportunity to object" before Dr. Egilman could comply with the subpoena was very ambiguous and therefore could not support a contempt conviction. Similarly, since the Secrecy Order was so ambiguous about how much time Lilly had to be given, there was no way they could prove any violation was clear and convincing. As to diligent attempts to comply, John pointed out that even though I wasn't subject to the Secrecy Order, I had repeatedly told Dr. Egilman he had to comply, and I'd even suggested he consult his lawyer to advise him on the issue. John also said that because I had come to New York to testify at the hearing, there was no reason to have a deposition. John is a terrific lawyer, and he wrote a terrific brief on very short notice by working all night on it.

When I arrived the most striking thing to me about the United States District Court building in Brooklyn was the view of the Brooklyn Bridge and downtown Manhattan from the foyer outside of the courtrooms. It was like a painting, the way the window framed it.

The legendary Judge Jack Weinstein had presided over the Agent Orange case—involving thousands of military service members claiming injury from the herbicide used to defoliate the jungle during the Vietnam War—and had literally written the rules for handling this type of mass tort (injury) case. He was in his mid-80s, and if he had lost a mental step it was not evident to me. Judge Weinstein didn't sit on the elevated and imposing judge's bench in the courtroom. Instead, he had everyone sit around a large conference table. He didn't need the elevated physical position to be in charge.

Dr. Egilman's lawyer was Ed Hayes. He was from Queens, although I thought Brooklyn at the time, as he was my idea of a classic Brooklyn lawyer, complete with a strong accent and loud sport coat. He and Judge Weinstein apparently had a long history together. A few months later, Judge Weinstein threatened to have Mr. Hayes arrested for failing to show up to testify about his representation of a police officer accused of committing murder for the Mafia.

There were rumors John Doe was in the courtroom. I was asked about that by my attorney, John McKay, but I didn't know who he was. Many years later, I learned he was Jonah Bossewitch, and he was the person who Will Hall had contacted to get the Zyprexa Papers out on the Internet through Tor and BitTorrent. Among other things, including being an expert on the Internet, Jonah is a journalist and has since received his PhD in communications from Columbia University. Ten years later, Jonah told me he had been there that first day but didn't come the second day because he was concerned that if he was unmasked, Judge Weinstein would slap the injunction on him.

Fred von Lohmann, representing Jonah as "John Doe," was a sharp-as-tacks, tall, thin young lawyer with socks that matched his tie. Fred insisted that was entirely coincidental.

Judge Weinstein started the hearing by suggesting I either give my deposition that day and the next or skip the deposition by giving testimony. John suggested I just give testimony, but only if Lilly had established that there was a violation of the Secrecy Order. Lilly lawyer George Lehner responded they wanted a chance to review all of the documents, not just the ones "Mr. Gottstein has chosen to provide the Court and the parties." Lilly also made a point of telling the judge that the Plaintiffs' Steering Committee in the Zyprexa MDL had jointly moved for extension of the injunction. Judge Weinstein told Lilly it had the burden of proof and they should present their case. Mr. Lehner then said they would call me as a witness and turned the questioning over to Sean Fahey.

Fahey started out by asking whether I was supposed to be honest with the court and parties and not abuse an attorney's subpoena power. Then he had me read part of the draft letter I had written to the Special Discovery Master about how I came to possess the Zyprexa Papers. Mr. Fahey kept trying to get me to say I was helping or assisting Dr. Egilman, and I kept testifying that he had his interests and I had my interests, and that in making the Zyprexa Papers available to the public, I had been pursuing my interests. He kept asking in different ways until he was finally satisfied he had gotten what he wanted:

Q So your sense was that Dr. Egilman called you so that you could help or he could help—you could help him make the documents public. That's what you just said, right?

A I'm trying to think exactly. One of the things is that I had my interests and he had his interests. So I don't know that I was really trying to help him at that point.

Q You both had an interest in publicizing the documents, correct?

A Yes, I have my interest. I really hesitate to speak for Dr. Egilman.

Q But your understanding based on your conversation with Dr. Egilman was that he called you so that you could assist him in disseminating the documents that were subject to a protective order, right?

MR. HAYES: I object. It calls for a state of mind of Dr. Egilman.

MR. McKAY: I also object because it—it states facts that aren't in the record. That's not what he said. It's predicated on a—

THE COURT: Excuse me. I'll deal first with the Egilman objection. What is your objection?

MR. HAYES: My objection is that it calls for his analysis of Egilman's state of mind.

THE COURT: That is overruled. The state of mind of the witness is what is in issue at the moment and his belief as to what Egilman wanted to do is admissible.

MR. HAYES: Yes, your Honor. Thank you.

THE COURT: Your objection, sir?

MR. McKAY: My objection is framing the question, he misstated what Mr. Gottstein's testimony was—

THE COURT: Sustained. Reframe your question.

Q Mr. Gottstein, your understanding based on the conversation with Dr. Egilman, your state of mind at the time was that you understood that the—that Dr. Egilman was calling you so that you would assist him in disseminating documents that were subject to a protective order, right?

A I think that is probably correct. I was pretty focused on my objectives not his objectives but it's hard for me to say that is not accurate.

Q And your sense was—we know that you wanted to get the documents made public, you've already said that, right?

A Correct.

Q And your sense was that Dr. Egilman shared your desire to make them public, correct?

A Well, what I said is that—it's my understanding that he also had that objective, and so did he share mine? I don't know but I think that was his objective.

The problematic part of my answer was saying "I think that is probably correct" in response to the question of whether Dr. Egilman was calling so that I would assist him in disseminating the documents. The question was whether that was Dr. Egilman's goal, not mine, but it was a great question because it made my answer look like I had agreed to assist him, when in fact, I was pursuing my own goals when Dr. Egilman made the opportunity available. This was problematic because if I had aided or abetted Dr. Egilman in violating the Secrecy Order, then I became subject to the court's jurisdiction and, potentially, subject to punishment.

Having gotten what he wanted, Fahey moved on to my not getting a copy of the Secrecy Order before I subpoenaed Dr. Egilman:

Q   And you never asked for a copy of the protective order, did you?

A   Actually I did ask for it.

Q   When?

A   Probably the first telephone call. It was pretty early on in the telephone conversations.

Q   On November 28th?

A   I don't remember the exact day.

Q   Was there a conversation before the 28th?

A   No, but it might have been in subsequent phone calls.

Q   But subsequent to Dr. Egilman sharing the documents with you, you asked for the protective order, correct?

A   Yes. [I misspoke—Actually, it had been before Dr. Egilman shared the documents with me.]

Q   And you didn't get it, right?

A   He said I didn't want it and I didn't push it.

Q   Why did he say you didn't want it?

A   Again, we're calling for his state of mind. My kind of sense of it was that if I didn't have it, then I wouldn't be charged with the knowledge of it but.

Q   And you wouldn't be here in a proceeding like this?

A   No, I don't think that is correct because he did read the relevant portions to me and I felt—first off, I felt and do feel that we followed the procedure set out in the protective order; and second of all, I feel that it was Dr. Egilman's obligation to comply. Now, subsequent to all of this coming out, I realize that I probably should have been more insistent on getting the protective order but I felt pretty confident that all I needed to do was comply with my part of the process.

Q   So essentially what you didn't know couldn't hurt you, right?

A   I really hesitate to answer that. I guess maybe that was his sense of it. Mine was I wasn't really concerned about that because I felt I had—he read [the part about subpoenaing documents] to me.

Then, the most critical exchanges, from my perspective, occurred when Fahey asked me about BB not having been given Zyprexa:

Q   There is no evidence that BB was ever taking Zyprexa?

A   There is no evidence, you mean in the record here?

Q   You haven't offered any evidence that BB was taking Zyprexa on December 6 when you issued the subpoena or at any time since December 6, is that correct?

A   That's correct.

Q   And so you found a case to issue a subpoena calling for Zyprexa documents and there is no evidence that the person involved in that case ever was taking Zyprexa, correct?

A   Well, again, it hasn't been produced in this proceeding yet. I'm not sure that he has never been. At this time I'm not sure that he has ever been. He certainly was potentially subject to it and Eli Lilly's apparently illegal marketing activity was certainly relevant to the question of whether or not he should be ordered to take this drug against his will.

Q   I understand what you are saying but I just want to make it clear that you have no evidence to present to the Court today that at any point from December 5th through today, you have no evidence to provide to the Court that BB was taking Zyprexa at any time during that period, correct?

A   Correct.

Q   And so you issued a subpoena, you found a case with someone who has no evidence of taking Zyprexa and you issued a subpoena to Dr. Egilman on December 6. Dr. Egilman told you he had Zyprexa documents, right?

A   Yes.

At the time, I thought I had said that even though I didn't have any proof, I was pretty sure BB had been given Zyprexa. Later, when John asked me if I wanted him to ask me any questions, I didn't tell him to ask me about that, because I felt certain I had already testified I was pretty sure BB had been given Zyprexa. This ended up being a big problem.

Then, Fahey asked me about not giving Lilly the amended subpoena:

Q   And earlier you said you had told Dr. Egilman repeatedly that he should send the second subpoena to Lilly, correct?

A   Yes.

Q   And you knew he planned not to send it to Lilly, correct?

A   Yeah, I think—he told me he didn't see that it made any difference.

Q   And you decided that it was not important for you to send the subpoena to Lilly either, correct?

A   My—my position is that it was his responsibility under the CMO [Secrecy Order] and not mine.

I then testified about copying and sending the documents out, and Fahey made the point that I was more interested in disseminating them than reading them. He then asked whether I wanted to prevent the court from stopping me:

Q   And you were anxious to get them out as quickly as you could, right?

A   Anxious, yes, I thought it would be good to get them out.

Q   Before the Court could enter an order telling you you shouldn't?

A   Well, I don't know. I mean I guess—I don't know that—you know, I knew that Eli Lilly would want to try to stop it.

Q   Right, and you wanted to get them out as quickly as you could to make that harder?

A   Well, I would say yeah, I wanted to get them out in a way that would make it impossible to get them back.

Q   Right. And I just want to confirm that you, sir, as an officer of the Court and an attorney in the State of Alaska, relied on a physician to determine the legal implications of a protective order, correct?

A   No, that is not precisely true. I advised him to get counsel repeatedly and I looked at it in terms of what my obligations were and that I didn't have any obligations under what is called CMO-3 here [the Secrecy Order], I think, the protective order, that I had to follow the rules. I felt that the protective order essentially provided a road map of how to do it and that I followed that road map.

Fahey continued to try to get me to admit that I had done something wrong, with me continuing to testify that I didn't think so:

Q   In paragraph 6 of that declaration, you wrote, and these are your words: Dr. Egilman indicated that three business days could be construed as sufficient notice to comply?

A   Yes.

Q   And you relied on Dr. Egilman's interpretation of the case management order and the procedures under which you were supposed to be operating as an officer of the Court and you never asked for the protective order and you never had a copy of the protective order before you pursued your course of action with Dr. Egilman?

A   There is a lot there and I'm kind of tired from everything, flying all night and stuff but you said as an officer of the Court. I was certainly an officer of the Alaska Court and followed those rules. I never did and I don't believe now that I am subject to—a party to that case management order. Now, I think really the guts of the question is what was reasonable notice. We discussed that and how—

actually, we discussed and I know more about the law now but how ambiguous that order was and so he said that he felt it could be construed that way. One of the things, for example, that we discussed was, and I mentioned it, that initially I assumed that I was going to get one of those AS 47.30.839 proceedings where the usual practice, which I think is an absolute outrage, is for the hospital to file a petition sometimes only an hour before the hearing and then go through and get a forced drugging order in the hearing that starts an hour from when the respondent was served. And that what is reasonable notice under those circumstances? And what I said, and I think I put it in my draft response, is that well, I'm not going to do a hearing under those conditions, and I always get a continuance [delay]. And so we talked about that and what it meant to be reasonable notice and we talked about that but I made it clear I was not his attorney and he needed to consult his own attorney and that it was his obligation to comply with the order.

The hearing that day ended shortly after this exchange, at 3:25 p.m., with arrangements being made for me to provide Lilly with all of the documents I had brought with me, most of which were on my computer. The hearing was set to resume the next day, January 17th, at 10:30 a.m. I was concerned about being kept up late that night and then having to testify the next morning. Judge Weinstein said they would accommodate me.

At Pepper Hamilton's office that night when we went to give them the documents, I think there were around twenty lawyers and paralegals set to work all night, going through the materials so that I could be confronted with them the next morning. I have to admit to some satisfaction in going up against so much firepower. It had to have been costing Lilly at least $10,000/hour. Of course, that was chump change to them, but Pepper Hamilton and other Lilly law firms did very well financially that night. True to my concerns, it was quite late by the time we got back to the hotel; I had a chance to get some, but not enough, sleep. I think I probably took a Halcion to make sure I got at least some sleep. I needed to take it early enough so it would clear my system by the time I was put on the witness stand again in the morning.

WEDNESDAY, JANUARY 17TH – DAY TWO OF THE TRIAL

I recollect getting to the courtroom a little early and listening to the tail end of a hearing at which I learned Medicaid was going to take about 30% of people's settlement money to pay for diabetes treatment it had provided to Zyprexa victims.

One of the first revelations in my testimony that day was Alex Berenson had called me and told me that if I sent the Zyprexa Papers to anyone else in the media, he wouldn't run the story, and that I had acquiesced because I knew having *The New York Times* break the story would be the best coverage. I also testified that once "Eli Lilly actually got moving on this," Dr. Egilman and I hadn't talked.

Q   You understood that both the Lanier firm and Lilly believed that the documents had not been produced pursuant to the protective order before they published in the New York Times?

A   I don't know what they believed but I know that's what they said.

Q   Let's ask it that way. You were told by the Lilly lawyers that they believed prior to the publication of the December 17th *New York Times* article that you had obtained those documents in violation of a protective order in this case, correct?

A   I got two threatening letters from Eli Lilly on the 15th. So I think that's probably right but I would want to look at them again to see what it was that they put in those letters.

Q   One of the letters was from me?

A   Yes, I guess it was, yes.

Q   And the other letter that you received was from the Lanier law firm saying that the documents were not produced pursuant to the protective order and that was before *The New York Times* publication of the documents on December 17, correct?

A   Can I look at that letter again?

Q   Sure.

A   That is not clear to me that they said that—

MR. HAYES: I object. The letter is whatever it is. He is characterizing it.

THE COURT: The witness is refreshing his recollection. He may.

A   I mean I'm just skimming it again. It says that Lilly's position was that it was provided in violation.

Q   Did you understand the Lanier firm to disagree with that position?

A   You know, how can I comment—they didn't say they disagreed. They didn't say they agreed.

Q   Did Dr. Egilman tell you that he had spoken with Rick Meadow on December 13 and that Rick Meadow had told him not to produce documents pursuant to the subpoena?

A   I don't remember him saying that.

Q   Did Dr. Egilman tell you that on December 13 he told Rick Meadow that he would not produce documents pursuant to the subpoena?

A   He did not tell me that.

So here, once again, Lilly was, at a minimum, misleading when Mr. Fahey stated the Lanier firm said the documents had not been produced pursuant to the protective order. Rick Meadow's letter actually said:

> Please further note that by providing a copy of this letter to Mr. Gottstein concerning Lilly's position that such materials were provided in violation of a court order, I am demanding the return of such materials to the PSC and I am further conveying Lilly's demand that no disclosure of such materials be made until such time as Lilly has had the opportunity to file its motion and be heard on this matter by Judge Weinstein of the Eastern District of New York.

Mr. Meadow's letter clearly said it was Lilly's position, but he didn't say what position he himself had, if any. What I missed is the letter also states, "The only person to whom Dr. Egilman has provided confidential materials, *if such materials are deemed confidential*, is James B. Gottstein" (emphasis added). So the Lanier firm, which represented some of the plaintiffs in the Zyprexa MDL, clearly didn't even take a position on whether the Zyprexa Papers were confidential.

It seems worth mentioning that Judge Weinstein did not tell Mr. Fahey to stop misstating the facts in his questioning. I don't think many judges would. It is part of our adversarial system to allow lawyers to try to trip up witnesses.

Fahey then started going through the people to whom I had sent the Zyprexa Papers.

> Q I want to talk to you a little bit about the people that you distributed the documents to once you received them. And yesterday I believe you said you spoke with Mr. Whitaker before he received the documents?
>
> A Yes. . . .
>
> Q What did you tell him?
>
> A That I had gotten these documents pursuant to a subpoena and that I was sending them to him.
>
> Q What did he say?
>
> A Thank you. I don't know exactly, but thank you, I think he indicated he would be interested in them.
>
> Q And you understood that he would disseminate them to others?
>
> A No.
>
> Q You didn't?
>
> A No.
>
> Q What did you think he was going to do with them?
>
> A He is an expert on the treatment of schizophrenia. He wrote a book that I think is the best book in the last 50 years on the subject called *Mad In America, Bad Science, Bad Medicine and the Enduring Mistreatment of the Mentally Ill.* And so he is the one that got the FOIA documents, Freedom of Information Act documents on the approval that showed what I would consider kind of the way that the studies were kind of misrepresented or cooked or something that

resulted in the approval of Zyprexa. And he—and that was part of, it was in the book and anyway so he was an expert.

Q Let me bring you back to my question. What did you think he was going to do with the documents that you were going to send him? That was my question.

A I thought he would be very interested in them and he very well might write an article. He has a continuing interest in this as an author and journalist so I thought he would be interested in them.

Q You thought he would publish the documents, right?

A I didn't know if he would—that he might.

Q And he might communicate them to others?

A Well, I didn't think that he would. I didn't think that he would do that but I don't know.

Q So let me understand this. You were sending documents to a person who had published information about Zyprexa in the past and you're telling us today that you thought you were going to send those documents to him and that he was just going to leave them in a desk in his office and not communicate them to anyone?

MR. McKAY: Objection.

A I didn't say that.

THE COURT: He didn't say that. Can't you move ahead. Are we going to go through each person?

This is an example of why we wanted to just give testimony instead of a deposition. In a deposition, for all practical purposes, Lilly would have been able to ask as many questions as it wanted and go as long as it wanted, although the process was supposed to be supervised by the Special Discovery Master.

Fahey had to move on, so he started asking me questions about my communications with Alex Berenson.

Q What caused him to call you three days after your conversation with Dr. Egilman?

A   This would be around what? The second of December or something?

Q   Early December.

A   What caused him to call me?

MR. HAYES: Objection. First, he has to establish that he knows he talked to him. Objection.

THE COURT: Overruled.

A   I think he was working on a story on this.

Q   Why did he call you? What did he tell you when he called you?

A   He told me that he had given Dr. Egilman my name.

Q   Alex Berenson had given Dr. Egilman your name?

A   Yes.

Q   Is that how Dr. Egilman came to contact you on November 28.

A   I think so.

Q   And you said that he had told you that he had given Dr.— Help me understand that. What did he say?

A   He said that Dr. Egilman had some documents that he wanted to get to *The New York Times* and that he had, you know, thought that I might be someone who would subpoena them.

Q   You could help get Dr. Egilman to have the documents or—strike that. Alex Berenson told you that Dr. Egilman thought you would be someone who would help him, meaning Dr. Egilman, get the Zyprexa documents to *The New York Times*, right?

A   Well, I don't—I wouldn't—what I said was that he thought I was someone who might subpoena the documents.

Q   And so how—so Alex Berenson gives Dr. Egilman your name, correct, that's what he said?

A   That's what he said.

Q   Then Dr. Egilman calls you on November 28 and says I have some documents you might want to subpoena, right?

A   Did he say that exactly? I think that's the import of it.

Q   And did the two of you when you were talking on November 28 talk about this relationship you both had with Alex Berenson?

A   I may have mentioned that I tried to contact him before, that I might have tried to contact him before.

THE COURT: Him is who?

THE WITNESS: Mr. Berenson.

Q   Did you tell Dr. Egilman that you had spoken with Alex and that you understood that he had given Dr. Egilman your name?

A   Yes, I think at some point that was communicated one way or another.

Q   So in fact the call was not as you said in your letter out of the blue, right?

A   It was out of the blue.

Q   But you knew it was coming?

A   No, no, Dr. Egilman called me first. That was out of the blue.

Q   Okay. That is a fair point. But after the November 28 letter you learned that it was not out of the blue, it was actually orchestrated by Dr. Egilman and Alex Berenson, right?

A   Well, I don't know how that is inconsistent with what I wrote in my letter. It was out of the blue.

Q   It was out of the blue for you, right?

A   Yes.

Q   But it was not out of the blue for Dr. Egilman or Alex Berenson?

MR. MILSTEIN: Objection, your Honor. The question is just argument at this point.

THE COURT: I don't believe it is.

A So I mean out of the blue—I mean—it seemed that—it's like I said, what Alex Berenson told me was that he had told Dr. Egilman that I might be someone who would subpoena the documents so I don't know where out of the blue comes into that.

THE COURT: Move to something else.

One thing to note here is that even though Judge Weinstein overruled Alan Milstein about it just being argument by Fahey, he shut down that line of questioning after the very next question.

I testified that when Special Master Woodin had directed me to return the Zyprexa Papers, I hadn't because I didn't think I was subject to his directives, and I had immediately tried to clarify this with him. I testified I had already stopped disseminating the Zyprexa Papers, after receiving Jamieson's letter a couple of days before Special Master Woodin's order. I testified about my efforts to get the Zyprexa Papers returned to Special Discovery Master Woodin after the temporary injunction had been issued, including by asking Alex Berenson to give them back. I would have been flabbergasted had Mr. Berenson returned them, of course.

Judge Weinstein asked what other witnesses were going to be called, and Jonah Bossewitch's concern about coming back the second day proved warranted:

MR. FAHEY: We believe John Doe was here yesterday and we are not sure if he is going to return but if he does return, we'd like to call him.

MR. HAYES: John Doe?

MR. FAHEY: Yes.

THE COURT: He is not in the courtroom today as far as you know?

MR. FAHEY: He is not here today.

Fahey then moved to asking me about an e-mail from Will Hall that was among the hundreds of e-mails I had given them the night before. You'll recall Will was the person who got the Zyprexa Papers out on the Internet through the untraceable Tor and didn't want to be identified as such. I was hoping I wouldn't be asked the right question that would force me to reveal his identity.

Q I'm going to show you the next document which I believe is Petitioner's 4?

THE COURT: Yes. (So marked in evidence Petitioner's Exhibit 4.)

A Okay.

Q Have you read the document, sir?

A Yes, I've looked at it.

Q That is a document you produced to us last night, correct?

A Yes.

Q Can you just describe the document for the record.

A It's a forward—it's an e-mail. It appears to be an e-mail from Will Hall forwarding an E-mail that he had received.

Q What does the e-mail relate to?

A It's got—the only thing it has is a website.

Q Can you read the website into the record?

A Http://cyber.law.harvardedu/briefings/dvb/.

Q What is the re line of the E-mail or the title?

A Subject?

Q Diebold versus?

A Versus the Bloggers.

Q And the date of that—let me back up. Will Hall is one of the recipients of documents from you, correct?

A Yes.

Q And Will Hall sent this E-mail to you on what date December 13, right?

A The one down below says December 13 which is when he got it but I'm not sure when it was forwarded to me. It looks like December 13th but it's pretty confusing.

Q   I agree that the format it was produced in is confusing. We'll stipulate to that but at the top it says received?

A   Yes, okay.

Q   Okay, December 13?

A   That's what it looks like.

Q   And the issue of the Diebold case is that document[s] had been leaked on the internet and the argument was that they were so broadly disseminated that they should not be subject to any further protection, correct?

A   I don't know. I'm not sure I clicked on that link. I don't know that I clicked on that link. That's all I can say.

Q   Regardless whether you clicked on the link, you understand what the Diebold case is all about?

A   Not necessarily, no.

Q   What does not necessarily mean?

A   I'm not that good on case names so I don't really know.

Q   You didn't understand the E-mail when you got it?

A   Well, there is a link and I understood that there was a link. I get a lot of E-mails and I just can't read them all. So—and to click on something, I don't necessarily click on all the links. So I don't remember clicking on this link.

Q   Did Will Hall provide any message to you or—what did he say in his E-mail?

A   He didn't say anything.

Q   So he just gave you this link?

A   Yes.

Q   And the link again is related to Diebold versus what?

A   The subject line if I can find it here is basically the original message that he forwarded, the subject line yes, the subject line is forward Diebold versus the Bloggers. And the only thing in there is a forwarded message that has a link.

Q   That was on December 13, correct, that you received that link?

A   It appears to be.

THE COURT: Do you want that in evidence too?

MR. FAHEY: Yes. And if I have not already asked for P3 to be in evidence, I would ask for that as well.

THE COURT: Admitted. How long is this going to take?

To my great relief, Fahey moved on to something else and never asked the question or questions that would have identified Will as the person who put the Zyprexa Papers on the Internet in a way designed to prevent Lilly from blocking their availability.

Then Lilly finished its initial questioning of me by having me read from an e-mail I had sent out to the PsychRights e-mail list:

Q   I'd ask that you read into the record the paragraph beginning with "in terms of" on page 3 of the documents. . . .

A   "In terms of where things go from here, Eli Lilly is fully capable of crushing me with legal actions but I hope they will realize they have bigger problems and that doing so will give them a huge public relations nightmare (I hope). They have threatened me with criminal and civil contempt sanctions. It has already cost PsychRights $15,000 in attorney's fees to deal with the aftermath. This, of course, is very cheap considering what was accomplished but has significantly reduced PsychRights' bank account. Any and all contributions to help will be appreciated."

From my perspective, this was a good way to end Lilly's interrogation.

ED HAYES' CROSS-EXAMINATION

Then, Dr. Egilman's lawyer, Ed Hayes, cross-examined me. He had informed us Dr. Egilman was going to "take the Fifth," meaning refuse to testify, as was his right under the Fifth Amendment to the U.S. Constitution, on the grounds it might incriminate him. Mr. Hayes was irritated with me for not doing the same. But there was just no way I was going to take the Fifth. I didn't feel I had done anything wrong, and I felt taking the Fifth would be very detrimental to my reputation—far more detrimental than whatever I might say on the witness stand.

Mr. Hayes asked me whether I was the person who'd made the Freedom of Information Act requests to the FDA regarding Zyprexa:

A   No.

Q   Who did that?

A   There were two separate FOIA requests that I posted on the internet. One was the internal—correspondence with Eli Lilly with the FDA about the approval of Zyprexa and the other was the adverse events—it wasn't a database actually, I put it into a database, that Ellen Liversidge whose son was killed by Zyprexa had FOIAed for all of what they call the atypical neuroleptics.

MR. FAHEY: I would object to the characterization of somebody dying from Zyprexa. There has been no evidence of that.

THE COURT: Strike it.

This is from the official transcript of the hearing, so even though Judge Weinstein "struck" this testimony, it remains part of the official record. However, having it "struck" meant we couldn't make any arguments based on it, and Judge Weinstein would not consider it for his decision.

Most importantly, that Zyprexa may have killed Ellen Liversidge's son was not something Judge Weinstein or Lilly considered relevant to the hearing. This is an example of what can happen because our legal system puts everything into categories. Because of the way Lilly framed this particular proceeding—which we were not able to get beyond—the only issues were whether Dr. Egilman and I had violated the Secrecy Order and, if so, what should be done about it. How many people might have been killed by the secrecy and how many might not be killed by the Zyprexa Papers having been made public was not relevant.

Mr. Hayes asked me questions about my and PsychRights' efforts to make information available to doctors and the public about psych drugs and the FDA's failure to do a proper job in investigating the negative effects of certain drugs, as well as drug company dishonesty in presenting information to the FDA. He also asked me about my personal observations of Zyprexa's negative effects on people, and he questioned me regarding my knowledge about Lilly deliberately withholding negative information about Zyprexa from the public and the FDA:

> Q   In this particular case involving Zyprexa, at the time you subpoenaed Dr. Egilman, had you the impression that Eli Lilly had deliberately withheld from the public and from physicians adverse side effects of Zyprexa?
>
> A   Absolutely.
>
> MR. FAHEY: Objection, foundation.
>
> THE COURT: I'll allow it.

When Mr. Fahey objected, it was for lack of foundation, which meant he was saying it had not been established that I had any knowledge that would form a basis for me legitimately testifying on that subject.

Mr. Hayes also asked me about BB.

> Q   BB—describe BB to us. Who is BB? Not give us the name but give us an age, a health situation, their mental capacity.
>
> A   He is probably in his 50s. He has been in and out of the psychiatric hospital many times. He is currently under a full guardianship order that allows the guardian basically complete control. They said that he couldn't even authorize me to look at his records because only the guardian could do that. He also has been subjected to numerous Court ordered involuntary psychiatric druggings.
>
> Q   Now, do you know anything about the other issues with regard to BB's health? Was he an overweight man or an obese man?
>
> A   No.
>
> Q   Do you know if he suffered from diabetes or suffered from high blood sugar?
>
> A   No, I never saw his record.
>
> Q   You have not seen his health records?

A   Correct.

Q   But you do know that he had been the subject of involuntary druggings?

A   Yes.

I had already testified that I had been prevented from seeing his records, but it would have been good for me to repeat that here.

ALAN MILSTEIN'S CROSS-EXAMINATION

This is the entirety of Alan Milstein's cross-examination:

CROSS-EXAMINATION BY MR. MILSTEIN:

Q   I represent Vera Sharav. Again it was your impression there were thousands of cases involving harm to people from Zyprexa, is that right?

A   Yes.

Q   And that Lilly was in the process of settling those cases?

A   Yes.

Q   So why is it that you wanted these documents out there?

A   To protect people from this drug.

MR. MILSTEIN: That's all I have.

PETITIONER'S EXHIBIT 7

Just after lunch, while they were waiting for me to get back (oops), Judge Weinstein wanted to deal with the large number of e-mails Lilly had brought into the court from what I had provided the night before. This included the self-destructing e-mails from Dr. Egilman I had preserved. Judge Weinstein phrased it as "authenticating" the documents. Authentication is different from admitting, and it only means confirming they are genuine and are what they claim to be. My lawyer, John McKay, said he didn't have any problem with just authenticating them, but he didn't want them all admitted without having a chance to go through them himself. Then, the judge just admitted them all, saying we could move to strike documents later. Thus, 1,305 pages of e-mails were admitted in one fell swoop. This meant that in any subsequent briefing, Lilly could cite any of these e-mails. All of the e-mails during the period in question I quote are part of Petitioner's Exhibit 7.

JOHN McKAY'S CROSS-EXAMINATION

After I arrived, John McKay began questioning me. I testified the BB case was a real case and not a subterfuge, and I would spend a considerable amount of time on it. I testified I had told Dr. Egilman to give Lilly a copy of the subpoena immediately. Then:

> Q ... [Y]ou indicated you have considerable knowledge about Zyprexa and other similar drugs. Do you represent clients who are injured by Zyprexa or other similar drugs in litigation for monetary damages?
>
> A No.
>
> Q So your interest is in protecting their interests as patients of the mental system rather than pursuing monetary gain, is that correct?
>
> A The focus of PsychRights and my focus is fighting unwarranted court ordered forced psychiatric drugging but of course when you represent a client, you get all of their interests. So there may be other interests that go along with that. So I represent my clients to the best of my ability.

I testified Lilly's general counsel had received a copy of the subpoena on December 6th, the same day it was issued.

I testified Dr. Egilman's transmittal letter gave all of the items required by the Secrecy Order, including his address, phone numbers, and e-mail address, and Lilly's general counsel had received it the same day I had given it to Dr. Egilman.

> Q If Dr. Egilman—did Dr. Egilman tell you that he had received any word from Eli Lilly in response saying don't send this out, don't send these documents out?
>
> A In what timeframe?
>
> Q Good question. Obviously, not after all of this came up. Let's start at December 6, the day that they received it.
>
> A No.
>
> Q Did they call him back and say don't send this out?

A   He didn't tell me that, no.

Q   The next day?

A   No.

Q   The following day on Friday, did he do that?

A   No.

Q   We know from this case they work Saturday, Sunday, around the clock but anything on the weekend?

A   No.

Q   Monday?

A   No.

Q   So at least after more than three full business days had passed, he had not received any word, they didn't pick up the phone, say don't send these out or wait until you hear from us or anything?

A   He didn't tell me of anything like that.

Q   Was it your understanding that the protective order requires reasonable time to object?

A   Yes.

Q   It doesn't require them to get a Court order keeping somebody from sending it out, it requires that they be given time to object?

A   Yes.

Q   If Lilly, anybody from Lilly had called Dr. Egilman during this period and said don't do anything until you hear from us or we object or anything of that nature, would you have taken the documents from Dr. Egilman had he given them to you?

A   Not if I was aware of that.

Q   And I've already asked you if you were a party to the multi-district litigation. Before this, were you familiar with who the counsel were in this case or specifically did you have—had you had dealings with any of the plaintiffs' or defendant's law firms regarding this matter?

A No.

Q But your information also was supplied on the subpoena and the notice of deposition that was attached to Dr. Egilman's December 6 letter and transmitted to Lilly, is that correct?

A Yes.

Q And they didn't call you on Wednesday or Thursday or Friday or Saturday or Sunday or Monday?

A Correct.

Q The following week you after the documents were transmitted to you by Dr. Egilman and you sent them out, you've described the circumstances of that you were contacted, I believe you received a letter that you received on the 15th from Brewster Jamieson representing Lilly, is that correct?

A Yes.

Q Did he indicate to you an objection to distributing or using these documents?

A Yes, I mean I didn't think it was really a proper way to do it but yes, he did.

THE COURT: What day are you talking about?

THE WITNESS: It was faxed to me I think after business hours the 14th but I didn't get it until the 15th.

MR. FAHEY: I think we have a copy of that if you want to enter it into evidence.

THE WITNESS: I think it's an attachment to my declaration, too.

Q It was faxed to you after the close of business and you received it the follow morning on December 14—you received it December 15th?

A Yes.

MR. FAHEY: Can I put an objection. I think the document when it was faxed speaks for itself. I think that it's P1 or P2 already in evidence.

THE COURT: Let me look at the document. . . .

THE COURT: This is Lane Powell's letterhead?

THE WITNESS: Yes.

THE COURT: Dated December 14, 2006?

THE WITNESS: Yes.

MR. FAHEY: Yes, your Honor.

THE COURT: And that was faxed to you?

THE WITNESS: Yes, I believe it was Chanukah and I went home earlier than I normally do.

MR. FAHEY: The time on it just for the record, the time on the fax strip is 18:05.

THE COURT: 18:05 of what?

MR. FAHEY: On the 14th.

THE COURT: Of what time zone?

MR. FAHEY: Alaska time.

MR. McKAY: So if I—I realize that New York hours and Anchorage hours, to say the close of business was not meant to be a legal conclusion. When I said after the close of business, I thought that was a fair characterization of after 6:00.

THE COURT: It arrived at your office at 6:05 and you saw it the next morning?

THE WITNESS: Yes.

THE COURT: What time?

THE WITNESS: A little after midnight. I should explain, right? When I—we now have a fax machine that automatically scans E-mail stuff to me. So I happened to wake up and check my E-mail and I saw it.

Q When this letter came from Eli Lilly's counsel, first of all, that was the first time that they had either told you by phone or by letter we do not want you to send these documents out, is that correct?

A Yes.

Q At that time, whether they knew it or not the documents had already been not only provided to you but sent out by you?

A Yes.

Q And you've described yesterday that you felt that you were proper in doing that. I'm not going to go over that now again. At that time [were] the documents already out?

A Yes.

Q But you still had other people asking you for the documents?

A Yes.

Q You said when I first asked you the question, you qualified your answer saying you weren't sure that the way they requested it was proper, yes or no?

A Yes.

Q Shortly after this you got a request, just as an example, from Senator Grassley's office for copies of these documents, is that correct?

A Yes.

Q Did you decline to give those to Senator Grassley's office because Lilly had at that time asked you not to even though you say you question whether that was an appropriate request at that time?

A Yes.

Q And in fact, once Lilly communicated to you that it didn't want these documents out, without waiting for a Court order and without challenging this further until this was resolved, you made no further distribution of these documents, is that correct?

A   That's correct.

Q   In fact, since that time you have not assisted or tried to get these documents out to other people, is that correct?

A   Correct.

Here, John was asking questions to establish that the Secrecy Order had been followed to the letter. Judge Weinstein was pretty sharp to ask when "the next morning" I had seen Brewster Jamieson's letter; otherwise, the impression would have been left that I had seen it when I got to the office the next morning. I think I lost some credibility with Judge Weinstein there, but overall, he felt I was very honest in my answers. I'm sure I didn't earn Brownie points for not further disseminating the Zyprexa Papers after receiving Jamieson's letter, because everyone knew I had already accomplished my main objectives for dissemination before Jamieson sent me the letter.

I didn't want it to come out that I had told Dr. Egilman about Jamieson's telephone call a few days before the letter, triggering Dr. Egilman to send me the Zyprexa Papers and then me to send them out. Of course, John knew and was careful not to ask a question about this. The issue was whether anyone else was going to ask the right question to get that information. I don't think Jamieson ever told Lilly he had called me a couple of days before he sent the letter. I suspect he realized the call had been a big mistake. In fact, at the end of the day, that is what caused the Zyprexa Papers to be released. The voice mail alerted us Lilly was moving and Dr. Egilman needed to act fast. In other words, if Lilly had sent the letter before I had received and then disseminated the Zyprexa Papers, I would not have done so until the court in BB's guardianship case said I was entitled to enforce the subpoena. Even if the court had ruled I could enforce the subpoena, Lilly could have moved for a protective order restricting or prohibiting further distribution. I would have fought the imposition of a protective order in the guardianship. What would have ultimately happened is unknowable, but one thing is clear: it would not have happened very fast.

TED CHABASINSKI'S CROSS-EXAMINATION

Ted Chabasinski then cross-examined me telephonically. He established I had not discussed the plan to obtain and distribute the Zyprexa Papers with any of his clients—David Oaks and Judi

Chamberlin or anyone else from MindFreedom, or Robert Whitaker—before I sent the documents out, nor had I told them what I wanted them to do with the documents.

SEAN FAHEY'S REDIRECT EXAMINATION

Sean Fahey then had a chance to question me again on "redirect." I really messed up right off the bat:

Q   Mr. Gottstein, I'm a little confused about two points. One, yesterday you testified that Dr. Egilman told you enough about the documents to know that they were in your words hot, right?

A   I'm not sure that I said that he told me enough about them.

Q   You knew before you had the documents that they were "hot," you said that yesterday, right?

A   I'll take it that I did.

Q   And then—

A   But he didn't really tell me very much really about the documents if anything really.

Q   Enough to know that they were quote hot"?

A   I knew that he had documents that I was interested in.

Q   Because they were "hot"?

A   Yeah.

Of course, one slang meaning of "hot" is stolen, and this was almost certainly the impression Fahey was intending to give.

My actual testimony earlier that day had been:

Q   Could you tell me what Dr. Egilman told you about the Zyprexa documents that were produced in the Zyprexa litigation?

A   He said that he had some documents and they—he really didn't describe them that much but that—you know, that they contained some alarming things in them. I don't really remember the specifics of it or that he really told me very much about them but I got the impression that they were what I would consider hot or very—they would be of great interest to me.

So it was clear from earlier testimony that what I meant by "hot" was "they would be of great interest to me." But had I ultimately left the judge with the impression that I'd thought I was trying to acquire stolen property?

Then Mr. Fahey had me testify about sending the first subpoena out on December 6th, which called for the production of documents on December 20th, and then about the amended subpoena issued on December 11th, which called for production prior to December 20th. I testified Dr. Egilman had sent me the documents on the 12th, and I had sent them out the same day. This was Lilly's main complaint. The Secrecy Order required the notice to Lilly to include "the date on which compliance with the subpoena is requested," and they had been told it was December 20th. I told Dr. Egilman he should give Lilly the amended subpoena for that reason, but he wouldn't. I considered it Dr. Egilman's obligation, not mine, as I'd told Magistrate Judge Mann on December 18th.

In any event, Fahey ended his questioning for Lilly after again making the point, through my testimony, that Lilly had not been told the true date the documents had been requested. At this point, I thought I was through. But that proved not to be the case, with dramatic events soon to unfold.

VERA SHARAV'S DIRECT BY GEORGE LEHNER

Vera Sharav was questioned by a different Lilly lawyer, George Lehner. Vera testified the Zyprexa Papers had been mailed to her on December 14th, she hadn't received them before December 18th, and she had them with her. She also testified she had received word from Robert Whitaker that the documents had been posted; she'd then tried to get them and when she couldn't, e-mailed me for them.

> Q Did you have any conversation with anybody about what these documents may be that were in the mail on their way to you between the 14th and the time they arrived at your home?
>
> A I think you have to understand that many of us were quite aware that the documents had first been obtained in what is now referred to as the Zyprexa 1 trial, the one in which

there were 8,000 plaintiffs and Lilly paid some $690 million which we regard as money to keep the documents out of the public domain. And so there was guessing as to what was in them. We also know from documents from the FDA and from pre-clinical—before the drug was approved as to some of the problems and the fact that diabetes is now an epidemic—

Q What I want to really focus on are the conversations that you had about how you learned what was in these documents. You said you became aware even before the time the documents were on their way to you what was in those documents. How did you become aware of that?

A As I just explained, the adverse events that have been observed in clinical practice—

Q So—

A I would also like not to be interrupted.

Q The first time I did it and I apologize.

A The fact that patients are getting diabetes, cardiovascular dysfunction, hyperglycemia, that people are dying, this is what is really the issue here. People are dying from this drug. So getting documents that validate the clinical evidence is very important to us.

Vera was not answering the question, and Lehner tried to cut her off, but she was having none of that. Vera was brilliant in making almost every answer an indictment of Eli Lilly and the harm it had caused through lying about Zyprexa.

Q The documents arrived in the mail, what did you do at that point with this disc? It's a computer disc?

A I had it. I didn't do anything with it but I got some calls.

Q Did you load it up on your own computer?

A Yes.

Q And you tried to open it?

A Yes.

Q And were you able to open it?

A   Yes, I was.

Q   Did you print up any of those documents?

A   Yes.

Q   And did you then distribute the documents that you printed to anybody or give them to anybody?

A   I read the documents or some of them.

Q   Did you give them to anybody else?

A   I had calls from a couple of press people and two came, borrowed the disks, made copies and returned them. I didn't do it.

Q   Who were these people?

A   *Wall Street Journal,* Bloomberg News. . . .

Q   Were you aware when you received these documents that they had been the subject of what has been described here and you've heard the testimony of a protective order that had been entered into this case?

A   I don't know about a protective order about the case. What I was given to understand is that the documents were obtained legally, that certain legal procedures were undertaken and that's it and I accepted that. And of course by the time I got them, they had been in *The New York Times* so I figured that is the public domain.

Q   Who had given you the understanding that they had been obtained legally? Who told you that they had been obtained legally? You said you had been given an understanding?

A   That would be Jim Gottstein.

Q   So you spoke to Jim Gottstein over the weekend?

A   I spoke to him when I couldn't open the link. Remember. I couldn't, in other words, download it myself so I said can you send me it.

Q   So you called Mr. Gottstein, said I'm trying to download these documents from a link I have, I'm not able to open them and you had a conversation with Mr. Gottstein at that time?

A   Yes.

Q   During that conversation you were led to believe that these documents had been obtained legally?

A   Yes.

Q   And that understanding was provided to you by Mr. Gottstein, is that correct?

A   It was validated in my mind when they appeared on Sunday in *The New York Times* front page, then again on Monday on the front page. Then of course the editorial calling for congressional hearings about the content of the documents and that is really my interest. My interest is the content because the documents document the fact that Eli Lilly knew that the—that Zyprexa causes diabetes. They knew it from a group of doctors that they hired who told them you have to come clean. That was in 2000. And instead of warning doctors who are widely prescribing the drug, Eli Lilly set about in an aggressive marketing campaign to primary doctors. Little children are being given this drug. Little children are being exposed to horrific diseases that end their lives shorter. Now, I consider that a major crime and to continue to conceal these facts from the public is I think really not in the public interest. This is a safety issue.

MR. LEHNER: I move to strike as being nonresponsive to my last question and I would like to ask the court reporter if he is able to—I think I remember my last question. I'll repeat my last question. Nonetheless, I'll make a motion to strike the last answer.

THE COURT: Denied.

Q   Now, I'll ask that this be marked as Petitioner's number 7, please—8.

THE COURT: You are offering it in evidence?

MR. LEHNER: I am, your Honor.

THE COURT: Admitted. (So marked in evidence Petitioner's Exhibit 8.)

Q   Have you had an opportunity to review what has been marked as Petitioner's 8?

A   Yes.

Q   And if I'm correct, this is an E-mail that was sent from Mr. Jim Gottstein to Veracare. Is that your E-mail address?

A   Yes.

Q   And it was sent on Tuesday December 19th?

A   Yes.

Q   And it's copied to Mr. Gottstein and Mr. McKay and Mr. Woodin, somebody at the Lanier law firm, an address emj@lanierlawfirm, an address rdm at the Lanier law firm, gentleman at the law firm of Lane Powell?

A   These weren't familiar to me, of course.

Q   The only name that is familiar on there I take it is Mr. Gottstein?

A   Yes.

Q   He sent you this E-mail on December 19 and if you would read the first two lines of the E-mail.

A   "I mailed you two DVDs with some documents on them pertaining to Zyprexa and have been orally ordered to have them returned to . . . ."

Q   Now you indicated earlier on that you received one DVD. Did you receive one or in fact receive two?

A   2.

Q   So you received two DVDs?

A   Yes.

Q   Have you brought both of these DVDs with you here today?

A   Yes.

Q   You brought both of them here with you today?

A Yes.

Q My questions earlier on about opening the documents loading them on your computer, my understanding was we were talking about one DVD but did you in fact open up both DVDs and copy both DVDs onto your computer?

A I did one. I assumed they were duplicates.

Q Did you look at the second DVD to determine if it was a duplicate?

A No, I didn't have time. This is very laborious.

Q Was there something in the package to indicate to you that these were duplicates of one DVD? Was there anything in the packet itself that suggested that these were duplicates of the same DVD?

A No, I had asked for two copies.

Q Who did you ask for two copies?

A From Jim.

Q So you had a communication with Jim?

A That was the same communication that I referred to earlier. When I couldn't open it and download it myself, I indicated that to him.

Q And what was your interest in having two copies?

A I wanted to take one to the New York State Attorney General.

Q Now, this E-mail goes on and gives the address to whom Mr. Gottstein has been asked to send these DVDs back. And it gives a link to the proposed order in the case. Did you open up that link and read the order?

A No, I didn't, actually because I noticed that he said he was orally ordered and I didn't think that orally ordered was a Court order and I wanted to hear that there would be a hearing or some sort of thing in court and then I would of course follow that. But when it says I've been orally ordered, that sounded peculiar to me. It didn't sound like an order from the Court. . . .

Q Would you go on and read the rest of the E-mail after the address. The address—we'll stipulate the document says to Mr. Peter Woodin. Then it gives a website, but if you would read that paragraph that begins starting with a copy.

A "A copy of the proposed written order is posted at PsychRights—that is the organization and so forth—with a comment about certain language which I strenuously disagree with and we are trying to get eliminated from the signed order.

Q Would you read the next paragraph?

A "Regardless, please return the DVD, hard copies and other copies to Special Master Woodin immediately. If you have not yet received it, please return it to Special Master Woodin when you do receive it. In addition, please ensure that no copies exist on your computer or any other computer equipment or in any other format, websites or FTP sites or otherwise on the internet. There is a question in my mind that the Court actually has jurisdiction over me to issue the order. I believe I came into the documents completely legally but the consequences to me if I am wrong about the jurisdiction issue are severe so I would very much appreciate your compliance with this request."

Q I take it that you did not return the DVD to Mr. Gottstein or to Special Master Woodin, is that correct?

A That's correct.

Q And you did not return the hard copies or any copies of the hard copies that you made to Special Master Woodin, is that correct?

A That's correct.

Q And I take it that you did not check your computer to make sure that no copies of the documents once you had opened them on your computer existed, is that correct?

A That's correct.

Q Why not?

A   In the meantime, I also had word that there would be a hearing.

Q   When did you first get word that there would be a hearing?

A   I don't know the exact date but this was very much in tandem because the first thing I heard, I think the first communication was from your co-counsel.

Q   What's his name?

A   It's not listed here. Fahey. So that there were cross-signals going on and I did see that there would be a Court hearing and I decided to wait for that.

Q   Was there anything in the notice that you received about the court hearing that suggested that the order that had been given here to return these documents was somehow being withdrawn?

A   As I say, this is coming to me not from the Court, it's coming from James saying that he was ordered orally and telling it to me. That is not direct instruction from the Court.

Q   But the same time as you testified, you didn't feel it was necessary to even push on the link here where you could read the order yourself, that was your testimony?

A   It's—

Q   That was your testimony, isn't that correct?

A   Jim posted many documents during this time. I did not go to each one because I was busy also with other things. The Zyprexa thing, as important as it is, was not the only thing that I had to deal with during this period. So no, I did not go and download each of the documents. They were coming fast and furious.

Q   Let's go back and look at the website address to see whether that might have heightened your concern about what this particular document was. That website address reads http://PsychRights.org/states/Alaska/caseXX/Eli Lilly/proposedorder. Is that correct?

A   Proposed order.

Q And you read that? . . .

MR. LEHNER: Just for housekeeping, I think we did move the admission of Petitioner's 8.

MR. MILSTEIN: I have no objection to the admission of the order. I object to his characterization. He characterized the order as saying it required the return of the documents. The order requires no such thing. . . .

Lehner then questioned Vera about posting on her blog the temporary injunction signed by Judge Cogan on December 29.

Q The—why don't you just read that paragraph through to the end, please.

A "See the court injunction several of us received below but the internet is an uncontrolled information highway. You never know where and when the court's suppressed documents might surface. The documents appear to be downloadable at—and it provides two websites that I'm unfamiliar with. Do you want me to read them?

Q No, that is all right. We'll note there are two websites here in the documents but these are website addresses that you wrote put in this document that directs people to go to the documents, is that correct?

A If they chose, yes.

Q And you were aware, however, that the order that you put on the—and posted in this blog and had copied in there suggested that those—suggested or not or ordered that the temporary mandatory injunction requires the removal of any such documents posted at the website?

A We did not have them at our website.

Q You read the order, is that correct?

A Yes.

Q And you understood that the order itself required that the mandatory injunction required the removal of any such documents posted at any website?

A Yes, but I have no control over what people put on their websites.

Q But you did feel that you had not only the opportunity but I guess you felt you had the obligation to direct people toward the websites where you believed at least they could find these documents which the Court had ordered to be removed pursuant to the order of December 29th, is that correct?

A That's correct.

Mr. Lehner then moved on to ask Ms. Sharav about her coordination with me, asking about an e-mail she had sent me.

Q Why don't you just tell us the dates on which this E-mail was sent and received?

A It was sent on Sunday December 17th, the day that the first article on the front page of *The New York Times* appeared and I wrote a note to Jim: "Hope I get the copies." I still hadn't had the copies. "I intend to call New York State Attorney General Andrew Cuomo tomorrow to deliver, then will send to other attorneys general. I think that is ground-breaking. Lilly is finally having a PR disaster. I'd like to coordinate with you when you write up the summary of threats, et cetera. Forward so that I can incorporate into infomail and then P.S. your portrait is a third of the page."

Q After you talked to Mr. Gottstein, you had asked him to send you the DVDs because you had not been able to download them from the link, is that correct?

A Yes.

Q And you signaled to him your intention then that it was your desire to disseminate and spread this information as broadly as you could at this point?

A In particular to the New York State Attorney General after I read in *The Times* what was in the content of the documents.

Q Before you read *The Times*, other than what you testified to earlier about your suppositions of what might be in these documents, did you have any other information that led you specifically to believe—that led you to a specific belief about what was in those documents?

A As I explained, there have been—

Q Let me strike that question and ask more particularly. Did you and Mr. Gottstein when you talked to him that day discuss the content of the documents?

A No.

MR. LEHNER: I have no further questions at this time.

CROSS-EXAMINATION BY ALAN MILSTEIN

It was then the turn of Ms. Sharav's lawyer, Alan Milstein, to ask her questions. While I had not been able to read much of the Zyprexa Papers before being ordered to return them, Vera had.

Q And what did the documents show with respect to the practices of Eli Lilly?

MR. LEHNER: Objection, your Honor.

THE COURT: I'll allow it.

A In my opinion, this is about the worst that I have seen. It borders on indifference to human life. Eli Lilly knew that Zyprexa causes hypoglycemia, diabetes, cardiovascular damage and they set about both to market it unlawfully for off label uses to primary care physicians and they even set about to teach these physicians who were not used to prescribing these kind of drugs to, they taught them to interpret adverse effects from their drug Prozac and the other antidepressants which induce mania and that is on the drug's labels. They taught them that if a patient presented with mania after having been on antidepressants, that that was an indication for prescribing Zyprexa for bipolar which is manic depression. That is absolutely outrageous and that is one of the reasons that I felt that this should involve the Attorney General.

Q What else did the documents say about the way Lilly marketed its products?

A They marketed it, as I said, for off label uses which is against the law. They told doctors—they essentially concealed the vital information that they knew from the prescribing doctors and covered it over, sugar coated it which you can see the sales. The sales of a drug that was approved for very limited indications, for schizophrenia and for bipolar. Each one of these is about one to 2 percent of the population. But the reason the drug became a four and a half billion dollar seller in the United States is because they encouraged the prescription for children, for the elderly, for all sorts of reasons. The drug is being prescribed irresponsibly because doctors have not been told the truth and major study by the National Institute of Mental Health validates this. It's called the CATIE study. It has been published and they corroborate to such a degree the harm that this drug is doing and the other so-called atypical antipsychotics that leading psychiatrists who had been fans of these drugs are now saying we were fooled, we didn't realize. It isn't just weight gain. They are blowing up and it is calling what is called metabolic syndrome, which is a cluster of life-threatening conditions. This drug is lethal and many doctors now say it should be banned.

MR. LEHNER: Let me move to strike the testimony again as being nonresponsive to the question that was being asked.

THE COURT: It shows her state of mind. . . .

Q When you reviewed the documents, was there anything in those documents that you viewed as trade secrets or confidential information the way that phrase is usually construed?

A Absolutely not.

MR. FAHEY: Objection.

A What it showed me was why they were willing to pay so much money to keep them concealed.

MR. LEHNER: Same objection, no foundation for which she could answer that question.

THE COURT: I'll allow it. It shows state of mind.

When Alan Milstein had finished asking Vera questions, Lilly's lawyer had the right to question her on redirect examination. He did not want to do so but asked that the two DVDs with the Zyprexa Papers she had brought with her be turned over to the Special Discovery Master. Judge Weinstein asked whether there were any objections.

> MR. MILSTEIN: We have an objection. That is what this hearing is about, whether or not this Court will issue a preliminary injunction ordering a person who did not act in concert with nor did she aid or abet the distribution of these documents by Dr. Egilman, whether this Court can order this witness to return these documents.

> MR. VON LOHMANN: Let me also just note for the record, your Honor, none of the non-parties have been ordered by this Court or any other Court to return these documents. The January 4th order that your Honor signed also asks simply that they not further disseminate the documents. There is nothing in the January 4th order just as there was nothing in the December 29 order suggesting that the Court is ordering the return of those documents. So what counsel here is asking for is not the enforcement of a prior ruling, what counsel is asking here is something entirely new.

> MR. LEHNER: This Court asked Mr. Gottstein to retrieve the documents and return them to Mr. Woodin, have people return them directly to Mr. Woodin. That request was based particularly with respect to the first order. She says she has them. Other people felt compelled to comply with that request.

> MR. MILSTEIN: It's a temporary restraining order that was issued. If the court issues a preliminary injunction order then Ms. Sharav is prepared to give the documents or the DVDs to the special master. If the Court dissolves the confidentiality order with respect to the documents, as we have requested, or decides not to issue a preliminary injunction, then she can continue to hold on to these documents and she can post them on her website and distribute them to the public which needs to see them to prevent further harm.

THE COURT: The order of December 18 from Judge Cogan orders them returned, I believe.

MR. VON LOHMANN: I believe that order orders Mr. Gottstein to request their return but especially considering none of the parties are named in the order, I think it's certainly—I can't speak for—none of these non-parties even had seen this particular order at the time.

MR. MILSTEIN: And they did not request *The New York Times* return the documents.

THE COURT: We don't have *The New York Times* here. We have your client.

MR. MILSTEIN: I understand that.

THE COURT: Unless you want to represent *The New York Times*—

MR. MILSTEIN: *The New York Times?*

THE COURT:—and expand the orders to include it. We can talk about the witness before us.

MR. MILSTEIN: *The New York Times* is noticeably absent from the request of Eli Lilly to be ordered to return these documents.

THE COURT: I understand. Well, the order of December 18th requires Mr. Gottstein to attempt to recover the documents.

MR. MILSTEIN: To request and she has refused Mr. Gottstein. It doesn't order her. It orders Mr. Gottstein to ask her and she says "no, I'm going to wait until the Court orders me if the court can order me."

MR. McKAY: And Mr. Gottstein complied with respect to that order.

THE COURT: He is here in court. Paragraph 4 says: "Mr. Gottstein shall immediately take steps to retrieve any documents subject to this order regardless of their current location and return all such documents to Special Master Woodin." Come forward, sir. Did you ask the witness to return the documents?

MR. GOTTSTEIN: Are you asking me if I did?

THE COURT: Yes.

MR. GOTTSTEIN: Would you return the documents?

THE WITNESS: I will return them if the Court orders it.

THE COURT: You refuse to turn them over at his request?

THE WITNESS: Yes.

THE COURT: I'm ordering you to turn them over to your attorney to hold them in escrow.

MR. MILSTEIN: I'll do that, your Honor.

THE COURT: Give the envelope to the attorney. Are those all of the documents you have?

THE WITNESS: Yes.

THE COURT: You can seal it. Sign it. We'll hold them in escrow subject to—you'll hold them in escrow subject to the order of the Court.

With that dramatic turn of events, Vera Sharav's testimony ended. She was one brave woman. Chutzpah in the best sense of the word. A true heroine.

RICK MEADOW'S DIRECT BY SEAN FAHEY

The next witness was Rick Meadow, the managing attorney for the New York City office of the Lanier law firm, which had hired Dr. Egilman as an expert witness. On being questioned by Fahey, Meadow testified he had told Dr. Egilman on December 13th not to comply with the subpoena, and Dr. Egilman did not tell him he already had complied. When Meadow found out, Dr. Egilman was fired, but only for the Zyprexa case.

ED HAYES' CROSS-EXAMINATION OF RICK MEADOW

Mr. Hayes, Dr. Egilman's lawyer, started out his cross-examination of Mr. Meadow by establishing the Secrecy Order had been negotiated by the plaintiffs and Lilly, and was then signed by the judge. The Secrecy Order required that before anyone be allowed access to the Zyprexa MDL documents, the person requesting access had to sign what was called an endorsement agreeing to comply with the Secrecy Order.

Mr. Meadow testified Dr. Egilman had tried to add "unless release is needed to protect public health" to the initial endorsement he'd signed (which said he would only use the material for the purposes allowed by the Secrecy Order), but he'd been told that was unacceptable. Judge Weinstein then pointed out that Dr. Egilman had signed another endorsement in which he had added the words "unless this conflicts with any other sworn statement." To this, Meadow testified he'd thought that was okay, based on Dr. Egilman's explanation, and hadn't notified Lilly. Meadow also testified Dr. Egilman was very highly regarded as an expert witness by Mark Lanier, the head of the Lanier law firm, having been a key witness in a number of cases, and Lanier wanted to be able to keep him. Mr. Meadow testified he had observed Dr. Egilman, and in his opinion the doctor was an excellent witness.

That Dr. Egilman had modified the endorsement to permit him to release documents came as a complete shock to me because it showed, or at least suggested, he had intended from the beginning to make public documents subject to the Secrecy Order. I was also surprised Dr. Egilman had gotten access to the database only a couple of weeks before calling me. He'd acted fast. As I write this, I wonder whether he had spoken to Alex Berenson even before being given access to the documents.

ALAN MILSTEIN'S CROSS-EXAMINATION OF RICK MEADOW

When it was his turn to question Mr. Meadow, Alan Milstein got right to the point.

> Q This is Alan Milstein. How many documents approximately did Lilly produce in your litigation?
>
> A Millions, I think.
>
> Q And what percentage of the millions of documents that they produced to the plaintiffs' attorneys in the litigation did they mark confidential?
>
> A I think all of them.

This illustrates the pervasive abuse of the protective order provision in the court rules. Case law is very clear these sort of "blanket protective orders" are not favored and the courts should (1) make clear that only documents for which such protection is warranted are covered and (2) look out for the public interest, because the parties don't. The defendants, such as Eli Lilly here, of course want to keep as much secret as possible. The most important thing to the plaintiffs' lawyers is access to the documents so they can try and make their case. The defendants won't agree to turn them over without secrecy, so the plaintiffs' lawyers usually go along. The public is not given a chance to express their view, so only the courts are in a position to protect the public interest. Normally, they don't. First, they tend to be concerned only about arguments between the people in front of them, so if they have reached an agreement, the courts are unlikely to say, "Hey, wait a minute, we're not going to keep the public from being able to see documents that show great harm without sufficient justification," even though that is exactly what is required. Second, the judges don't want to throw a monkey wrench into getting cases resolved.

Ironically, in a 2000 *Journal of Law and Policy* article, Judge Weinstein had written:

> Mass tort cases usually involve serious public concerns in terms of safety and the prevention of future injuries from harm. Yet, many of these cases terminate in some form of secrecy agreement that reduces protection against future harm to the parties. The private litigant is not required to take into account public safety in vindicating his or her rights. . . .

> If the court is faced with the question of whether to seal documents, it should engage in a balancing test, weighing the interests of the parties in keeping the information confidential against the interests of the public in publishing it. [Jack B. Weinstein, "Secrecy in Civil Trials: Some Tentative Views," *Journal of Law and Policy* 9 (2000): 53–65.]

Mr. Milstein finished up his cross-examination of Richard Meadow by asking about the information in *The New York Times*.

> Q You did have occasion, did you not, to read the *New York Times* articles about the Zyprexa—about Zyprexa which discussed the documents which Dr. Egilman had turned over to Mr. Gottstein, correct?

A   Yes.

Q   And the information in the *New York Times* articles was consistent with the facts that you developed, you and your firm developed during the course of the litigation, correct?

MR. FAHEY: Objection, foundation.

THE COURT: I'll allow it. . . .

A   Yes.

Q   It's your belief, is it not, sir, that at least some of your clients suffered harm because they or their physicians did not have access to the information in the documents that Dr. Egilman produced to Mr. Gottstein? Do you want me to repeat that?

A   Yes, would you please.

Q   It's your belief, isn't it, sir, that at least some of your clients suffered harm because they did not have access to the information in the documents produced by Dr. Egilman to Mr. Gottstein?

MR. FAHEY: Objection, no testimony Mr. Meadow knows which documents have been produced by Mr. Gottstein.

Q   I'll rephrase. It's your belief, sir, that some of your clients suffered harm because either they or their physicians did not have access to the information revealed in the *New York Times* article?

A   Possibly.

This is how Mr. Milstein finished his cross-examination of Mr. Meadow.

It is shocking to me that Mr. Meadow, who represented quite a number of plaintiffs in the Zyprexa MDL charging they had been harmed because Lilly had hidden from doctors that Zyprexa caused diabetes or other metabolic problems, only testified that his clients had "possibly" suffered harm. I wonder whether this is why Mr. Milstein ended his cross-examination when he did. Mr. Meadow, who was supposedly on the side of people who had been harmed by Zyprexa, joined with Lilly in the motion for the injunction against allowing the public access to the Zyprexa Papers. I think this shows how much plaintiffs' lawyers rely on secrecy agreements to more easily obtain the documents they need to achieve the settlements that are so lucrative for them.

This exchange is also another example of Lilly trying to prevent witnesses from testifying about the harm caused by Zyprexa and about Lilly hiding the information from doctors. Mr. Fahey objected there had been no testimony indicating Meadow knew what documents were given to *The New York Times*—but Fahey knew that Meadow did know, since Meadow had provided a list of the documents to Fahey's law firm.

JOHN MCKAY'S CROSS-EXAMINATION OF RICHARD MEADOW

My lawyer, John McKay, also had some questions. Mr. Meadow testified he had never spoken, written, or communicated with me but had copied me on his December 15th letter in which he said that by copying me he was conveying Lilly's demands against me. John also got Meadow to testify that documents could only be classified as confidential under the Secrecy Order if there was a good-faith basis for confidentiality. John then asked about the settlement that had just been reached a couple of weeks before.

> Q   I think you said, and I'm sorry we're having trouble hearing, it's a bit garbled in the courtroom, but did you just say that Zyprexa 2 has settled but it's subject to a confidential order?
>
> A   With my client, yes.
>
> Q   That's what I was asking. How recently did that occur?
>
> A   Do I have to answer these if I am subject to a confidential order?
>
> THE COURT: You do not.
>
> Q   And I apologize because I am not as familiar with the litigation. So the question I have and you can tell me if I'm permitted to ask this given the confidentiality order, my question is simply does whatever settlement that you have entered into on behalf of your client contain a provision that says that the documents that are at issue here may not be released?
>
> A   Judge—. . .

THE COURT: I don't see the relevancy of this, so I'll cut it off. Do you have anything else?

MR. McKAY: No.

Thus, the concern Dr. Egilman had expressed in the first phone call—that he needed to get the documents to me quickly, before he lost access to them because of an impending settlement—proved justified.

FAHEY REDIRECT OF RICHARD MEADOW

Sean Fahey then just had Mr. Meadow testify that his declaration (affidavit) was true when he said he understood the Secrecy Order, and he accepted Dr. Egilman's explanation that his modification of the endorsement was to make sure the Secrecy Order would not preclude him from providing testimony to the FDA or Congress.

ED HAYES' RE-CROSS OF RICHARD MEADOW

Ed Hayes, Dr. Egilman's lawyer, had Mr. Meadow testify the Secrecy Order did not require Dr. Egilman to notify his law firm or any of the plaintiffs' law firms on receipt of a subpoena, and it did not give an address to which reasonable notice had to be given.

DAVID OAKS' TESTIMONY

David Oaks was up last and was questioned by Lilly lawyer George Lehner. He testified he hadn't received any of the DVDs I sent out, nor had he ever posted them on MindFreedom's website, but he had posted links to them.

CROSS-EXAMINATION BY MR. CHABASINSKI

When David was cross-examined by his lawyer, Ted Chabasinski, he reiterated he hadn't received the Zyprexa Papers from me and had immediately taken down links to them once the temporary injunction was issued. He testified he'd never had any conversations with me regarding what to do about the Zyprexa Papers, and he had first found out about them when the *Times* article came out. After David's testimony, the evidentiary part of the hearing was closed (finished).

ALAN MILSTEIN'S RULE 50 MOTION

At that point, Alan Milstein made what he termed a Rule 50 Motion, arguing Lilly had not presented evidence sufficient to establish its right to a permanent injunction.

MR. MILSTEIN: This is Alan Milstein. First, with respect to David Cohen, there is absolutely no evidence that he aided and abetted Dr. Egilman in allegedly violating the protective order. As to Vera Sharav, there is no evidence that she aided and abetted Dr. Egilman in violating the protective order. And as to the Alliance For Human Research Protection, there is no evidence that that organization aided and abetted Dr. Egilman in violating the protective order.

Therefore, this Court cannot enjoin them since they did not assist, aid or in any way are they complicit in the violation of the protective order.

In addition, we'll rely on our brief with respect to the other issues. I think the Court, the foundation of Eli Lilly's motion for TRO and preliminary injunction is that these documents are trade secrets and yet in all of the papers they filed, all they do is say, without any kind of support, that they are trade secrets. And the Court has had occasion to look at the documents or at least has had occasion to read the *New York Times* article. What is abundantly clear is that they are not trade secrets. Lilly in no way fears dissemination of these documents to their competitors, to Merck or to Glaxo.

What Lilly wants to prevent is the public at large, the consumers of its products, from seeing these documents and learning the truth about the product that Lilly produces and the way it markets it.

Documents like that are not confidential and should not be marked confidential. You heard the testimony of the plaintiffs' attorney who said to his knowledge, that virtually every document produced by Lilly in this case is marked confidential.

That is not the purpose of a confidentiality order and it's not what is set forth in CMO-3 and so these documents which are now in the public record and are critically important to save human lives, to prevent human suffering, these documents need to be released from this protective order and this Court should in no way assist Lilly in keeping them from the public.

And so for that reason we say that Lilly has presented no evidence that would allow this Court to issue a preliminary injunction.

THE COURT: As I understand your position, you are not moving yourself or for any of your clients to be released from CMO-3 for the reasons stated in CMO-3 that permit relief.

MR. MILSTEIN: We had filed a separate motion, your Honor. What I have made here is a Rule 50 motion. In addition, we have filed a separate motion as a third-party not otherwise subject to CMO-3 to modify the protective order to allow dissemination of these documents by the three clients that I represent because it is in the public interest to do so and they should not be sanctioned by this Court to be kept secret from the consumers of these products because that can only cause more and more harm.

THE COURT: There are two problems. One, what should be done with respect to the injunction as it relates to your clients? That's what your Rule 50 motion is directed to, correct?

MR. MILSTEIN: Correct. And with respect to that question, it's my position that my clients are not and should not be subject to any preliminary injunction because there is no evidence that they aided or abetted or in any way were complicit in the violation of that protective order.

And so for that reason we say that Lilly has presented no evidence that would allow this Court to issue a preliminary injunction.

THE COURT: I will rule on that. You may brief it if you wish. We'll get a briefing schedule and I'll rule on it in connection with the evidentiary hearing we have just held.

Now, if in addition you want to proceed pursuant to CMO-3 for the independent release of documents, you can do so, but I don't consider sufficiently formal your papers in the present procedures to raise those issues in the clear cut way that they should be raised.

So I'm not ruling on that but if you intend to proceed along those lines as for example was done in the Agent Orange case where the Court issued an order unsealing, then I suggest you do it in a formal way. I'm not satisfied to approach such an important motion by the informal papers I have now.

MR. MILSTEIN: I'll do that. I think if the Court denies the preliminary injunction as to my clients, then we can do what we want.

THE COURT: I don't care what you do. I'm just telling you what your position is.

I think the judge was either disingenuous or hadn't looked at Mr. Milstein's motion, because Mr. Milstein had filed a formal motion. In any event, Judge Weinstein set a briefing schedule, ending February 12th, where the parties could make their arguments about what the court should do based on the evidence that had come in. Judge Weinstein directed Lilly to include in its brief which of the Zyprexa Papers constituted trade secrets or were otherwise entitled to secrecy under Civil Rule 26(c) and how their release harmed Lilly.

At this point, Fred Von Lohmann of the Electronic Frontier Foundation, representing John Doe (Jonah Bossewitch), objected there was no basis for continuing the injunction against his client, to which Judge Weinstein responded he was not going to disturb the *status quo*, meaning things would stay where they were until he made his decision, but Mr. Von Lohmann could appeal that decision if he wanted. An appeal would normally take at least a year, although maybe this type of appeal would be shorter. In any event, the right to appeal was not much of a remedy. The judge did say he wanted to make his decision quickly, which he did.

DR. EGILMAN, THREATS OF CONTEMPT CHARGES, AND THE FIFTH AMENDMENT

Then Nina Gussack, Lilly's chief lawyer in the case, told Judge Weinstein Dr. Egilman's deposition had been postponed until the next week because they needed to obtain deleted e-mails. Ed Hayes said unless Lilly would commit to not seeking criminal contempt, Dr.

Egilman might take the Fifth Amendment at such a deposition. Lilly responded that if the facts supported both civil and criminal contempt, it would pursue both. Judge Weinstein said that "contempt is a quagmire" and "it is a difficult and perplexing series of problems which had occurred to me with respect to [Dr. Egilman]."

Judge Weinstein said he thought the deposition should be restricted to injunction issues, which Mr. Hayes had noted was not an issue for Dr. Egilman because he was not objecting to it being made permanent. Nina Gussack reiterated that Lilly wanted to create a factual record to support sanctions, to which Judge Weinstein responded, "I really must say that we had a fairly full revelation of what he did and said. I don't know what is going to be added."

My lawyer said we wanted to know whether Lilly was going to seek contempt against me and, if so, whether it would be civil or criminal contempt (or both). The judge said Lilly should let us know as soon as possible and then said he thought I had testified fairly, fully, and openly. Ed Hayes said, "to make it simple," Dr. Egilman was going to take the Fifth if there was any possibility Lilly would seek criminal sanctions. The judge then said he didn't think there was any point in having a deposition, and that a letter saying Dr. Egilman was taking the Fifth Amendment would be sufficient. Then there was more discussion about contempt proceedings against Dr. Egilman and me.

> THE COURT: When are you going to inform Mr. Hayes?
>
> MS. GUSSACK: Your Honor, I believe the evidence that we heard yesterday and today provide a basis for seeking sanctions against Mr. Gottstein as well as against Dr. Egilman.
>
> THE COURT: He wants to know if you are going to proceed with criminal contempt. Actually, of course, the concept of criminal and civil contempt is so vague and overlapping that it doesn't make any sense from a conceptual point of view with respect to the issue you are raising. I think anybody who has been in this field knows that but nevertheless, he said that if you don't commit yourself not to proceed with a criminal contempt sanction, his client will plead the Fifth Amendment. So if you don't want to give him that assurance, tell him that immediately, as soon as

you can. He will give you a letter and then that simplifies matters.

MR. McKAY: I'm still asking can they say at this time whether they are not going to pursue criminal contempt against Mr. Gottstein.

THE COURT: They are not in a position to tell you that because he is theoretically in the same position as Mr. Hayes' client.

John then wanted to make sure that my testimony was sufficient and there was no reason to subject me to a deposition and take my computer. Judge Weinstein agreed. The hearing closed with Judge Weinstein saying, "It's a pleasure to have such distinguished counsel before me." With that, John and I headed back to Alaska after watching *Spamalot* on Broadway from the nosebleed section, through most of which I slept.

Ch. 8. Weinstein's judgment

On January 23rd, Mr. Hayes wrote Lilly's lawyer that Dr. Egilman was refusing to testify, under the protection of the Fifth Amendment.

On January 25th, Judge Weinstein issued an order that the motion to declassify would not be heard until after the injunction proceedings and related contempt proceedings, if any, were completed.

On January 29th, Judge Weinstein issued an "Invitation and Order" to Alex Berenson, giving him the opportunity to address my testimony at the January 16–17th hearing. On February 5th, George Freeman, Assistant General Counsel for *The New York Times*, wrote Judge Weinstein that the newspaper respectfully declined the judge's invitation for Mr. Berenson to testify.

On January 31st, Lilly filed its brief in support of continuing the injunction, opening with the following paragraph:

> Dr. David Egilman, an experienced expert witness widely retained by plaintiffs' firms, and attorney James Gottstein, who was willing to manufacture a case in order to issue a sham subpoena, sought to harm Eli Lilly and Company ("Lilly") by selectively releasing documents in a calculated breach of this Court's Confidentiality Order. Egilman and Gottstein both fully appreciated the significance of the Court's Order, but chose to disregard it, in order to advance their own agendas. On the eve of settlement of thousands of cases, with trials in other cases fast approaching, Egilman and Gottstein released a biased selection of confidential documents to the media and collaborators in their plan. They were aided by a group of individuals all too ready to assist them in disseminating these confidential documents quickly and broadly so that Lilly could not cure the harm. Even when caught, members of this group continued to violate the injunctions that followed

From my perspective, this was absurd. Public interest lawyers such as I was are allowed to seek cases to achieve their public interest goals. That is what public interest lawyers do. The complaint that Dr. Egilman only released negative documents is laughable. Of course relevant documents out of the hundreds of thousands of documents had to be selected. Lilly could have tried to rebut them but never even tried—presumably because they couldn't. I certainly didn't consider myself to be disregarding the Secrecy Order. I do think it was fair enough to say a group of people got the Zyprexa Papers out broadly so Lilly couldn't suppress them any longer.

Lilly next said it was impossible to undo the harm to Lilly, and "punishment for the violation of the Court's Orders must await separate contempt proceedings," but the injunction should be continued to prevent further harm to Lilly by everyone who had aided and abetted the violation of the Secrecy Order. However, they weren't seeking such an injunction. They didn't even think of going after *The New York Times*. They also didn't go after Pat Risser, presumably because it was clear they couldn't intimidate him.

Lilly submitted proposed findings of fact that were full of lies, just as it had in previous filings and during the trial. Perhaps the most important lie was the Zyprexa Papers were no longer available on the Internet.

As to the guardianship case, on February 2nd, I filed motions to remove the Alaska Psychiatric Institute from the case on the grounds it was not a party, and to stay (delay) Lilly's motion to intervene, because whatever happened in the Zyprexa MDL might, as a practical matter, resolve Lilly's motion to intervene. That same day, the Office of Public Advocacy, Mr. Bigley's guardian, filed a non-opposition to Lilly's intervention, meaning it had no objection to that intervention.

On February 5th, Judge Weinstein issued an order that everything pertaining to the Zyprexa Papers injunction be put into a different case file than the Zyprexa MDL. It was assigned Case Number 07-CV-0504.

On February 7th, citing the *Times* articles occasioned by the Zyprexa Papers, the United States Psychiatric Rehabilitation Association and a number of other organizations and mental health professionals moved to intervene in the Zyprexa MDL to declassify the Zyprexa Papers and contest the confidentiality designations of documents under the Secrecy Order. Judge Weinstein on February 12th denied this motion to intervene, citing the pending injunction proceedings, but said they could renew the motion after the completion of the injunction proceedings and possible related contempt proceedings. I don't see how this was a proper reason to deny their motion.

On February 7th, Ed Hayes, along with Alexander Reinert, filed their brief on Dr. Egilman's behalf, opposing Lilly's. It was focused on the argument that the court should not make factual findings that would prejudice (harm) Dr. Egilman's defense against Lilly's threatened contempt motion against him. They also argued against Lilly using Dr. Egilman's "taking the Fifth" as giving them "free rein to imagine facts that were not inconsistent with the evidence." The problem they were trying to avoid is that while exercising one's right not to self-incriminate oneself under the Fifth Amendment to the United States Constitution cannot be used against one in a *criminal* trial, it can in a *civil* case.

Because Lilly's proposed factual finding that Dr. Egilman had willfully violated the Secrecy Order would inevitably lead to a contempt finding, they discussed the criteria for establishing contempt. These included that to establish civil contempt, there must be clear and convincing evidence the person had deliberately violated a "clear and unambiguous" court order, while for criminal contempt, Lilly had to prove this beyond a reasonable doubt. As they had in December, they argued that Lilly should be made to actually file for contempt to give Dr. Egilman notice of exactly what he was being charged with.

They pointed out that Lilly should not be allowed to complain that Dr. Egilman had not notified Lilly's Zyprexa MDL lawyers, or the law firm that had hired Dr. Egilman, when the Secrecy Order Lilly had drafted only required Dr. Egilman to notify Lilly—which he had promptly done. Dr. Egilman's brief also pointed out Lilly had not followed the court's order to provide the specific information about why each of the Zyprexa Papers was entitled to court-ordered secrecy.

On February 7th, Ted Chabasinski filed a brief on behalf of MindFreedom, David Oaks, and Robert Whitaker to modify the Secrecy Order, amounting to a full-scale attack on the Secrecy Order for hiding knowledge of the harm caused by Zyprexa from the public. He also documented Lilly's despicable behavior in other cases and pointed out that our system of litigation against giant corporations for damaging people isn't working. Ted's brief made an eloquent plea to Judge Weinstein that he not participate in keeping from the public the great harm Zyprexa was causing individuals diagnosed with mental illness.

On Wednesday, February 7th, my lawyer asked for a short extension—to February 12th—to file our brief, and none of the other lawyers, including Lilly's, objected. Such motions are routinely granted. However, Judge Weinstein denied the extension, saying, "The court's schedule regretfully does not permit further delay," and ordered our brief be filed on Friday, February 9th by 5:00 p.m..

John did a tremendous job getting it filed, digging out damning information surrounding the Secrecy Order, despite Lilly being obstructionist. John was able to reveal that hundreds of documents Lilly had designated as confidential, substantially overlapping with the Zyprexa Papers, had lost their confidentiality in December of 2005. A group of entities known as the Third Party Payors had notified Lilly the documents should be "declassified" under Paragraph 9 of the Secrecy Order, and Lilly had had twenty days to object and then forty-five days after that to file a motion to keep them secret. Lilly had failed to meet the forty-five-day deadline, so under the terms of the Secrecy Order, the documents automatically lost their confidentiality protection. However, the Third Party Payors did not act on the automatic declassification, and Lilly tied them up for years in litigation, preventing the documents' release.

On March 23rd, Tom Sobol—one of the attorneys for the Third Party Payors—wrote to Judge Weinstein about the situation as of that date. He advised the judge that even though the Third Party Payors believed these documents had lost their confidentiality under the explicit terms of the Secrecy Order, "we agreed, in good faith, not to take any steps toward disseminating documents prior to January 16, 2006." This was exactly a year before I was put on trial for releasing what were basically the same documents. In other words, most, if not almost all of the Zyprexa Papers, were no longer protected under the Secrecy Order when I subpoenaed them. By definition, then, my receipt and distribution of them could not have been a violation of the Secrecy Order, and the injunction against dissemination should not have been granted. Nonetheless, Lilly kept being able to tie the issue up, and it was not until three years later, in May of 2009, that Judge Weinstein finally ruled on the Third Party Payors' de-designation motion. By that time, most of the documents had already been introduced into open court, though, and had lost their confidentiality in that way.

To my mind, this demonstrates a couple of things. First is the timidity of many lawyers. Why didn't they simply act on the documents' automatic declassification? They just allowed Lilly to tie them up. Second is the way defense lawyers can stall things in litigation for a long time. As a general rule, litigation is not a speedy process. Utilizing all of the opportunities to assert rights, with the other side having a chance to have their say, and then waiting for the court, followed by the possibility of appeals can really drag things out.

Back in our case, the other bombshell John uncovered was a draft of the Secrecy Order when it was being negotiated, which said Lilly had to be given ten days' notice of a subpoena before documents could be produced. This meant one would know how long a person such as Dr. Egilman had to wait after giving notice before any subpoenaed documents could be produced. Changing it to a "reasonable opportunity to object" had two important effects. First, it meant there was no way to know how long was long enough. Second, and more importantly—and probably why Lilly wanted the change—it meant no matter how long someone waited, Lilly could argue it hadn't been given a reasonable opportunity to object.

John's brief didn't start with these two revelations, however. Instead, he began with a familiar theme brilliantly stated:

> Sometimes a fact is just a fact. Goliath failed to duck in time, though he had reasonable notice. The Israelites were legitimately entitled to the benefits resulting from this, however unanticipated.

After noting Dr. Egilman and I had complied with the terms of the Secrecy Order by giving Lilly a reasonable opportunity to object, John launched a full frontal assault on the Secrecy Order itself. He argued it should be voided

> because it impermissibly reverses the presumption of Rule 26 and allows a party to enforce a secrecy regime on documents of critical importance to the nation's debate on health, safety, and other issues of immense public interest.

Under Civil Rule 26(c), only documents for which there are legitimate reasons ("good cause") for confidentiality should be allowed to be kept secret. The Secrecy Order acknowledges this when it defines confidential discovery materials to mean only "information [Lilly] in good faith believes is properly protected under [Civil Rule 26(c)]." Documents that show a product is extremely harmful to the public, such as Zyprexa, are supposed to clear a very high hurdle if they are to be kept secret. Instead, as John pointed out, just the opposite was true in practice under the Secrecy Order, with Lilly designating everything as secret, even newspaper articles. This was expedient and "greased the wheels" for the parties to the lawsuit but was very detrimental to the public. The practice of allowing defendants to negotiate such secrecy orders has often been criticized by appellate courts.

We also filed a motion to dissolve the injunction because I had gotten the Zyprexa Papers legally, in accordance with the Secrecy Order, and they had lost their confidentiality for that reason.

Lilly filed its reply brief on February 12th, saying the Secrecy Order "was designed to allow the parties to litigate these cases in Court, not the media." Since the Zyprexa MDL lawsuits were over the huge amount of harm caused by Zyprexa, Lilly was essentially saying the Secrecy Order was created to continue to hide this harm from the public. Lilly argued the Zyprexa Papers presented a distorted view of Zyprexa. But again, there was nothing to prevent Lilly from trying to rebut this "distorted view"—something they never did. Instead, they went after the messengers, saying "the First Amendment does not compel this Court to allow the enjoined parties to make a mockery of its Orders."

Lilly argued the proposed injunction was "content neutral," because in such cases free speech concerns are much less than when an injunction enjoins specific content. It seems ludicrous to say enjoining the Zyprexa Papers—which demonstrated the great harm caused by Lilly and by its illegal promotion of the drug—was content neutral. The enjoined contents were specific documents. How much more content specific could an injunction be?

As usual, Lilly misrepresented the facts and law in their reply brief, but I have to say I think it was a pretty good brief. That's why Lilly's lawyers get paid the big bucks. In any event, it seems Judge Weinstein was just indulging the lawyers by having the parties file briefs after the trial. It was clear the briefs had no impact on him because he issued his seventy-eight-page Memorandum, Final Judgment, Order & Injunction early in the morning on February 13th, the day after Lilly's reply brief was filed.

THE DECISION

Judge Weinstein started the decision with:

> This case raises intriguing questions of when it is appropriate to conduct aspects of civil litigation in secrecy, and of what are appropriate limits on civil disobedience by newspaper reporters, forensic experts, and attorneys.

He said the guardianship case had been a pretense to issue the subpoena. While I did take that case to issue the subpoena, the case itself was no pretense and had legitimate objectives in addition to the subpoena.

But, he said, while he was entering an injunction against me and Dr. Egilman, as well as those to whom I had sent the Zyprexa Papers (except *The New York Times*, National Public Radio, and Congressional staffers), "No newspaper or website is directed to do anything or to refrain from doing anything. No person is enjoined from expressing an opinion or speaking or writing about the documents."

Judge Weinstein referred to me as a "conspirator" who as such "should be enjoined to deter further violations of this and other courts' orders."

> Those whose rights have been abused by the conspirators in violation of the court's protective order include Lilly and tens of thousands of plaintiffs and their attorneys who depended upon CMO-3 and sealing orders of the court to effectively prosecute this important litigation without unnecessary breach of the parties' privacy. It is significant that both the [Plaintiffs' Steering Committee] and Lilly support the issuance of the injunction now being issued.

He wrote that individual plaintiffs' medical and personal information had been sealed and should be kept private. However, the Zyprexa Papers contained nothing of that sort, only information about Zyprexa's harm and Lilly's illegal behavior. It wasn't the plaintiffs who wanted that information kept secret, it was Lilly. The plaintiffs' lawyers agreed because Lilly required the secrecy for them to get paid, or more charitably, to make litigating the case much easier.

Judge Weinstein also wrote:

> Conspirators Egilman and Gottstein took particular pains to deny Lilly an opportunity to prevent the breach; they made the documents public before Lilly could move to preclude their release, after they had in effect assured Lilly that it had time to protect itself in court before any release would occur. Egilman, in violation of his obligations under CMO-3, did not inform Lilly about a second subpoena procured by Gottstein that contained an accelerated production date.

I do think Lilly had a legitimate complaint about not being given the amended subpoena requesting the documents be provided before the December 20th deposition date. I just didn't believe it was *my* obligation to inform Lilly. It was Dr. Egilman's, and I had told him he should. My and PsychRights' interest in the Zyprexa Papers was independent of Dr. Egilman's, and I never viewed myself as assisting him, but as both of us having the desire to make known what the Zyprexa Papers revealed. Judge Weinstein didn't see it that way, though as his term "conspirators" indicates.

He went on to say:

> It is not necessary now to decide whether in the long run the public was better served by this conspiracy to flout CMO-3 than by seeking direct and open revelation through amendment of the court's protective order. Even if one believes, as apparently did the conspirators, that their ends justified their means, courts may not ignore such illegal conduct without dangerously attenuating their power to conduct necessary litigation effectively on behalf of all the people. Such unprincipled revelation of sealed documents seriously compromises the ability of litigants to speak and reveal information candidly to each other; these illegalities impede private and peaceful resolution of disputes.

Judge Weinstein was also very critical of Alex Berenson and *The New York Times*, noting Berenson had been "deeply involved in the effort to illegally obtain the documents" and then saying that "affirmatively inducing the stealing of documents is treated differently from passively accepting stolen documents of public importance for dissemination." Judge Weinstein made these observations even though he was not enjoining Berenson or *The New York Times*.

Suffice it to say it did not comfort me that Judge Weinstein said obtaining and distributing the Zyprexa Papers as I had was a crime.

In establishing our "conspiracy" to violate the Secrecy Order, Judge Weinstein cited my testimony that Dr. Egilman's intention in calling me had been to enlist my assistance in disseminating the Zyprexa Papers. He didn't acknowledge my other testimony that while that may have been Dr. Egilman's intent, it wasn't mine—I'd had my own objectives.

The questioning by Lilly, and Judge Weinstein's citing of this testimony, illustrate two things. First, parties in litigation will seize upon snippets of testimony taken out of context to make untrue points. It is easy to see why lawyers do that for their clients, but it is less easy to see why judges do. However, judges are making the case for their decisions just as lawyers are making the case for their clients. Trial court decisions are subject to appeal, and judges like their decisions to be upheld on appeal. However, my sense of Judge Weinstein forty years into his time on the federal bench is he made decisions in the way he thought they should be made, regardless of whether the Court of Appeals might overturn them. I think that was his reputation. Still, he wanted his decisions to be perceived as fair. I leave it for you to judge.

It is important to keep in mind the distinction between "findings of fact" and "conclusions of law." The jury in jury trials, and the judge in "bench trials," determine the facts after weighing the evidence, including the credibility of witnesses. These findings of fact are rarely overturned on appeal and only when the evidence cannot be reasonably interpreted to establish the facts in question. Questions of law, on the other hand, are subject to much more scrutiny on appeal. The higher court takes a fresh look at these and will substitute its judgment for that of the trial court on questions of law, including how the law applies to the facts.

In addition to finding as a fact I had assisted Dr. Egilman in violating the Secrecy Order, Judge Weinstein found I had deliberately misled Lilly and violated the terms of the Secrecy Order by not informing Lilly about the amended subpoena. He also found I had "conspired to steal" the Zyprexa Papers. Again, Judge Weinstein described my subpoenaing and releasing of the Zyprexa Papers as a criminal act.

Judge Weinstein found that people to whom I had sent the documents "began devising schemes to evade court orders to return [them] even before such orders had been issued." Judge Weinstein singled out MindFreedom and associated Judi Chamberlin with MindFreedom's efforts because she was on its board of directors. There was no coordination between Judi and MindFreedom. In fact, as far as I know, Judi didn't do anything with the DVDs. The disks with the Zyprexa Papers didn't reach Judi until sometime in January, by which time she had already been ordered not to disseminate them.

Judge Weinstein cited David Oaks' December 25th e-mail alert informing people where the Zyprexa Papers could be downloaded and stated that the people putting the Zyprexa Papers on the Internet had been "counting on the fact that many courts are closed today [on Christmas]." Judge Weinstein also singled out Robert Whitaker for, according to the judge, offering his gratitude to those who had helped disseminate the Zyprexa Papers in violation of court orders, citing only the following two sentences from a longer January 2nd e-mail sent by Mr. Whitaker: "Kudos should go to others who have helped get this information out—Will Hall, David Oaks, Vera Sharav, MindFreedom. This is a fight much worth fighting."

Bob's e-mail had been in response to me e-mailing an apology to the people to whom I had sent the Zyprexa Papers, including Bob, for getting them in the middle of things without asking them first. Bob's full e-mail reads:

> Dear Jim,
>
> I understand that any email to you may not remain private, and I am writing this with that knowledge. I have cc'd a couple of people—Will Hall, David Oaks, and Vera Sharav—whom I don't think will mind receiving this email. If they want to share it with others who received the documents, that is fine with me.

You mentioned in your email that you were "sorry" to get us involved. Please remember that you have done a very fine thing by getting these documents to *The New York Times*. It will be an act that you will always look back on with great pride.

We are talking about the dissemination of knowledge that will save lives. It isn't simply that Zyprexa causes diabetes. It clearly causes a broader kind of metabolic dysfunction that manifests in several ways—diabetes, obesity, the high blood sugars, etc. In other words, it interferes with the basic processes that allow a person to physically live and thrive.

And this drug, of course, has been marketed to millions of people, including very, very young children. Every single person who stays on olanzapine "indefinitely" will have his or her life shortened. The drug, in essence, gives them a metabolic disease.

The fact that *The New York Times* printed those articles will cause some doctors to refrain from prescribing Zyprexa, and certainly from prescribing it to children. Unfortunately, not all doctors will be so moved, but many will. And that means your actions will have saved many lives, including the lives of many children. And let us remember too that Zyprexa is regularly given to foster children to make them more "manageable"— such children will benefit too from your actions.

There is no finer action than to get out information like this that will achieve such an end as saving the lives of the innocent. I'm sorry that you are having to suffer the expense of defending yourself from Eli Lilly's attacks. The fact that the company would continue in this vein is beyond comprehension; it puts them in the position of wanting to continue to cover up the fact that it has misled the public about the harm that its drug regularly causes. even as it promotes it to children. The immorality of that is mind boggling.

The same kudos should go to others who have helped get this information out—Will Hall, David Oaks, Vera

Sharav, MindFreedom. This is a fight very much worth fighting.

That's all, Jim. Just wanted [you] to know that I'm sorry to know that Eli Lilly is causing you such trouble, but that you should be very very proud of what you did. What you did was the very definition of a moral act: You did the right thing, even though, as I'm sure you probably knew when you did it, it was going to cause you some trouble.

Happy New Year, and thank you for sending me a copy of the documents.

Bob Whitaker

Bob of course was being courageous because he knew it was fairly likely Lilly was going to get the e-mail. And he did incur the ire of Judge Weinstein for it.

The judge also noted in his decision that on AHRP's website, Vera Sharav had posted a link to where the Zyprexa Papers could be accessed, after she had been enjoined from dissemination.

In discussing the law about what a court may properly order be kept secret in discovery, he wrote, "courts balance the need for information against the injury that might result if uncontrolled disclosure is compelled," and that such balancing "requires taking into account litigants' privacy rights as well as the general public's interest in the information." He then went on to say, "Discovery involves the use of [a] compulsory process to facilitate orderly preparation for trial, not to educate or titillate the public." In other words, since the parties are required to provide the information under court rules, they have the right to keep secret information for which there is a legitimate claim for confidentiality. But what about information regarding the massive amount of harm being caused, as Mr. Whitaker described in his e-mail? Do companies have the right to keep this information secret? Information that should never have been secret in the first place?

After asserting the court's power, right, and authority to order such documents be kept secret, Judge Weinstein noted that courts have the inherent authority to enforce their orders and "the equal power to punish for a disobedience of that order," and court orders apply not only to the person(s) specifically identified as being subject to the order, but also to those "in active concert or participation with them who receive actual notice of the order," meaning those who know about and are violating the order jointly with the person subject to the order. Judge Weinstein also wrote that even an improper order must be complied with unless and until it is modified or overturned, and he had the power to order people to return the "stolen" documents. Judge Weinstein held the court could bind non-parties where such action is necessary to preserve its ability to enforce its own prior decisions.

Judge Weinstein held the injunction was "content neutral" because it wasn't the content of the Zyprexa Papers that resulted in the injunction, it was them being unlawfully obtained. He went on to say that even though it was not required, the injunction was the least restrictive means available to protect Lilly, the plaintiffs, and the court. It is easy to understand in what way the injunction was said to protect Lilly, even though that was illusory. It is also easy to understand that the court wanted to protect its power, but how the injunction protected the plaintiffs deserves a little comment. The plaintiffs had agreed to the Secrecy Order in order to move the litigation along. They agreed to maintain the secrecy to facilitate getting paid for the harm they'd suffered by taking Zyprexa, because Lilly insisted on keeping the information on this harm secret. In other words, when they settled, they agreed to accept money for themselves (through their lawyers) in exchange for allowing harm to be inflicted on other, unknowing, victims.

One of Judge Weinstein's justifications for the injunction was the Zyprexa Papers contained information that would give Lilly's competitors an advantage. Even had this been true, which was dubious, it is almost inconceivable these competitors had not obtained the Zyprexa Papers within a few days of their appearance on the Internet, if not in a matter of hours. Another justification Judge Weinstein gave for the injunction was the Zyprexa Papers were a "selective and out-of-context disclosure [that] may lead to confusion in the patient community," saying "what appears damning may, in context after difficult proof, be shown to be neutral or even favorable." Leaving aside the questionable premise that the Zyprexa Papers were misleading, to me this is immoral. Lilly should have been forced to address what the Zyprexa Papers revealed. As Robert Whitaker's e-mail showed, Zyprexa was causing immense harm, including shortening the lives of those who took it long-term. Why shouldn't Lilly have been forced to address what the Zyprexa Papers showed? They were making billions of dollars on Zyprexa every year. Why should the court help Lilly profit through hiding from its potential customers the great harm caused by Zyprexa?

In deciding whom to enjoin, Judge Weinstein created a number of categories, with some overlapping. Lilly did not ask for an injunction against some of the people to whom I had given the Zyprexa Papers, and Judge Weinstein did not enjoin them. Judge Weinstein identified these as Alex Berenson of *The New York Times*; Snigdha Prakash of National Public Radio; Steve Cha, the Congressional staffer for Representative Waxman; my office neighbor, Jerry Winchester; Dr. Grace Jackson; the Alliance for Human Research Protection; Emelia DiSanto; and MindFreedom. Judge Weinstein mistakenly included Emilia DiSanto and MindFreedom in this category. Emilia DiSanto did not receive the Zyprexa Papers from me and, as far as I know, from anyone else. Contrary to Judge Weinstein's finding, MindFreedom had not gotten them from me but had downloaded the Zyprexa Papers from the Internet.

Emelia DiSanto never received the Zyprexa Papers because she asked for them after I had received the letter on December 14th from Brewster Jamieson and I had de-activated FTP access through the Internet. When she called because FTP access wasn't working, I wouldn't send them to her.

Judge Weinstein also did not include in the injunction people who had returned the Zyprexa Papers. These were Dr. Breggin, Steve Cha, my wife (Terrie), Will Hall, Dr. Grace Jackson, Dr. Stefan Kruszewski, Bruce Whittington, Jerry Winchester, and Laura Ziegler.

Lilly had not asked to enjoin Pat Risser, and Judge Weinstein did not enjoin him.

Judge Weinstein did enjoin people against whom Lilly had asked for an injunction who both received the Zyprexa Papers and had not returned them. These were Judi Chamberlin, Dr. David Cohen, David Oaks, Vera Sharav, Eric Whalen, and Robert Whitaker. I hadn't sent the Zyprexa Papers to Eric Whalen; he had downloaded them from the Internet. Lilly's threats against him have previously been described. Judge Weinstein included David Oaks in the injunction because he said it was highly likely he had gotten them from me or someone else, implying David had not testified honestly. However, David testified while he had not gotten them from me, "like apparently thousands of people, we did click and download."

Judge Weinstein did not enjoin any websites, saying it was unlikely the court could effectively enforce an injunction against the Internet, and it would be a dubious manifestation of public policy were the court to attempt to do so. This is worth a comment. An injunction can only be granted to prevent irreparable harm—in this case, purportedly to Lilly. However, if websites were not enjoined because the injunction against them would be impossible to enforce, what harm against Lilly was being prevented?

In spite of this Judge Weinstein permanently enjoined me and Dr. Egilman from possessing or further disseminating the Zyprexa Papers, saying he was not satisfied we could be counted on to return all copies of the Zyprexa Papers we might have in our possession or control. Judge Weinstein held Lilly would suffer irreparable harm for the following reasons:

> Publication of the protected documents has already created irreparable harm to Lilly by revealing its trade secrets, confidential preliminary research, and merchandising techniques. It has made settlement of the remaining MDL and state cases and trials more difficult by creating probable prejudice largely irrelevant to the issues posed by the pending cases and by making impartial juror selection more difficult. It may have adversely affected prospective plaintiffs who may be less willing to sue if their intimate medical problems can be revealed through violation of the court's protective orders. And, of course, flouting the court's orders weakens the judicial structure.
>
> . . . [T]here remains the substantial probability of further abuse of [the Secrecy Order] by the conspirators and individuals who have not returned the protected documents. This danger constitutes a continuous overhanging threat of harm which is likely to affect Lilly's standing in the marketplace and the value of the corporation as a whole.

The idea that potential plaintiffs would be deterred because their sensitive medical records might be revealed is just plain fabrication.

The Zyprexa Papers were released to expose Lilly's lies about Zyprexa being safe. The Zyprexa Papers did not contain any medical records, and there was no reason to think anyone was going to release anyone's medical records.

Then Judge Weinstein wrote, "There has already been sufficient revelation in *The New York Times* so that if Congress, the Food and Drug Administration, or the Federal Trade Commission wish to investigate or act they have grounds for doing so, subpoenaing protected documents as necessary for their purposes." This was the only real acknowledgement in his decision that the Zyprexa Papers exposed information important to the public welfare.

In any event, I lost big-time, with Lilly saying they were going to file for criminal contempt against me, and Judge Weinstein all but ruling I had committed a crime. Lilly had also threatened to seek to have me disbarred. Lilly could even sue me for the loss of income they had suffered as a result of me subpoenaing and releasing the Zyprexa Papers. To say all of this was alarming would be a gross understatement. However, even if all of this were to happen to me, I felt it would be worth it because I had saved thousands of lives, if not tens or hundreds of thousands, and improved the lives of more. There was no doubt Lilly could crush me financially. I was extremely worried about all of this, of course, especially its impact on my family. At that point, having achieved the objective of exposing the great harm caused by Zyprexa, my goal was to avoid or reduce these extremely negative consequences. I definitely was going to appeal Judge Weinstein's decision, which had to be done within thirty days. And it looked like Lilly was going to seek criminal contempt against me in roughly the same time frame.

In the meantime, things were heating up in Bill Bigley's guardianship case, with a status conference scheduled for the following Thursday, February 22nd.

Ch. 9. *Alaska v. Lilly,* Capitulation, and Betrayal

Since Judge Weinstein had permanently enjoined me from possessing or disseminating the Zyprexa Papers, on February 15th Lilly filed its opposition to our motion to stay (put on hold) Lilly's motion to intervene in the guardianship case. That same day, API filed its opposition to our motion to drop API from the case. On February 21st, I filed (1) a reply to Lilly's opposition to having its motion to intervene stayed, (2) a reply regarding dropping API from the case, and (3) a response to API's "Motion to Appoint a Visitor." With respect to the last, I argued that having a court visitor who was paid by OPA to make recommendations about whether to terminate or replace OPA as guardian was a conflict of interest, and such a visitor was not likely to be neutral or to fully explore alternatives.

The status conference in the guardianship case was scheduled for the next day, February 22nd. I filed a withdrawal of my motion to disqualify Master Duggan, because I had been convinced he was not regularly bypassing the *Myers* decision by authorizing guardians to consent to the drugging of their wards against the wards' will. As it turned out, my decision was premature. Before the status conference, the head of OPA suggested to me that I not represent Mr. Bigley as vigorously as I was. I was outraged and offended and of course rejected the suggestion, but to me what it most clearly showed was that the lawyers appointed to represent people against whom guardianship proceedings are filed were not expected to put up a vigorous defense on behalf of their supposed clients. However, I do know some who do.

Under Alaska statutes, the Superior Court has jurisdiction over guardianship cases in Alaska, which are randomly assigned to Superior Court judges. But pretty much all the cases are referred to the Probate Master, who makes recommendations to the judge. At that time, as with involuntary commitment and forced drugging cases, virtually all guardianship cases in Anchorage were referred to Master Duggan. Except for certain procedural questions, Master Duggan could only make recommendations to the Superior Court judge. Objections to the master's recommendations could be made to the Superior Court because technically, the Superior Court judge assigned to the case made the decision. However, the lawyers assigned to people facing involuntary commitment and forced drugging orders virtually never objected to whatever recommendations the Probate Master made. I suspect the same was true for guardianship cases, but don't know for sure. Lawyers in private practice are appointed, so it may be different. A request for a new trial could also be made, but judges rarely granted them.

Superior Court Judge Christen decided to handle all the motions rather than have Master Duggan make recommendations. My guess is, based on her experience of me in Faith Myers' case, she knew I would be objecting to Master Duggan's recommendations and thought she might as well handle it from the outset. Judge Christen was the presiding (head) judge of the Anchorage trial courts at that time. She was appointed to the Alaska Supreme Court two years later and then to the Ninth Circuit Court of Appeals just three years after that, in early 2012.

The status conference was fairly contentious. I wanted all of Mr. Bigley's API records, and API didn't want to give them to me because they were so voluminous, since he'd had almost seventy admissions at that point. They didn't want to go into storage to retrieve his older records. To me, though, the first few admissions were crucial to understanding what had put Bill on the path of becoming a lifelong psychiatric patient, and the last few were crucial for understanding his current situation. It is important to note that psychiatric hospital records should not be taken at face value because they are written in a way to support involuntary commitment and forced drugging. There is a legal principle that documents prepared "in anticipation of litigation" are not to be given a lot of credibility, but the courts tend not to recognize psychiatric hospital records as falling into this category. Nonetheless, there would be good information in the records. I could see Judge Christen was not inclined to order API to provide all the records, even though Mr. Bigley was entitled to them, so I agreed to accept the records for his first two admissions, all of the summaries, and from June 2004 to the present.

When I received the records a short time later, I confirmed Bill had indeed been drugged with Zyprexa as recently as a week before I'd had the subpoena issued. Then, Bill had been hauled into API for his sixty-ninth admission the same day as the status conference, and during that admission he had been held down and given at least one shot of Zyprexa against his will.

As for the Zyprexa Papers, in a decision I regret, I felt I needed a high-powered New York law firm able to handle the appeal and contempt cases at the same time. A law school friend of mine recommended a lawyer who worked for the firm Bracewell & Giuliani (Bracewell, for short), as it was named at that time. When I called Bracewell, their primary concern was whether I could pay. Their attorney rates ranged from $345 to $695 per hour, and they insisted on a $50,000 retainer. Three attorneys worked on my case in what seemed like one for the price of three. They prepared the appeal paperwork, and their billing was breathtaking. I hired them on March 2nd, and their bill for March *just to file the appeal* was over $66,000! This wasn't for the briefs; it was only for the paperwork to start the appeal. As it turned out, their concerns about me being able to pay were completely justified, and I had to find someone else.

Based on Laura Ziegler's recommendation, I was able to hire Steve Brock of Berkman, Henoch, Peterson & Peddy for the appeal. Steve wanted to represent me *pro bono*, but his law firm wouldn't go for it. I greatly appreciate all the work Steve did on my behalf.

From virtually the moment Judge Weinstein's decision came out, setting the stage for Lilly to obtain a contempt judgment against me, John McKay went to work trying to reach a settlement. I had mixed feelings about settlement because I knew the great value of the public platform I had for publicizing the tremendous harm being caused by psychiatric drugs in general, and neuroleptics such as Zyprexa in particular. Lilly bringing contempt charges against me could continue to give me a platform that would reach a large number of people. On the other hand, the prospect of defending against contempt charges with the potential of being put in prison while having to deal with the appeal at the same time was, to say the least, very concerning. I was looking at financial ruin from the legal fees alone and had a family to consider. Lilly was also threatening to ask the Alaska Bar Association to take away my license to practice law. I was therefore open to a settlement but was willing to do only so much.

One of Lilly's goals was to shut me up, but we tried to convey that Lilly was no more my target than any of the other drug companies making psychiatric drugs, and pointed out that keeping this going forced me to focus on Lilly. In a March 21st letter to Lilly, John also pointed out the facts would look a lot different at a contempt trial, with me being able to testify Mr. Bigley had been drugged with Zyprexa against his will shortly before I'd had the subpoena issued. John also pointed out most of the Zyprexa Papers had lost their confidentiality almost a year before I'd had them subpoenaed as a result of the Third Party Payors' de-designation under the Secrecy Order. John said Lilly was at a high point, with Judge Weinstein having vindicated its position and painted Lilly as a victim, while Lilly pursuing me would be a public relations negative. John wrote: "Without wishing to seem flippant on this very serious matter, Mr. Gottstein's feeling is that Lilly enhancing his stature by making him a martyr will be appreciated." John also wrote that "giving up a goldmine of publicity for [the PsychRights] cause in order to extricate himself from the problems created when he found himself with the Zyprexa Documents before Lilly objected, is not an easy choice."

The elements for settlement would be that Lilly stop pursuing the contempt charge and seeking the revocation of my law license, and that I drop the appeal. I had talked to Alaska's Bar Counsel, the person in charge of ethics enforcement against lawyers, and while he couldn't make a ruling without a complaint being filed, he wasn't very concerned about the situation. Even though the prospect of a criminal contempt charge was extremely worrying to me, I thought it unlikely because of the negative publicity about Zyprexa Lilly would likely get from filing such charges. That didn't stop me from worrying about it, though, and even if the odds were pretty low, the consequences to me would be severe if they did file contempt charges and win. Even if they didn't win, the cost of defending myself would probably bankrupt me.

Lilly also wanted to restrict my ability to subpoena their documents in the future. This was probably not allowed under lawyer ethics rules, and it proved extremely complicated, with John and Lilly going back and forth about it. Lilly also insisted I pay money to a designated charity. They wanted $250,000, which wasn't even in the realm of possibility for me, and we responded with $50,000.

Dropping the appeal was a big deal for me because I didn't want Judge Weinstein's decision that I had acted illegally to stand, and I hoped I would win the appeal. I knew unless his decision was reversed on appeal, for the rest of my legal career it would be dredged up to argue I was not trustworthy. This has proven true. Fortunately, except perhaps in one case, it has never seemed to negatively affect judges' decisions, I think because of my reputation and these judges' experiences with me. On the other hand, avoiding the expense of the appeal was a significant issue for me, and winning would be an uphill battle. I figured the appeal would cost at least $50,000 more than I had already paid, so $50,000 to resolve everything, including potential contempt charges and a challenge to my law license, made economic sense.

Shortly after John sent the letter to Lilly about possibly settling, I was contacted by a journalist who wanted to know what I thought about Lilly's argument that the Zyprexa Papers had been taken out of the context of a much larger production of documents. My response included the following, to which the journalist then asked Lilly to respond:

> That is no excuse for hiding them. Of course [Lilly] buried the plaintiffs with fifteen million pages of documents, and so of course you want to go through and find the relevant ones. And if they've got other information that they say rebuts it, then they can bring that up, and the public will benefit by a public discussion of that, of all the facts, rather than hiding the facts. And they've also said that they're under, that this [Secrecy Order] prevents them from really bringing in these other documents, and that's not true. They have every right to release any of the documents they want to. And the [Secrecy Order] even says so. . . .

> Then, if you talk about the subpoena that I had issued and what went wrong, is that Lilly waited too long. They had, under the [Secrecy Order], they had the right to be notified and given a reasonable opportunity to object. And also, Dr. Egilman was required to cooperate with Lilly. And all they had to do was call Egilman, or write him, or e-mail him, or fax him, they had all those ways of communicating with him and instructing him to object to the subpoena. At that point, which is what I really expected to happen, is, I would have been arguing in the Superior Court in Alaska why my client should have access to these documents, and Lilly would be arguing why they shouldn't. And the court would decide. So from that perspective what happened, what went wrong, is that Lilly didn't object in time. They had a reasonable

> opportunity to object, and then didn't. And once I got
> them, as far as I was concerned, they had lost all
> protection.

I wasn't making things easy for John, and on April 6th, one of Lilly's lawyers wrote to him, complaining that I was on a "high visibility offensive" and saying the above quote had caused Lilly to direct them to cease negotiating and, instead, promptly file a contempt motion. He then wrote that he doubted there was any way to salvage the negotiations, but John should feel free to make any suggestions.

So that was definitely a mixed message, and John continued to engage them in long-drawn-out negotiations while we put the appeal on hold. I suspect Lilly never had any intention of filing contempt charges against me, because things would look a lot different and they would suffer bad public relations, but at the same time, they wanted to intimidate me into being quiet. To my shame, they were successful about a year later.

On September 7, 2007, Dr. Egilman settled with Lilly. He paid $100,000 to a charity and avoided contempt charges being brought against him. It was rumored he had a backer who funded his payment. Most of the settlement was secret, and I am pretty sure Dr. Egilman agreed to never communicate with me again. I think this because I have called a few times over the years and e-mailed once or twice, receiving no response. I do see he has continued to do good work trying to protect the public from unscrupulous giant companies.

On January 30, 2008, Alex Berenson published a story in *The New York Times*, titled "Lilly in Settlement Talks with U.S.," in which he reported federal prosecutors were discussing a settlement of a secret civil "whistleblower" case and criminal investigation into Lilly's illegal marketing of Zyprexa that could result in Lilly paying more than $1 billion. Mr. Berenson reported the people involved in the investigation said it had "gained momentum" after *The New York Times* reported on the Zyprexa Papers I'd subpoenaed and released to him in December of 2006.

Under the federal False Claims Act, anyone can sue on behalf of the federal government for fraud committed against the federal government and receive 15–30% of the recovery, if any. These cases are filed in secret to prevent jeopardizing a criminal investigation that might already be underway. They are only supposed to be kept secret for thirty days, but the secrecy is almost always extended, and on average they're kept secret for over a year. A number of whistleblowers had filed such secret lawsuits about Zyprexa, the first of which was in 2003, so by 2008, that one had been kept secret for more than four years. Mr. Berenson found out about these settlement discussions because one of the lawyers involved inadvertently e-mailed him when he meant to e-mail someone involved in the case whose last name was also Berenson. Oops.

Ten states, including Alaska, had sued Lilly over the harm Zyprexa caused that Lilly had kept secret, resulting in them having to pay extra Medicaid costs, and another thirty-three were jointly investigating Lilly about Zyprexa. *Alaska v. Lilly* was the first of these set to go to trial, in early March of 2008. That made it very important because it could set a precedent for all of the other states. I had planned to be pretty visible during the trial and expected to generate a fair amount of news coverage in furtherance of PsychRights' mission. For example, I thought it the height of hypocrisy that the state of Alaska was suing Lilly for Zyprexa causing extra Medicaid costs but was still drugging people with Zyprexa against their will. *The New York Times* was sending Alex Berenson to cover the trial, and he wanted to research a story about me and my PsychRights work while he was in Anchorage.

Lilly insisted I neither attend the trial nor talk with any media people about the trial, especially Mr. Berenson, if they were going to settle. They continued to threaten me with contempt charges. I was very reluctant to agree and certainly wasn't going to go along without an agreement to settle all of the things they had hanging over my head. John and Lilly kept going back and forth on a potential settlement. We finally came to an agreement on the terms, but by then the trial in *Alaska v. Lilly* was imminent and Lilly said it wanted to focus on the trial and put the settlement in final written form after that. We agreed to put off finalizing and signing the agreement until after the trial. I lived up to my end of the bargain by not attending the trial and not talking to any reporters about it. I told Alex Berenson about what was happening, and he was disappointed but understood.

The trial for *Alaska v. Lilly* was split into two parts, the first part being liability, which was whether Lilly had done anything wrong that harmed the State of Alaska. If so, there would be a second part to decide how much money Lilly had to pay (damages). This is called "bifurcation" (splitting in two) and is not all that unusual, but it was done in *Alaska v. Lilly* because the State of Alaska had not yet given Lilly a copy of its Medicaid database from which the amount of damages could be calculated. Alaska also had not officially informed Lilly how much it was seeking for in damages, but Assistant Alaska Attorney General Ed Sniffen said that damages could rise to the hundreds of millions of dollars if the state won and was awarded treble (triple) damages for the cost of care it had provided.

After a couple of days of preliminary matters and jury selection, opening statements were made to the jury on March 5, 2008. Being the plaintiff, the State of Alaska went first, with an opening statement from Mr. Allen, one of its attorneys. One of the things he told the jury was that the *Times* stories about the Zyprexa Papers I had subpoenaed and released in December of 2006 had caused the Food and Drug Administration to write Lilly just a few weeks later about failing to provide it with important safety information, resulting in inaccurate information on Zyprexa being given to doctors and patients.

In Lilly's opening statement, Nina Gussack—who had also been involved in the Zyprexa Papers trial against me the previous year—pointed out that while the State of Alaska was suing Lilly for the harms caused by Zyprexa, it was still going to court to force patients to take Zyprexa against their will. I'm afraid I had given Lilly this point during our settlement negotiations.

Following opening arguments, the trial was conducted over fourteen days, revealing very damaging information about Lilly not telling the FDA or doctors about the harm it knew Zyprexa caused. The exhibits introduced into evidence in open court by the state included some of the Zyprexa Papers, which lost whatever secrecy protection they might still have had as a result. There were also a number of exhibits that as far as I know were not part of the Zyprexa Papers. Some of the most interesting were the "call notes" of Lilly's sales representatives, documenting their interactions with doctors.

For example, in the very first such exhibit, on May 17, 2002, drug representative Margaret Williams wrote she had reminded the doctor that Zyprexa "is a great mood stabilizer, especially for patients whose symptoms were aggravated by an SSRI." "SSRI" stands for selective serotonin reuptake inhibitor, a class of drugs marketed as "antidepressants." It has come out in the last few years that antidepressants basically don't work, and cause fairly serious negative effects, including sexual dysfunction that for many people doesn't get better even after quitting the drug. Also, for many they are very difficult or impossible to quit.

One very interesting thing to me about this call note is Lilly acknowledges SSRIs cause some people to become manic. This was well-established even then but suppressed by mainstream psychiatry and the drug companies. This continues. The other interesting thing is Lilly suggests the response to someone who has become manic as a result of a so-called anti-depressant is not to withdraw the person from that drug but to add Zyprexa. This process of someone becoming manic from an SSRI and then being put on a neuroleptic such as Zyprexa, which converts them from a person with what was likely a temporary problem to a lifelong patient (and customer) with serious mental illness is well documented in Robert Whitaker's book *Anatomy of an Epidemic*. That drug companies, such as Lilly did here, would recommend adding their neuroleptic drug is understandable, since they profit from doing so, but that doctors ignore common sense and go along with this is extremely disturbing.

It is very important not to stop SSRIs abruptly. It is also well established that SSRIs cause some people to suicide or become violent, even in some cases to commit murder, and the most dangerous time is when there is a dose change. This includes increasing, decreasing, starting, or stopping an SSRI. *Medication Madness*, by Dr. Peter Breggin, documents this effect for SSRIs as well as other psychiatric drugs that cause people to commit otherwise inexplicable violence. If you want to quit an SSRI, it is generally recommended to taper off slowly. Pay close attention to whether you're experiencing an extreme mood state and, if so, go back up to the dose where you didn't. Since it is very hard for most people to recognize when their thinking is not right, I believe it is very helpful to enlist someone you trust to observe what is going on and let you know if they feel your thinking is getting questionable. Dr. Breggin also wrote a book about getting off psychiatric drugs, *Psychiatric Drug Withdrawal*, and there is a very good free download on the Internet titled *The Harm Reduction Guide to Coming Off Psychiatric Drugs*. Will Hall was one of the principle authors of the *Harm Reduction Guide*.

The call notes introduced in the Alaska trial also document calls to doctors where Zyprexa was recommended as a "mood stabilizer" for patients who "fail" on an SSRI. The Lilly sales representatives told doctors that Zyprexa is very safe, which is a lie.

In a June 27, 2002 office visit by Kristen Clouthier to the Anchorage Neighborhood Health Clinic office, a Pam Engle was concerned about Zyprexa because of weight gain by her patients. Kristen noted: "But we discussed proper diet and the fact that if patients are feeling better they will be able to actually exercise." This was a classic example of what Alex Berenson wrote in his Zyprexa Papers exposé regarding Lilly deflecting concerns about weight gain caused by the drug.

That same day, Kristen visited Dr. Scott Mackie's office, bringing a Zyprexa bag of goodies, including chocolates and dried fruit, and showing him fishing pictures (fishing is big in Alaska). In a July 11, 2002 visit to promote Zyprexa, the call note states Kristen "discussed elderly and SSRI patients." Zyprexa was used on elderly patients who had not been given any diagnosis of mental illness, especially in nursing homes to disable them so they were easier to manage. This is still rampant in spite of various exposés about this form of elder abuse, although as I understand it, these days it is more likely to be Seroquel or Risperdal than Zyprexa. There is a "black box" warning on all of the second-generation neuroleptics, including Zyprexa, that they double the mortality risk in the elderly. In 2011, the Inspector General of the United States Department of Health and Social Services released a report about the rampant drugging of the elderly with neuroleptics in nursing homes. This report criticized the Centers for Medicare and Medicaid Services (CMS) for paying for this off-label prescribing, which is not allowed under Medicare. CMS astoundingly responded it did not have the authority to enforce the restriction against paying for prohibited off-label prescriptions.

In another call note, on July 12, 2002, Kristen responded to a question from Dr. Timothy Coalwell about Zyprexa causing diabetes by saying that it didn't—it might, she said, increase appetite, which could lead to obesity, but no causal relationship had been established between Zyprexa and diabetes, and anyway, there was a high risk in this population, she said. All of this was untrue. Dr. Coalwell asked for a confirmation letter from Lilly, but Kristen said he was satisfied with her response instead. The call notes entered into evidence cover a couple of years and continue in this vein for twenty-one pages, showing the Zyprexa reps deflecting a lot of questions about weight gain and diabetes.

The state tried to introduce an e-mail from the then-incoming CEO of Lilly, encouraging sales reps to discuss using Zyprexa in children and teenagers, but the judge disallowed it because illegal off-label promotion was not part of the case he'd allowed to go forward.

The trial ground on, with Lilly taking a beating. This included the revelation that the Japanese government had required Lilly to issue a warning about Zyprexa causing diabetes, which caused a 75% drop in new patients being prescribed Zyprexa there, yet Lilly had not given doctors in the United States a similar warning.

On March 14, 2008, Bill Bigley was facing yet another involuntary commitment and forced drugging trial in the same courthouse where the *Alaska v. Lilly* trial was being held. I wasn't representing Bill in that particular case, but I had gotten the public defender who was representing him to ask Bill whether he wanted it open to the public, and he did. Bill always wanted his trials open to the public.

I let Alex Berenson know about the trial, and he attended. I was there too, and it is the only time I have talked to him in person. He wrote about both the *Alaska v. Lilly* and the Bigley trials in an article titled "One Drug, Two Faces," published by *The New York Times* on March 25, 2008:

> Two courtrooms, two floors of the Nesbett Courthouse, two views of Zyprexa.
>
> In Courtroom 403, lawyers read corporate memorandums to a jury that must decide a lawsuit brought by the state of Alaska, which claims that the drug maker Eli Lilly hid the dangers of Zyprexa, Lilly's best-selling schizophrenia medicine.
>
> At the same time, in Courtroom 301, William Bigley had his own opinions on Zyprexa, and all the other drugs he has taken since 1980 to battle demons that only he can see. On this day, March 14, a state court judge would decide whether Mr. Bigley should be held for 30 days in a psychiatric hospital.
>
> Mr. Bigley, 55, told the judge that the drugs were "poison" and that he did not need them. "I'm fine," he said. His words were sadly undercut by his regular pronouncements that he knows President Bush, owns a

private jet and has seen flying saucers. Of all the facts at issue in the two courtrooms, one is beyond debate. Mr. Bigley is not fine.

Even so, Mr. Bigley's hearing—which had an unexpected outcome—offered a textbook illustration of the agonizing choices faced by mentally ill patients as they consider taking Zyprexa and similar medicines, called antipsychotics.

By calming the hallucinations and delusions that plague people with schizophrenia, drugs like Zyprexa allow many patients to live outside psychiatric institutions.

But the documents being discussed in Room 403 offered plenty of evidence that Mr. Bigley, whatever his delusions, has good reason to dislike the medicines. . . .

Mr. Bigley's case illustrates why psychiatrists and patients feel they have no choice but to use Zyprexa, whatever its side effects. Mr. Bigley, a thin man with greasy black hair, cloudy eyes and a salt-and-pepper beard, has been hospitalized more than 70 times since his first breakdown in 1980.

Psychiatrists say he has paranoid schizophrenia with symptoms of mania. Over the years, he has been medicated with Zyprexa, Risperdal, Haldol, Thorazine and many other psychiatric drugs, despite his objections.

Exactly how many times Mr. Bigley has been put on Zyprexa over the years is unclear. But medical records from his hospitalization in December 2006 refer to his complaints that Zyprexa was making him hungry—a common side effect. Psychiatrists took him off Zyprexa and gave him Seroquel, another antipsychotic, in its place. . . .

The records also show that neither Zyprexa nor any other drug has given Mr. Bigley any lasting relief, and that he always stops taking his medicines after being released from the hospital. Unmedicated, Mr. Bigley is jittery and quick to anger. In conversations with a reporter, he was nearly incomprehensible, spewing complaints and curses about the way he is treated. But Mr. Bigley has never been known to be violent or suicidal. Despite his psychosis, he has survived Alaska's harsh winters. He bounces among apartments, group homes and the Alaska Psychiatric Institute, the state-run mental hospital in Anchorage, mumbling about the Secret Service and other favorite topics to anyone who will listen.

But he makes one point with absolute clarity: He does not want to be medicated or hospitalized.

On March 14, he repeated that request to state court Judge Jack W. Smith, who was hearing the psychiatric institute's request to confine him.

There was little reason to believe that Judge Smith would side with Mr. Bigley. Hearings like his usually last only a few minutes. Psychiatrists and advocates for the mentally ill say that judges prefer not to second-guess doctors and typically rubber-stamp the requests of hospitals to confine and medicate patients.

As he sat before Judge Smith, Mr. Bigley—who had asked that his hearing be open to the public—hardly seemed like a good candidate for release. He fidgeted and interrupted the proceedings as his lawyers shushed him. He had been brought to the Alaska Psychiatric Institute on Feb. 23, after squabbling with housemates at his group home, where a resident called the police.

Dr. John Raasoch, a doctor at the hospital who treated Mr. Bigley, said that Mr. Bigley had irritated the staff and other patients.

"He's yelling, swearing on the unit, he hit the door," Dr. Raasoch said. Antipsychotic medication would calm Mr. Bigley and make him more cooperative, the doctor said.

"There's no point to have a psychotic individual in the hospital and not be able to treat him," he said. "I think he's suffering severe distress."

But Judge Smith appeared worried about both the side effects of antipsychotic medicines and that Mr. Bigley's history suggested he would not benefit from them.

"We're getting a short-term fix that doesn't change Mr. Bigley's underlying condition," he said.

Under Alaskan law, a person cannot be forced to take medicine against his will simply because a psychiatrist says he is unhappy or delusional. Mr. Bigley could be confined and medicated only if Judge Smith found he was violent, suicidal or a grave danger to himself because of his mental incompetence.

Mr. Bigley was not violent or suicidal, Dr. Raasoch said. But the doctor said he was in grave danger because he might irritate other people, including police officers, to the point where he might end up being hurt.

"He's very inappropriate," Dr. Raasoch said. "He gets up in people's faces. I think the majority of people would just punch him."

Elizabeth Brennan, the public defender representing Mr. Bigley, agreed that Mr. Bigley can be difficult. But Mr. Bigley is not in grave danger simply because he is a nuisance, and confining and medicating him would not help him, she said.

"The hospital has not shown that treatment will improve him," she said.

After nearly an hour of testimony, mainly from Dr. Raasoch, Judge Smith appeared troubled by the thought of confining or medicating Mr. Bigley against his will.

"It sounds like aside from getting in and out of the hospital, he gets by," the judge said. "That's a choice that he should be allowed to make."

And so Judge Smith ordered the hospital to release Mr. Bigley, though he acknowledged that Mr. Bigley was likely to be picked up again in a few weeks, or months at most.

"I don't find by clear and convincing evidence he's gravely disabled," Judge Smith said.

Though the decision was unusual in such cases, Mr. Bigley did not seem overly surprised, or even pleased.

"There's nothing wrong with my head in the first place," he said to the judge, inserting a seven-letter epithet. Within a few seconds, he began to hector Steve Young, his state-appointed guardian, demanding that he be given a hotel suite. "He's going to give me a dirty place," Mr. Bigley complained.

With that thought, Mr. Bigley headed for the street, his brain in chaos but his body free from the side effects of the medicines he will not take. One floor up, lawyers for Lilly and the state argued on, debating whether Zyprexa's benefits outweighed its risks—a choice Mr. Bigley, sound mind or not, had already made.

In a subsequent commitment proceeding, a psychiatrist testified that Bill saying *The New York Times* had written a story about him was proof he was mentally ill.

Just two days later, on March 27, 2008, the State of Alaska agreed to settle its Zyprexa case against Lilly for $15 million. This was after it said its damages could rise to hundreds of millions of dollars. The state said they accepted such a low number because they were concerned a pending Supreme Court case by the name of *Wyeth v. Levine* might decide federal law pre-empted (superseded) state law.

The pre-emption doctrine is based on the Supremacy Clause of the United States Constitution, which provides that federal law is the "supreme law of the land." If a state law does not conflict with federal law then it is valid, but if it does conflict it is invalid. The courts have to decide whether a state law conflicts with federal law. The ultimate question is what Congress' purpose was—or, put another way, whether Congress intended to pre-empt state law in the circumstances of the case being decided. If the federal law is so exhaustive or complete on a topic that it "occupies the entire field," then no state law on that topic is valid.

In the *Medtronics* case decided February 20, 2008, which was just a couple of weeks before the start of the trial in *Alaska v. Lilly*, the U.S. Supreme Court decided the Medical Device Amendments of 1976, amending federal law to include FDA regulation of medical devices, did occupy the field, and therefore a person who claimed they had been harmed by a faulty balloon catheter during a heart operation could not sue the manufacturer under state law. That federal statute states:

> [A] State shall not "establish or continue in effect with respect to a device intended for human use any requirement . . . (1) which is different from, or in addition to, any requirement applicable under [federal law] to the device, and . . . (2) which relates to the safety or effectiveness of the device or to any other matter included in a requirement applicable to the device under" relevant federal law.

In interpreting this language, the Supreme Court held Congress had intended to pre-empt state court damages actions against medical device manufacturers. This is what the statute says.

In contrast, with respect to drugs, which was the issue in *Wyeth v. Levine* and *Alaska v. Lilly*, the statute has a specific provision indicating a state law would only be invalidated upon a "direct and positive conflict" with the FDA statute. Here, the statute clearly did not occupy the entire field.

The real reason the State of Alaska settled for the paltry $15 million is it was unable to retrieve from its computer system the cost of treating patients for diabetes and other medical problems caused by Zyprexa. This was a huge break for Lilly because the *Alaska v. Lilly* settlement formed the basis for the settlement of a large number of the other states' lawsuits against Lilly. The other states didn't know the real reason Alaska had settled for $15 million. A few months later, in October of 2008, Lilly settled lawsuits by thirty-three other states for only $62 million. Six months later, in early March of 2009, the Supreme Court decided *Wyeth v. Levine*, holding that state lawsuits against drug companies were not pre-empted by the federal Food, Drug and Cosmetic Act.

Once the *Alaska v. Lilly* case was over and I had given up my chance to get more publicity against forced psychiatric drugging and electroshock, Lilly reneged on its agreement to settle with me. I was angry with Lilly, of course, but mainly upset with myself for being duped. I knew Lilly and its lawyers were not to be trusted.

On January 15, 2009, the Department of Justice announced a $1.415 billion settlement of criminal and civil charges against Lilly for its illegal off-label marketing of Zyprexa in the False Claims Act cases that had "gained momentum" as a result of the Zyprexa Papers' release. The "whistleblowers" who had brought lawsuits over this under the False Claims Act received almost $79 million. John McKay called at least one of the lawyers to see whether they would be willing to help with the legal fees I was facing from defending myself against Lilly for releasing the Zyprexa Papers—which, after all, had played a substantial part in their clients receiving almost $79 million. My legal fees ended up being almost $300,000, over $115,000 of which I was not able to pay, even counting the $46,000 people donated to the Jim Gottstein Legal Defense Fund, established by what is now the International Society for Ethical Psychology and Psychiatry (ISEPP). Neither the whistleblowers nor their lawyers helped with my legal fees.

We continued to negotiate, never able to reach an agreement. At that point, convinced Lilly would not file contempt charges against me, I felt the main benefit of settling was avoidance of additional legal expenses, including the costs for my appeal. We kept putting the appeal on hold, but the court didn't like that, and I figured having the appeal move forward was going to be the only real deadline for settlement. As we got farther along, more expenses had already been incurred and the benefit to me decreased correspondingly. We had been able to get the amount I was to pay to charity down to $10,000 but couldn't reach agreement on the other issues. This went on until the middle of 2009, with the case being put on hold pending negotiations and then taken off hold. Finally, once I had incurred all the costs for the appeal briefing, I told Lilly they should pay me $10,000 instead of me paying $10,000. They were shocked and, of course, refused. I just didn't see any benefit to settling at that point, convinced as I was they would not file contempt charges and I would be giving up my chance to win the appeal.

Oral argument on the appeal was held February 2, 2010. Twenty or so supporters showed up, and about the same number held a rally outside the courthouse in subfreezing weather. The presiding judge for the three-judge appeals panel, Reena Raggi, was extraordinarily hostile at the oral argument, and I knew we were unlikely to win the appeal.

Eight months after the oral argument, in August of 2010, the 2nd Circuit ruled against me. The only thing the 2nd Circuit said about the harm exposed in the Zyprexa Papers was, "some [of the twenty million schizophrenia patients who have taken Zyprexa] allege [it] has produced negative side effects purportedly known to, but not disclosed by, the drug's manufacturer, Eli Lilly Co." The great harm exposed by the Zyprexa Papers was simply not considered relevant. We had asked the Court of Appeals to take into consideration that Bill had been drugged with Zyprexa against his will shortly before I had issued the subpoena. The Appeals Court refused because I didn't know at the time I had the subpoena issued that Bill had been given Zyprexa. As I said above, I was pretty sure he had been given Zyprexa, and I thought I had testified to that effect at the trial. This goes to show how one mistake at a trial can have disastrous consequences. I can't say for sure that Judge Weinstein's or the Second Circuit's decisions would have been different, but they very well might have because my being unable to testify that Bill had been given Zyprexa was central to their decisions against me.

In any event, immediately after the 2nd Circuit handed down its decision, I issued the following statement:

> Today, the United States Court of Appeals for the Second Circuit affirmed the District Court's injunction issued against me in connection with the subpoenaing and distribution of documents produced in the Zyprexa Products Liability Litigation. I am disappointed in the ruling. The Court of Appeals held the District Court did not abuse its discretion in finding the subpoena was a sham. This is not the case. I believe I acted properly, but understand why both courts would believe this. Ultimately, I feel I did not adequately explain my actions to the District Court and it was understandably offended by what it thought was a deliberate violation by me of one of its orders. My explanation was hampered at the time because critical information had been withheld from me, such as my client having been drugged with Zyprexa pursuant to a forced drugging

court order shortly before I took his case. I certainly intended no disrespect to the District Court.

So the Zyprexa Papers affair ended with a whimper. However, my representation of and relationship with Bill Bigley continued quite intensely.

Ch. 10. Bill Bigley & Me

The first time I met Bill was December 5, 2006, when I was looking for someone for whom I could subpoena the Zyprexa Papers. From then until 2009, I represented him in ten trial court cases and five appeals to the Alaska Supreme Court. One of those Alaska Supreme Court cases resulted in very important precedent for psychiatric defendants' rights.

I got to know Bill and about him, and was really struck that there but for the grace of God go I. He was born just two months before I was. He was first hospitalized in April of 1980, when he was 27. I was hospitalized two years later and was lucky not to have been made permanently "mentally ill," as he was.

Bill had four- and five-year-old daughters and a good job as a heavy equipment operator at the Sitka, Alaska lumber mill when his wife divorced him and obtained crushing child support and housing payments. According to his hospital file, when asked why he thought he had been brought to the hospital, "he said he had just gotten divorced and consequently had a nervous breakdown." Bill was given Haldol, a first-generation neuroleptic. During that first stay in API, it was noted Bill responded well to the hospital routine and participated in activities. He was said to have improved rather rapidly, showing no further indication of hallucinations or delusions. By the time he was discharged he was said to be pleasant and cooperative. His treating psychiatrist noted on discharge that his prognosis was somewhat guarded, depending on the type of follow-up treatment Bill received in dealing with his recent divorce.

That psychiatrist was Robert Alberts, who two years later saved me from becoming a lifelong mental patient. Unfortunately for Bill, he did not get to continue seeing Dr. Alberts after his discharge from that first admission to API. He was not given help dealing with his divorce. So he came back into the hospital for a second time that September. He was again put on Haldol and released after thirty days with no observed symptoms of psychosis. He was reported to have been pleasant and cooperative.

His third admission to API was in February of 1981. He had been referred from jail for acting strangely after being picked up for failing to answer a traffic citation and refusing to leave the jail because he thought people outside of the jail were going to harm him. The psychiatrist for this admission noted he had been slow to respond to the drugs during his first two admissions—which contradicted what Bill's medical record shows—and they weren't working very well on this one. So he increased the dose. This is typical in psychiatry: if what's being done doesn't work, do more of it. In a 2008 trial in which I represented Bill, Dr. Grace Jackson testified he was given such high doses of Haldol in that admission that it was guaranteed to cause Parkinson's disease and was the beginning of his long decline.

Because Bill wasn't improving in the eyes of the staff, API obtained a court order to keep him there against his will. The hospital file states:

> Mr. Bigley was furiously angry that he was deprived of his right to freedom outside the hospital, but despite his persistent anger and occasional verbal threats, he never became physically assaultive, nor did he abuse limited privileges away from the locked unit.

By this time, the pattern had been set that was to continue for the next quarter-century, before I met him. One of the things that comes through clearly from the records and from my conversations with him is Bill was devastated by losing his two daughters and never got over it. He continually tried to have a relationship with them, but this became more and more difficult as the number of psychiatric hospitalizations increased and the state took more control of Bill's life.

In 1996, the state Office of Public Advocacy (OPA) obtained conservatorship over Bill, which in Alaska meant it had complete control of his money. This understandably made Bill angry. In April of 2004, OPA was awarded full guardianship over Bill, taking all decision making away from him. This essentially put him in the same legal status as a child under the complete control of their parent. Bill was livid. This was the case in which I began representing Bill in December of 2006, and for which I subpoenaed the Zyprexa Papers. Interestingly, the court visitor in the guardianship case noted hospitalizing and drugging Bill didn't really change Bill's behavior. My observation was in line with the court visitor's—that drugging didn't make much of a difference.

The twenty-five years of psychiatric force naturally made Bill angry. The United Nations has determined psychiatric imprisonment, euphemistically called involuntary commitment, and forced psychiatric drugging can constitute torture. Bill expressed his anger in ways that could be frightening, even though he was very small. To my knowledge, he was never violent, even if provoked. To be psychiatrically imprisoned legally, he had to be found "mentally ill" and as a result of such "mental illness" a danger to self or others. He was never a danger to others. The prime example of "danger to self" is someone who is suicidal. To my knowledge, Bill was never suicidal, just as he was never violent.

There is also the concept that someone might be so disabled they can't take care of themselves. In *O'Connor v. Donaldson*, the United States Supreme Court allowed this as a justification for psychiatric imprisonment, holding:

> [E]ven if there is no foreseeable risk of self-injury or suicide, a person is literally "dangerous to himself" if for physical or other reasons he is helpless to avoid the hazards of freedom either through his own efforts or with the aid of willing family members or friends.

The court went on to say it is unconstitutional to confine someone if they are dangerous to no one and can live safely in freedom. The U.S. Supreme Court also said:

> May the State fence in the harmless mentally ill solely to save its citizens from exposure to those whose ways are different? One might as well ask if the State, to avoid public unease, could incarcerate all who are physically unattractive or socially eccentric. Mere public intolerance or animosity cannot constitutionally justify the deprivation of a person's physical liberty.

But for a reason not very different from this, if at all, Bill was psychiatrically imprisoned 100 times before he died. He was never a danger to others and didn't need to be locked up to survive. A number of times, the rationale was he might upset someone so much by what he was saying that he would be assaulted. In my view, that is just not a proper or constitutionally valid basis for locking someone up, especially when one considers it had to be proven by clear and convincing evidence that Bill wouldn't *survive* the "hazards of freedom."

It is obvious to me the approach the mental health system had taken with Bill, largely against his will after the first two API admissions, had never worked. Instead of considering taking a different approach, API not only continued the failed approach but escalated it.

Picking things up from a bit before we met, from April of 2005 until October of 2006 Bill was voluntarily going to the hospital for long-acting injections of Risperdal, a second-generation neuroleptic. Then, when API decided the Risperdal was no longer enough, they decided to add Zyprexa and Depakote and got a court order to force him when he resisted. Depakote is an anti-seizure drug that has also been marketed as a "mood-stabilizer." Bill complained the Zyprexa made him too hungry, so they switched to Seroquel. This was a week before I subpoenaed the Zyprexa Papers.

To keep Bill taking the drugs, his guardian had hatched a plan with the hospital to drug Bill up in the hospital with long-acting shots to "stabilize" him, and then instead of discharging him, give him an "early release," which meant he was still technically committed and subject to the forced drugging court order even though he wasn't in the hospital. This way, Bill would be dragged back into the hospital to be shot up with the drugs when he quit taking them, without the hospital having to go back to court. That is what had happened the week before I met Bill. It was not legal to haul Bill back to the hospital for not taking the drugs; it was only legal to haul him back if he became a harm to self or others or gravely disabled.

Bill was in API on a ninety-day commitment through this illegal but court-facilitated procedure when I first met him in early December of 2006. As I wrote above, my entry into his case and demand for a jury trial if they filed for continued commitment messed up their plans, though, and they simply discharged him on January 3, 2007, when the commitment expired. On January 22, 2007, he was hauled back into API. A commitment petition was filed on January 23rd, and he was committed for thirty days on January 27th. I was still dealing with Lilly in the Brooklyn Zyprexa MDL and wasn't able represent him, so he was represented by the Public Defender Agency and lost.

By the time they filed for a ninety-day commitment on March 21st, I was available to represent him. Just my getting into the case became a little mini-drama. One of the court rules is a lawyer cannot just get out of a case whenever they want, because the courts don't want the person to be without a lawyer. If there is a new lawyer ready to step in, they normally file what is called a Motion for Withdrawal and Substitution of Counsel, which then has to be approved by the judge. This presents no problem in most types of cases, but commitment cases come up so fast even a day's delay can be very detrimental to a client. For one thing, in Alaska, commitment court files are confidential, and I would not be allowed to look at the file unless I was recognized as the person's lawyer.

There is another rule that all a lawyer has to do to represent someone is file what is called an Entry of Appearance. It is not unusual in civil litigation for a party to have more than one lawyer, each filing an Entry of Appearance. However, the Public Defender Agency is not allowed to represent someone who has their own lawyer. They don't have a problem with doing a withdrawal and substitution, but it does cause a delay. I also don't have any problem with a withdrawal and substitution as a general matter, but I can't tolerate any delay in being formally recognized as the person's lawyer in this type of case because of the short time frame. So I filed an Entry of Appearance on March 22nd to immediately get into the case.

The next day, March 23, 2007, the probate master on his own issued an order that I was not Bill's lawyer unless and until he approved the Public Defender Agency's withdrawal and my substitution as Bill's lawyer. Bill theoretically had the absolute right to choose his lawyer (more on that later), and it is a really big deal to deny someone the right to choose their own lawyer. The probate master fundamentally misunderstood and misapplied the rules regarding representation, so I tried to get him to correct his error by filing a motion for reconsideration later that day. The probate master immediately denied it.

One can't appeal a trial court order in Alaska until the case is completely over, but there is an escape valve to ask the Alaska Supreme Court to review a trial court decision before the end of the case if there are important reasons to do so, through what is called a Petition for Review. These are rarely granted in Alaska. Because of the important representation issue and the likelihood the issue would come up repeatedly without the Alaska Supreme Court having a chance to decide the question, I filed a Petition for Review on March 27th. It wasn't denied until May 25th.

Meanwhile, the Public Defender Agency filed a motion to withdraw, and I filed a demand for a jury trial. Unlike in January, when

API released Bill rather than go through a jury trial, this time API didn't drop it. Perhaps this was because they didn't want to be pushed around by me. In fact, there were a number of notes in Bill's chart (medical record) complaining about me representing Bill and his becoming uncooperative as a result. In other words, they didn't like Bill having effective legal representation.

Bill had been illegally hauled back to API after another "early release." If Bill had been illegally ordered back to API, there was no basis for them to file a new petition for commitment. The person who had illegally ordered Bill to be picked up dodged the subpoena I had issued. The judge didn't care and went ahead with the jury trial scheduled to start on April 2, 2007.

I took a couple of depositions before the trial, including of the psychiatrist. When I asked him at his deposition whether Bill was restrained in any way when he was given shots, he testified, "[H]e doesn't usually fight once the nurse comes with three or four staff. He usually just submits." If Bill didn't submit, the three or four staff members would hold him down, pull down his pants, and inject him in his butt with a drug he didn't want to take and knew was harmful to him. This is not therapeutic. It is also standard practice in psychiatric so-called "hospitals" around the world.

A couple of months before the jury trial, the Alaska Supreme Court had decided *Wetherhorn v. Alaska Psychiatric Institute*, one of my Alaska Supreme Court victories, holding unconstitutional the part of the Alaska Statutes allowing the state to psychiatrically imprison someone for being gravely disabled, if their previous ability to function independently would substantially deteriorate. Citing the United States Supreme Court *O'Connor* decision, the Alaska Supreme Court held the statute could only be constitutional "if construed to require a level of incapacity so substantial that the respondent cannot *survive* safely in freedom" (emphasis added).

The psychiatrist testified, "I don't really know what that means legally," but this didn't stop him from giving his "expert opinion" that Bill was gravely disabled. He testified that in his "expert opinion," getting arrested was not surviving safely. He testified he didn't think Bill was going to die within a week or a month, but he didn't think he was going to "safely survive." At the end of the State's presentation of evidence, I moved to dismiss the case on the grounds that neither the psychiatrist's testimony nor anyone else's was sufficient to prove Bill was gravely disabled under *Wetherhorn*. The judge didn't care. My take on this is judges don't want to be blamed if they let someone go and then something bad happens. So if a psychiatrist says the person should be locked up, they lock them up. That is why I have decided to always ask for a jury if I have the chance. Even though I don't have that much jury trial experience, my sense is juries take the rules way more seriously than judges.

An example is the burden of proof. In civil cases, such as contract disputes, to win you only need to prove your case by a "preponderance of the evidence," which means it is more likely you're right than you're not—in other words, more than 50% of the evidence supports your case. In contrast, in criminal trials, the government has to prove the right to lock someone up (convict) "beyond a reasonable doubt." In a 1979 United States Supreme Court case, *Addington v. Texas*, Frank Addington argued since the state wanted to lock him up like a criminal, the same beyond-a-reasonable-doubt standard should apply. The United States Supreme Court rejected this on the grounds that psychiatrists could never or virtually never prove someone was mentally ill and dangerous beyond a reasonable doubt. It did, however, rule the states had to prove the person should be committed by more than a preponderance of the evidence, requiring them to prove it by "clear and convincing" evidence. The court allowed the states to define exactly what that meant. In Alaska, "clear and convincing" has been defined to mean "highly probable." My experience is when there is no jury and only judges decide the facts, they ignore the higher "clear and convincing" burden of proof and just *say* the state proved its case by clear and convincing evidence.

During the jury trial, in addition to testifying Bill was gravely disabled even though he didn't know what that meant, the psychiatrist testified Bill had one of the most severe cases of mental illness he had ever seen. He testified Bill had more admissions to API than all but two people. He testified Bill was psychotic (crazy) all of the time, whether on the drugs or not, but he stayed out of the hospital "a bit longer" when on them.

I called George Gee, the owner of a coffee shop Bill frequented, to testify on his behalf. Mr. Gee testified Bill had been coming in for years, with breaks of different lengths. While Mr. Gee said they had needed to ask Bill a couple of times to not come in for a while, he painted a far different picture of Bill than the out-of-control monster portrayed by the hospital.

For Bill to be committed for ninety days, the jury had to find by clear and convincing evidence that Bill was mentally ill and as a result gravely disabled. Under the statute, since API had not alleged Bill was a danger to himself or others, the jury also had to find that Bill's mental condition would be improved by the course of treatment in the hospital, which the judge ruled they only had to find by a preponderance of the evidence (more than 50%). The jury did find that Bill was mentally ill and gravely disabled as a result, but did not find that his mental condition would be improved by the course of treatment API was proposing. This meant Bill won and was let go. So Bill had previously been locked up sixty-seven times, and the first time a jury had a chance to decide whether he met commitment criteria, the answer was no. This illustrates why I always ask for a jury when I have the chance. There is no doubt in my mind the judge would have ordered Bill locked up if it had been up to him.

A little over a month later, Bill was hauled into API again and committed for thirty days by the judge. I didn't handle the case because I was up to my ears dealing with the Zyprexa Papers appeal. I believe API pulled the same "early release" scheme, and when the ninety-day commitment trial came up thirty days later, I convinced the public defender to have a jury trial, at which I would testify. I did, the jury decided Bill did not meet commitment criteria, and he was let go again. So after seventy commitments, the first two times a jury was allowed to consider the evidence, Bill was found not to meet commitment criteria and was freed.

TUESDAY, AUGUST 28TH, 2007

By August 28th, Bill had gotten many people upset with him, including his guardian, who banned him from their offices. There were also concerns about his safety because he had reportedly been walking in traffic. There was a series of e-mails between OPA and me in which, among other things, I notified OPA I would be representing Bill against a forced drugging petition if one were to be filed. I had been appointed to a committee to make recommendations for mental health commitment and forced drugging court rules, and I had written a memo about it a few weeks before. Under Alaska statutes, any adult can file what is called an *ex parté* petition to have a person hauled into the psych hospital by the police, usually in handcuffs, to be evaluated for possible commitment. The *ex parté* petition is not provided to the person, so they don't have a chance to show why they shouldn't be locked up in the psych hospital for an evaluation.

In the memo, I made the point that the way *ex parté* orders were routinely granted was illegal. The memo points out there is often no exigency (emergency) that would justify orders to haul people in for evaluation without notice. In the *Heather R.* case I won in 2016, the Alaska Supreme Court ruled, based on the statute, that if it was reasonably possible, the court had to interview the person before issuing an order to haul that person in for a psychiatric evaluation.

I also pointed out in the memo the problems with representation, and that an attorney who files an entry of appearance is the person's lawyer as soon as it is filed. Another point I made was that referrals to the probate master should be eliminated because the short time frames did not allow for proper handling, resulting in people being illegally committed and drugged against their will before there was a valid Superior Court order. Because of the extremely short time frame involved if they were going to try locking up Bill, in my e-mail to OPA I demanded my e-mail with the memo be included in any *ex parté* petition OPA might file, so the probate master would have that information before issuing any order. I also sent an e-mail to Bill's mental health provider, requesting the same thing.

WEDNESDAY, AUGUST 29TH, 2007

On August 29th, an *ex parté* petition was filed against Bill by his mental health provider and a police officer. The wrong e-mail was attached, but the memo was included. An order to have Bill picked up by the police was signed that same day, and he was hauled into API.

THURSDAY, AUGUST 30TH, 2007

At 4:00 p.m. the next day, August 30th, I found out API had filed petitions for a thirty-day commitment and to drug Bill against his will, and the court had set the trial for the following day at 1:30 p.m.

FRIDAY, AUGUST 31TH, 2007

A little before 8:00 the next morning, I e-mailed API's lawyer and the public defender to say I would be hand-delivering some filings for the trial set for that afternoon, and no one— including hospital personnel—who might testify against Bill should meet with my client without me being present. The filings were:

1. Limited Entry of Appearance to represent Bill just for the forced drugging petition, including exhibits regarding what had happened before;

2. Motion to Dismiss the Forced Drugging Petition (throw it out of court) because the petition didn't provide a factual basis for being granted; and

3. A challenge to the practice of forcibly drugging people based on the probate master's recommendation prior to Superior Court approval.

The trial was held that afternoon starting at 3:15 in front of the probate master. The public defender said it was their policy that if I represented Bill for anything, I had to represent him for the whole case. The hospital's attorney was practically apoplectic. I pointed out there was a separate petition for the forced drugging, and the forced drugging statute specifically stated a patient had the right to an attorney of his own choosing, and the Public Defender Agency was only to be appointed if the patient couldn't afford an attorney. Since I was representing him *pro bono* (for free), Bill could afford me and therefore the public defender could not represent him for the forced drugging petition. In contrast, under a different statute, the public defenders are automatically appointed for commitment petitions.

This makes a certain amount of sense on the surface. When someone is hauled in for evaluation, the idea is that because they are being locked up pending a judge deciding such confinement is warranted, it is important to have such a decision very quickly, so a lawyer has to be immediately available. In other words, the person's right to be free of confinement has already been taken away, and there needs to be a speedy decision on whether the imprisonment is justified. In contrast, for forced drugging, the person's right to not have unwanted drugs forced into them is not taken away until there is a judicial determination it is legally justified. That allows for more time. The Alaska Supreme Court explicitly acknowledged this in *Wetherhorn*, although not with respect to the representation issue.

The probate master decided if the commitment petition was granted, *and Bill wanted me to represent him*, the public defender would withdraw and I would substitute in for the rest of the proceedings. This was incorrect but in the end didn't make any difference.

Over the years, API, the public defenders, and the court system had developed a process to get through the cases as quickly as possible, and part of that was to treat the commitment and forced drugging petitions as a single case. Administratively, they were assigned the same case number by the court system, and they were heard one right after the other. The trials were maybe fifteen minutes in total for both the commitment and the forced drugging petitions. That was how long it took for both petitions in *Wetherhorn* (I represented Roslyn Wetherhorn only for the appeal, not the trial). This is not as bad as some places, where they might be as short as five minutes, but people being committed and ordered to take drugs against their will in fifteen minutes are not getting fair trials.

Worse, the public defenders' attitude is often, "If my client wasn't crazy, he would know what the hospital wants to do to him is good for him." Thus, they often don't mount any real defense, not wanting their clients' pesky legal rights to get in the way of the government doing what it wants to them. The judges have the same attitude. But the truth is, locking people up and drugging them against their will is very harmful.

One of the interesting things at the hearing was that after the representation issues got sorted out to the extent they did, the public defender went off to talk to Bill before the commitment hearing commenced, and Bill told her he wanted the hearing in a real courtroom, not in the little conference room at the hospital, and he wanted the hearing open to the public. Alaska statutes provide that (1) the commitment hearing shall be open or closed to the public as the respondent (in this case, Bill) elects and (2) the trial shall be "in a physical setting least likely to have a harmful effect on the mental or physical health of the respondent, within practical limits." These are two things I always talk to my clients about, and I had done so with Bill before. So he was not so crazy he didn't remember these rights and ask for them.

I don't think the commitment trial lasted even fifteen minutes before the probate master declared he was recommending commitment. The hospital then wanted to immediately conduct the forced drugging trial. I said no. I needed time to prepare. I said I didn't have enough information to be able to defend against the petition, including even what drug(s) they wanted to force on my client. I said the judge hadn't ruled on my motion to dismiss. The probate master promptly denied the motion to dismiss but had no choice but to delay the forced drugging trial until Wednesday, September 5th.

API objected it wasn't going to be able to drug Bill during that time, and the probate master pointed out they could drug him under a different statute in an emergency. I viewed this as an invitation by the probate master to drug Bill against his will without a court order authorizing it.

TUESDAY, SEPTEMBER 4TH, 2007

The day before the forced drugging hearing was scheduled, September 4th, I filed a pre-hearing brief raising a number of issues:

1. The *ex parté* order was improper and therefore void.

2. When a probate master decided whether someone was not competent to decline the drugs, the Probate Rule giving this immediate effect before the Superior Court could approve or even consider it was improper and illegal.

3. There was no valid commitment order signed by a Superior Court judge, and therefore Bill's continued psychiatric imprisonment was illegal. Further, because a forced drugging petition can only be heard after someone has been committed, the forced drugging case should be dismissed.

4. The forced drugging hearing had to be postponed because I had not been given requested records about Bill's alleged recent actions, including at API.

5. The trial court's ruling in the *Myers* case—which established there was a viable debate whether the drugs API wanted to force Bill to take might harm him or worsen his condition—was binding on API and made it impossible for API to prove by clear and convincing evidence it was in his best interests. (There is a legal principle called *collateral estoppel* or issue preclusion that when someone has already lost on an issue in court they

can't get a second bite at the apple and try and win it in another case.)

6. Under the *Myers* decision, the court could only authorize API to drug Bill with specific drugs in specific doses.

7. Bill was entitled to require the manufacturers of the drugs API was most likely to try and force on him to provide suppressed research data so the court would have complete information about the harms caused by the drugs.

8. The combination of drugs API was expected to want to force on Bill was a prohibited experimental treatment because they had never been studied, let alone approved by the Food and Drug Administration.

9. There were less-intrusive alternatives to the forced drugging.

I proposed "wrap-around" services, housing, and Bill being able to come and go from API as he wanted as a less-intrusive alternative. This was very carefully thought out based on my by then pretty extensive interactions with and understanding of Bill.

I listed thirteen potential witnesses, plus submitted affidavits as "pre-filed testimony" from Robert Whitaker, author of *Mad in America*, and Ron Bassman, a PhD psychologist who as a teenager had been locked up, massively drugged, electroshocked, and subjected to insulin comas. Dr. Bassman has written the fabulous book, *A Fight to Be: A Psychologist's Experience from Both Sides of the Locked Door*. I highly recommend it.

WEDNESDAY, SEPTEMBER 5TH, 2007

Just before the September 5th hearing, API filed its own pre-hearing brief and a motion to strike (throw out) all of the exhibits I had filed with my pre-hearing brief. API argued all of the evidence I presented about neuroleptics being very harmful with little if any benefit, and my assertion there were effective non-drug treatments, were irrelevant to the court's determination of whether forcing the drugs on Bill was in his best interest and whether there were any less-intrusive alternatives.

When the hearing was held, my first point to the probate master was that the forced drugging petition did not allege sufficient facts to support granting it. Whether it is a civil complaint, or a criminal indictment or complaint, when someone brings a lawsuit, the allegations have to be sufficient that if true, the person filing it is entitled to what they are seeking. So, for example, if I were to allege that Fred had overslept, that wouldn't entitle me to recover any money from Fred unless he owed me some duty not to oversleep and unless his oversleeping cost me the money I was seeking. Why should it be different in forced drugging cases? This is more than theoretical.

The forced drugging petition filed against Bill was a pre-printed form with a checked box that said:

> Petitioner has reason to believe the patient is incapable of giving or withholding informed consent. The facility wishes to use psychotropic medication in a non-crisis situation.

This just parroted the statute, but in *Myers*, the Alaska Supreme Court had held this to be constitutionally insufficient. Now, over a year later, when they wanted to forcibly drug Bill, API hadn't taken any steps to follow the *Myers* decision. As far as I could tell, the public defender had done nothing to try to get them to follow it, nor had the court.

But I wasn't willing to let the *Myers* decision be ignored, and I raised it at the beginning of the hearing. My point was the petition had to allege facts sufficient to grant it, just like in all other types of cases. The legalese way of saying it is that I was moving for "judgment on the pleadings," meaning even if all of the facts alleged in the petition were taken as true, that was insufficient to grant it. The probate master's response?

> And a judgment on the pleadings? Well, that just doesn't make sense, frankly, because we have the State's—their petition, but that's only because that's the way it's always been done. A petition for court approval of administration of psychotropic medication. And those always result—have always resulted, since the law went into effect, in a subsequent hearing. As far as I know, there's never been a judgment on the pleadings concerning such a petition. So there is no expectation

that such a petition would be dealt with just by
pleadings.

To me, this was a clear statement that neither the trial court, nor API,
nor the public defender treated these as real legal cases. They were just
going through the motions.

That these weren't treated as real cases was reinforced by the court
visitor's testimony. In Alaska forced drugging cases, a court visitor is
appointed to administer a competency assessment instrument and
determine whether the patient had previously expressed wishes
regarding psychiatric drugs. I objected to the court visitor meeting with
my client without me, testifying telephonically, and not having
previously provided me with her report. The probate master incorrectly
ruled the court visitor would have to submit a written report, which she
testified would take her two weeks, and then

> if Mr. Gottstein wants me to complete—do a
> completely thorough investigation, I will have to put
> every other case aside that I have pending and work on
> this.

This is an explicit admission the court visitor did not normally do a
thorough investigation. The probate master refused to order the court
visitor to send me the capacity (competency) assessment instrument
the court visitors were using. To me, this was yet another example of
what a travesty these legal proceedings usually are.

Bill was refusing to talk to the court visitor, which made him look
crazy. But if the capacity assessment instrument was completely invalid,
he had every reason to refuse to talk to her, and likewise if it was not a
legitimate, impartial investigation, which it was not. Of course, I was
entitled to an advance copy of the capacity assessment instrument so I
could prepare for cross-examination. In any event, the probate master
got the court visitor to promise to submit her report Monday morning,
September 10th, and set that afternoon for her testimony.

The psychiatrist testified next, saying Bill was demonstrably not
competent because he complained of sexual dysfunction, stomach
problems, and nausea and believed the drug they wanted to give him—
a long-acting injection of Risperdal—was poison. However, Risperdal
does cause sexual dysfunction and nausea, and I don't doubt the other
negative effects of which Bill complained. In light of this drug's severe

negative effects, I also think it is fair to characterize it as poison. Nonetheless, all of this was cited as evidence Bill was crazy and incompetent to decline the medication. The psychiatrist did testify Bill had Tardive Dyskinesia—which is basically drug-induced Parkinson's disease—from the large amount of neuroleptics he had been given over a long time, that the Risperdal could make it worse, and that such damage is permanent. The psychiatrist testified the drugs could cause liver disease, and "if he starts looking sick, and he won't let us do a blood test, we might have to hold him down and obtain a blood sample." As for the benefit from the drugs, the psychiatrist testified, "It's not going to make him sane," but he would be able to function in the community. The psychiatrist asserted there was no way Bill could live in the community unless he was drugged.

By pure serendipity, a person from New Zealand I had met in Ireland a couple of years earlier at a conference of INTAR (the International Network Toward Alternatives and Recovery), Sarah Porter, happened to be in town and was only available that day. She was heading back to New Zealand before the trial would resume on Monday. When Bill heard that, he said, "Take me with you."

Ms. Porter is a former psychiatric patient who developed an acclaimed alternative program based on building a good relationship with the person in distress and supporting that person to recognize and come to terms with the issues that are going on in their life. This is done in a way that builds a therapeutic alliance, and is based on negotiation rather than the use of force or coercion. After having her testify about her experience and success, the probate master formally recognized (qualified) her as an expert on alternative treatments, although not necessarily on what was available in Alaska. Ms. Porter testified:

> A. [T]here is now growing recognition that medication is not a satisfactory answer for a significant proportion of the people who experience mental distress, and that for some people it creates more problems than solutions. . . .

> Q. Now, you mentioned—I think you said that coercion creates problems. Could you describe those kinds of problems?

A. Well, that's really about the fact that [there is] growing recognition—I think worldwide, but particularly in New Zealand, that coercion, itself, creates trauma and further distress for the person, and that that, in itself, actually undermines the benefits of the treatment that is being provided in a forced context. And so our aiming and teaching is to be able to support the person to resolve the issues without actually having to trample . . . on the person's autonomy, or hound them physically or emotionally in doing so. . . .

Q. And—and have you seen success in that approach?

A. We have. It's been phenomenal, actually. . . . I had high hopes that it would work, but I've . . . been really impressed how well, in fact, it has worked.

MONDAY, SEPTEMBER 10TH, 2007

The resumed trial was scheduled to start at 1:30 on Monday, September 10th, and I filed an emergency motion to the Alaska Supreme Court to stop the illegal "emergency" drugging of Bill early that morning after working on it all weekend. I had learned from Bill that he had been drugged against his will, which I thought would happen since at the August 31st hearing, the probate master had essentially invited API to drug him under the statute allowing drugging in emergencies. However, that statute only allowed such drugging "to preserve the life of, or prevent significant physical harm to, the patient or another person," with the justification having to be documented in his medical records. Each emergency drugging order is valid for only twenty-four hours, and only three such emergency drugging orders could be given without getting a court to authorize further emergency drugging. The Supreme Court issued an order for a response to be filed by 3:00 that afternoon.

At the 1:30 hearing, API announced it was working with the psychiatrist Bill had brought in and was going to let Bill go under this psychiatrist's care without drugging him. This was after API had testified under oath that Bill was so mentally ill and disruptive he could not survive outside of the hospital until he had been suitably drugged.

More than I have described went on in this particular forced drugging proceeding, notably the probate master taking extreme actions to try to remove what I had filed from the court records, but I think the above gives the idea and demonstrates two points. First, it shows what can happen when a lawyer treats this type of case as real and to be defended effectively. That leads into the second point, which is psychiatric hospitals have such an easy time getting psychiatric imprisonment (involuntary commitment) and forced drugging orders that they don't even try to work with the patient. If the patient doesn't immediately agree to do exactly what the hospital wants, they will just get a court order to force the person. It is the path of least resistance. If you can make it hard enough or, better yet, impossible to get such orders, they will look for alternatives. That is what happened in this case.

OCTOBER 2007 TO JANUARY 2008

In late October of 2007, Bill was arrested for trespass, but the charges were dismissed when he was hauled into API. I didn't represent him, and he was committed for thirty days and subjected to forced drugging. He was then recommitted for ninety days and discharged in January of 2008 to a group home in the woods an hour or so out of Anchorage.

MARCH 2008

Living in the boondocks was not to Bill's liking, and at the end of February 2008, he was brought to API for "causing a ruckus at a bar" after leaving the group home. I entered an appearance for the forced drugging petition only, accompanied by the affidavits of Robert Whitaker, Ron Bassman, and Paul Cornils, who had provided outpatient case management services to Bill for ten months with an organization I had co-founded named CHOICES. My entering an appearance created a big stir, as it had the previous time, with API and the court expending lots of time and effort to fight it. The judge even sent back the papers I had filed, saying I wasn't permitted to file them because I wasn't yet Bill's attorney. The court was wrong about that. The content of the court record was very important to me because in these cases, I am always trying to set up an appeal if we lose, and in only rare exceptions will an appellate court consider anything but what is in the official court record. The Alaska Supreme Court tends to be strict about this.

This issue about the record ended up not mattering because the judge decided Bill wasn't gravely disabled and let him go. Thus, we never got to the forced drugging petition. This was the same case Alex Berenson wrote about in his *Times* article "One Drug, Two Faces."

APRIL 16TH–21ST, 2008

On April 16, 2008, an *ex parté* order was issued against Bill to haul him into API for evaluation. His chart (medical record) made clear he was not to be drugged under the "emergency" statute. They had gotten the message. A thirty-day commitment petition was filed on April 17th. On April 21st, I filed a conditional entry of appearance that if a forced drugging petition were filed against Bill, I would be representing him on that. Accompanying the entry of appearance was documentation regarding representation, and the affidavits of Robert Whitaker, Paul Cornils, and Ronald Bassman. That same day, a hearing was held on the thirty-day commitment, and Bill was found not to meet the commitment criteria and let go. API had testified previously there was no point in having him in API if they couldn't drug him. This was an implicit admission he wasn't a danger to self or others or gravely disabled (the only legal reasons to lock someone up for being mentally ill), because if he had been, that would have been a reason to keep him in API even if they couldn't drug him into submission.

APRIL 25ST TO MAY 7TH, 2008

Four days later, on April 25th, Bill was hauled into API by the police for "creating a disturbance" at a bank and spitting on someone. At various times in the past, Bill had been arrested for trespassing when he had gone into a place that had banned him. The police couldn't hold him on the criminal charges, though, because the judicial system had decided he was not competent to stand trial and never would be. There is no doubt Bill could be disturbing and disruptive. "The System" was very frustrated when it couldn't get him out of the way through involuntary commitment.

In any event, on April 26th, I e-mailed all of the likely attorneys to tell them I would be representing Bill in any forced drugging proceeding. In that e-mail, I asked for Bill's hospital records. I also pointed out Bill had lost his housing, wasn't allowed at either of the shelters, there was a blizzard—and as a result, it was pretty likely Bill had acted that way because he knew how to get hauled into jail or API when he needed to get indoors for the night. I proposed a settlement whereby Bill be allowed to access API when he desired, and if he was brought in involuntarily, that he be let out on a pass during the day for at least four hours, with or without an escort. Not having heard anything back, on April 29th, I e-mailed the CEO of API and informed him I would be representing Bill with respect to any forced drugging proceedings going forward, and any forced drugging petition must be served (sent) to me. I also told him I needed a copy of Bill's chart (medical records), updated daily.

API filed a thirty-day commitment petition against Bill on April 28th, as well as a forced drugging petition. They weren't served on me, but I was given a copy of the April 29th order appointing the public defender as Bill's attorney in the forced drugging proceeding at 4:37 p.m. on April 29th. This order set the trial for the next morning at 8:30. First thing that morning, I filed a limited entry of appearance for the forced drugging petition only and a motion to vacate (reverse) the appointment of the public defender. One of the things I pointed out is that under the *Myers* Alaska Supreme Court decision, the forced drugging petition could not go forward unless and until Bill had been committed. Bill again elected a public trial.

The probate master held I would not be recognized as Bill's attorney unless and until Bill was committed, and my filings were rejected until the forced drugging petition was under consideration. This was wrong because a forced drugging petition had been filed and I had filed papers that I was Bill's attorney with respect to the forced drugging case. At the end of the trial, the probate master said she was going to recommend commitment. She also said she thought the Superior Court judge should conduct the forced drugging hearing because she assumed there would be an objection to whatever she recommended, and it would be more efficient. She was right about that.

On May 2nd, the probate master issued an order that because she was going to issue a commitment recommendation later that day, my entry of appearance would "be considered operative as to the medication petition." However, this was not sent to me, and I didn't receive it until after the trial on the forced drugging petition began on May 12th. On May 5th, the Superior Court judge issued a thirty-day commitment order, which also was not sent to me. On May 7th, because it had fallen through the cracks, API filed a motion to conduct the forced drugging hearing as soon as possible. That was sent to me. The case was transferred to a different judge, and the court set the trial on the forced drugging petition for Monday morning, May 12th.

MONDAY, MAY 12TH, 2008

I objected to the forced drugging trial going forward, because no commitment order had been issued by a Superior Court judge. Only then was I notified the previous judge had issued a commitment order. I then objected that I hadn't been given a copy of Bill's chart and needed time to conduct discovery. I asked for a settlement conference because Bill was entitled to a less-intrusive alternative than being drugged against his will, pointing out that after around eighty admissions to API, something besides the revolving door should be tried.

The judge told API to let me look at whatever they had brought of the chart and ruled she was going to have API present its case, even though I said I was not prepared to go forward and had just arrived from out of town at 1:00 a.m. that morning. She said she would figure out how much time to give me to prepare at the end of API's case. This ignored that preparation for cross-examination is standard in litigation (but not in these cases). I objected that Bill's Due Process right to meaningful notice and a meaningful opportunity to respond was being violated. This had no impact on the judge.

One of the things to which API's first witness, a psychologist, testified was that Bill's belief the drugs were poison showed he could not rationally participate in his treatment and made him incompetent to decline the drugs. API's second witness, a psychiatrist, agreed Bill would just quit taking the drug once he was let go. She also agreed it would be good to have a program that worked with people like Bill who chose not to take drugs when they were not in the hospital. Under the statute, API had to get court authorization to administer drugs if the person was incompetent to decide, even if they agreed to take them. The psychiatrist, however, testified, "If the patient agrees to take medication, why would I want to come to court?" This is another example of blatantly ignoring the law.

At the end of API's case, I moved to dismiss the forced drugging petition for two additional reasons that emerged in the testimony. The first was API admitting it would be good if he could be treated in the community without drugs, meant there was a less-intrusive alternative. The second was that by accepting Bill's decision to take the drugs in the past without court authorization, they were admitting he was competent to decide to take the drugs, and they couldn't turn around and say he was incompetent when he decided against taking them. And then I reiterated the court should order a settlement conference to work out a less-intrusive alternative. Despite my repeated protests that I needed more time, including that I had an oral argument before the Alaska Supreme Court the next morning, the judge ordered I had to file whatever I was going to file the next day, May 13th, and put on my case the day after that, on Wednesday, May 14th.

This was a nightmare scenario for me, because as previously mentioned, I have a pretty low tolerance for sleep deprivation. I had arrived from an out-of-state trip late the night before, only to learn about this trial first thing that morning, with an Alaska Supreme Court oral argument already scheduled for the next morning and the judge ordering I had to file anything for the recommenced trial by the next afternoon, which was the afternoon after my Supreme Court oral argument. Then I had to put on my case the morning after that. This was the sort of situation where I would normally take something to sleep to keep from going 'round the bend. I don't remember whether I did, but probably not, because I had the Alaska Supreme Court oral argument the next morning, and the sleep medication would have made me groggy. I just had to carry on the best I could and hope things didn't get too bad.

TUESDAY, MAY 13TH, 2008

Bill's chart was waiting for me when I got back from my Alaska Supreme Court argument. There simply wasn't time to do a proper job and prepare motions the way I normally would. All I was able to do by the end of May 13th was file the affidavits of Robert Whitaker, Ron Bassman, Paul Cornils, and Dr. Loren Mosher, and the prior testimony of Dr. Mosher and Sarah Porter. I called these pre-filed testimony. Other than my having done it in previous cases, this had never been done in forced drugging cases in Alaska. The other side, in this case API, has the right to cross-examine witnesses giving pre-filed testimony. There is an exception to this general rule, though, if the witness is unavailable, and if, in a prior case, the other side had had the opportunity and a similar motive to rebut the testimony. I invoked this principle for Dr. Mosher's testimony because he had died and for Sarah Porter because she was in New Zealand. Dr. Grace Jackson was willing to testify telephonically, and I sent her Bill's chart. Then I tried to prepare for the next morning's trial.

WEDNESDAY, MAY 14TH, 2008

Dr. Jackson had prepared a written report about how harmful and ineffective the neuroleptics are and the viability of other, non-harmful approaches, which I introduced as an exhibit. Since Robert Whitaker is a journalist, not a doctor, I first asked Dr. Jackson about his affidavit, and she testified it was very accurate and clear. She next testified psychiatrists receive very biased and inaccurate information from drug companies, as well as from medical schools. She testified it was an indoctrination. She then testified that while she had initially believed what she was taught, she could see in her patients it was not true. This led her to investigate the truth about the drugs. She also testified about additional reasons psychiatrists and other mental health professionals were ignorant about how harmful and ineffective the drugs were, including that medical journals had essentially become a marketing arm for the drug companies by publishing articles that were, at best, misleading, and by not publishing articles about the ineffective and harmful nature of these drugs. I know this is hard to believe, but even the former editor of the *New England Journal of Medicine*, Marcia Angell, published a book about this in 2005: *The Truth About the Drug Companies: How They Deceive Us and What to Do About It.*

Dr. Jackson testified to what I consider fraudulent drug company studies (described in the first chapter) and how these drugs, including the Risperdal API wanted to inject into Bill against his will, shorten life spans by twenty to twenty-five years. Dr. Jackson testified these drugs cause Chemical Brain Injury (CBI), and Bill was an example. She also testified these drugs cause cognitive and behavioral decline. The judge wanted her to focus on Risperdal, and Dr. Jackson testified Risperdal was particularly bad for causing brain and pituitary tumors, and sexual side effects, including men growing breasts. She also testified Risperdal causes diabetes, thyroid problems, strokes, heart attacks, leg clots, and fluid in the lungs. Dr. Jackson testified to other harm, including the likelihood it causes Alzheimer's dementia. She testified that while these drugs are called "antipsychotics," what they actually do is stop annoying behaviors, and they are in fact chemical lobotomies. She said the term antipsychotic was really an historical euphemism, once it became unacceptable to mention what these drugs were really doing.

Moving to Bill specifically, Dr. Jackson testified:

- The huge doses of Haldol he had been given during his first hospitalization had been enough to cause Parkinson's disease and was really the beginning of a long demise.

- Bill's psychotic symptoms hadn't gone away. In other words, the drugs never worked on Bill, yet the hospital insisted they continue to force them on him.

- All of the neuroleptics cause psychosis in some people.

- It is often withdrawal from these drugs, not any underlying mental illness, that causes psychotic symptoms.

- Because of this, people ought to be given a fair amount of time after withdrawal to see whether they can recover from the brain damage caused by the drug(s).

- The less-intrusive alternative plan set forth in Paul Cornils' affidavit "looked like a very solid and a very reasonable proposal." This less-intrusive alternative was essentially what I had proposed in my September 4th, 2007 pre-hearing brief, which I had been proposing ever since with more detail.

My final question to Dr. Jackson and her answer were:

Q What would you say about Mr. Bigley saying, "You just wanted to throw me in a cage, lock me up like an animal, take all my money, and try to poison me?"

A Well, if one just heard that without understanding the context or this person's history, one might think that sounds a bit outrageous or a bit extreme. But having read even the few notes from this person's medical history, I would say that sadly enough, that's exactly what has been happening to this man for 28 years.

On cross-examination by API's lawyer, Dr. Jackson testified, "There is also a high likelihood [Bill] is simply just going to die in the next five years if he is placed on [Risperdal]."

Next, I called psychiatrist Dr. Hopson, the medical director of API. Dr. Hopson disputed Robert Whitaker's and Dr. Jackson's testimony, citing a study that asserted neuroleptics reduced relapse rates by 50%. API was supposed to have notified me of any studies its witnesses were going to cite so I would have a fair opportunity to rebut them, but it hadn't. When he was asked about the proposed less-intrusive alternative that would allow Bill to leave the hospital during the day, he rejected it, saying, "That is not our mission. . . . [I]f we started housing patients and just letting them go out on pass all day, we would be full of patients like that, and we wouldn't be able to fulfill our mission totally." However, he testified, leaving API out of it, he thought the plan would be ideal, and it might be that Bill wouldn't ever have to come into the hospital again. We couldn't finish with Dr. Hopson that day, so the judge set the next morning to wrap up, telling me I had two hours and that was going to be it.

THURSDAY, MAY 15TH, 2008

Questioned by API, Dr. Hopson started out by testifying schizophrenia was decreasing people's life spans, and he didn't think forcing Bill to take Risperdal would shorten his life. Dr. Hopson also testified all of API's patients were there against their will.

When I had my chance to question him about the study he had cited the previous day, it was clear he didn't know anything about the study, and API agreed to strike his testimony about that, meaning the court would pretend he had never testified to that and supposedly wouldn't take it into consideration. I also got him to admit that even though API didn't normally provide outpatient treatment, they had for Bill. This was important because I was saying they should make an exception for Bill

Next, API cross-examined Paul Cornils, who as I mentioned was with CHOICES. I had left the board years before because CHOICES had been seeking funding from the State of Alaska, and I didn't think it would be successful if I was on the board and litigating against the state at the same time.

One of the things to which Mr. Cornils testified was he hadn't observed any difference in Bill being on or off the drugs other than the sedative effects, which resulted in him being less disturbing. Mr. Cornils testified to Bill needing almost 24/7 availability of someone who could pacify situations, and this had been a very successful strategy when funding was available. However, he testified the current medical director of CHOICES wouldn't support them working with any clients who refused to take medications against their doctor's recommendation. Uh-oh. Cornils' testimony was completely contrary to what I understood to be CHOICES policy, as I later confirmed with its executive director, but it was a huge problem for the trial. I tried to clean it up by making clear that if Bill had a psychiatrist willing to work with him without the drugs, CHOICES would help. Further, I got him to agree Bill didn't have a doctor recommending the drugs after he was discharged, undercutting the implication he was going against his doctor's advice. However, I knew Mr. Cornils' testimony—that CHOICES wouldn't work with Bill if he was not taking the drugs as prescribed—was going to be trouble for my less-intrusive alternative proposal. Then the judge asked whether he had tried to find a mental health provider for Bill outside of API. Mr. Cornils testified he was not aware of anyone willing to take the risk of something bad happening and them incurring the blame. Uh-oh even more.

I tried to clean that up with Mr. Cornils' testimony that as far as he was aware, Bill had never harmed anybody, and he'd never seen an indication Bill would. However, he testified to having been involved in a situation where he thought Bill would have been assaulted if Mr. Cornils had not intervened. He was my last witness and was a disaster.

Still, I felt API had not come close to proving by clear and convincing evidence that drugging Bill against his will was in his best interests, but knew the judge was likely to rule against him anyway. In that event, I would appeal the decision to the Alaska Supreme Court on Bill's behalf and attempt to prevent Bill from being drugged while the appeal was going on. Normally, when a judge issues a decision, it cannot be enforced for ten days, during which time one can move for a stay of the decision (delaying its taking effect) during appeal. However, the rule for forced drugging was such an order was effective immediately. This makes sense from the perspective that the state's whole idea is to get the person drugged into submission during the thirty-day commitment so they can then be let go.

The procedure for seeking a stay pending appeal is to ask the trial court first, so as a precaution, I moved the trial court judge for a stay in the event she granted the forced drugging petition. Often, even if the trial court is not going to grant a stay for the whole time an appeal takes, it will grant a short stay to allow the appellate court, in this case the Alaska Supreme Court, a chance to decide on the stay before the order becomes effective.

MONDAY, MAY 19TH, 2008

The next Monday, on May 19th, the judge granted the forced drugging petition, giving me only forty-eight hours to seek a stay from the Alaska Supreme Court.

STAY MOTION

On May 20th, I filed the appeal and moved for a stay of the forced drugging order. The basis for the stay was Bill would suffer irreparable harm if API were allowed to restart drugging him against his will. In addition to the evidence presented to the trial court, I filed a new affidavit by Dr. Jackson, detailing the irreparable harm caused by Risperdal. API agreed to delay shooting Bill up with Risperdal until noon on Friday to give it a chance to file its opposition, which it did on Thursday, May 22nd. On May 23rd, a single justice of the Alaska Supreme Court granted the stay, holding the evidence we presented supported our contentions, although it didn't necessarily mean API was wrong. This was a huge win, because it prevented API from drugging Bill while the appeal was going on, which normally would take well over a year.

API filed a motion for reconsideration to the full Alaska Supreme Court on May 28th. Under the Alaska appellate rules, if a motion is decided by a single justice, one has the right to file a motion for reconsideration, asking all five justices to decide it. API's motion for reconsideration was based in part on the argument that the stay would prevent API from drugging Bill against his will during his current or any future commitments. It also raised the specter of the stay order meaning every patient who lost a forced drugging petition could keep from being drugged for the extended time an appeal would take, merely by filing an appeal and moving for a stay. The full Alaska Supreme Court denied the motion for reconsideration on June 25th, 2008 without explanation. This is typical.

CHAOS ENSUES

This put "The System" in a pickle. API wasn't willing to have Bill there without being able to drug him. When they let him out, he was quite disturbing to some people, and the police would be called in to arrest him. Bill was arrested at least nine times between June 22nd and October 17th, 2008 for going to places he had been told to stay away from, including his guardian's office, as well as for yelling and some minor property damage. Not a single one of these alleged crimes was more than being disruptive. In any case, they couldn't keep him in jail because as I've mentioned earlier, it had been decided he was incompetent to stand trial and would never be competent to stand trial.

Normally, someone like Bill would have been involuntarily committed to API and drugged. However, because of the Alaska Supreme Court stay of the forced drugging order pending appeal, API didn't believe they could drug him and didn't want him there undrugged. They therefore wouldn't file commitment papers, and Bill would be released and then arrested again within a fairly short time. It all could have been avoided if they had just provided someone to be with Bill or available when things got tense, to engage with him and calm things down—the less-intrusive alternative we had proposed. This had been done successfully with a small grant from PsychRights to CHOICES as a test, but PsychRights didn't have the funds to continue. It certainly would have been less expensive than all of the criminal cases, with the police, jail personnel, court personnel, lawyers, etc. being paid to ineffectively deal with the situation, let alone all the trouble he was causing. They were stubborn. Bill was stubborn. I was determined, trying to force "The System" to provide him with adequate support.

District Court Judge Stephanie Rhoades was most often the judge handling Bill's criminal cases. The District Court handled minor criminal cases, and Judge Rhoades had started Anchorage's Mental Health Court to divert people diagnosed with mental illness from jail. From my perspective, Mental Health Court was really established to save the state money by reducing the number of people in jail, rather than to actually help the defendants. When it started, the Mental Health Court was a voluntary deferred prosecution program whereby misdemeanor defendants could get the charges dropped if they successfully engaged in recommended mental health treatment, stayed out of trouble, and "graduated." In practice, the program was "take your drugs or go to jail." It usually took years to get through, which was far longer than if people had simply been convicted and served their sentences. I found the program offensive because the defendants were treated like little children—given certificates and applauded if they were "good."

I also questioned whether it was a good option for defendants, because the Mental Health Court had control of their lives for years, and the psychiatric drugs are harmful and counter-productive. Later, the program was changed to a deferred sentencing approach where the defendant has to plead guilty and the sentence is suspended pending the person successfully navigating the program and graduating. If they don't, since they have already pled guilty they are sent to jail to serve the sentence. I see no benefit in this for most defendants and advise against participating in Anchorage's Mental Health Court.

Ch. 11.   The Last Big Battle

WEDNESDAY, OCTOBER 15TH, 2008

Judge Rhoades was livid about what was going on and leaned on API to get Bill committed, drugged, and out of circulation. Due to this pressure, API on October 15th filed an *ex parté* petition against Bill for him to be sent to API to be evaluated for commitment. An *ex parté* order to have Bill hauled to API was issued that same day. Thirty-day commitment and forced drugging petitions were filed on October 20th. Unlike the last forced drugging petition, in this one API also asked for permission to drug Bill on an emergency basis. That was because I had made such a stink about it the last time, even going to the Alaska Supreme Court on an emergency basis to have it stopped. Remember, API had dropped that forced drugging petition after they were caught illegally drugging Bill based on phony "emergencies."

TUESDAY, OCTOBER 21ST, 2008

The hearing on the commitment and forced drugging petitions was set for the next day, October 21st. At the beginning of the hearing in front of the probate master, I filed an entry of appearance for the forced drugging petition only. API put on a very weak case, saying Bill was a danger to others—even though he had never assaulted anyone, to their knowledge. They said he was a danger to himself because he might provoke someone to attack him, even though the worst they suspected had ever happened was him being pushed down and scraping his hands.

Remember, in its *Wetherhorn* decision, the Alaska Supreme Court had ruled someone could only be locked up for being gravely disabled if they "could not *survive* safely in freedom" (emphasis added). API said he was gravely disabled but admitted he was getting food and shelter. API was convincing in its argument that Bill was a royal pain in the ass, which was not disputed. That is not a legal reason for commitment, even though it is often the real reason. At the end of the hearing, the probate master said he found by clear and convincing evidence that Bill was a danger to himself or others and gravely disabled.

API wanted the forced drugging hearing to start right then, but I said it couldn't because the Supreme Court had held a forced drugging proceeding could only happen after commitment, and there was no commitment order. The probate master only had authority to make a recommendation to the Superior Court, and Bill had the right to make objections to the Superior Court. The probate master said he was going to hold the hearing so it would already be done in the event the Superior Court committed Bill. I said no. I had only found out about the forced drugging petition a few hours before and wasn't prepared to go forward. I had motions to file. I reiterated that under *Myers* and *Wetherhorn*, two cases I had won at the Alaska Supreme Court, the forced drugging petition could only proceed against a committed patient.

I also pointed out that in *Wayne B. v. Alaska Psychiatric Institute*, an Alaska Supreme Court case I had won just two months before, the Alaska Supreme Court ruled the Superior Court judge had to read a transcript of the hearing that had been held before the probate master, as required by the court rules, or at least listen to the recording of the hearing, before deciding whether to go along with the probate master's recommendations. The probate master called a recess and phoned the presiding judge to ask her what to do. The presiding judge had been the trial court judge in the *Myers* case. When the probate master came back, he said the forced drugging trial would be set when and if the Superior Court judge approved the commitment. I e-mailed API's lawyer that day, saying I would like to negotiate something that had a chance for things to work out for Bill. In that same e-mail, I said I needed a copy of everything in Bill's medical chart for 2007 and so far in 2008.

WEDNESDAY, OCTOBER 22ND, 2008

The next day, October 22nd, I filed a motion to dismiss the forced drugging petition. My first argument was that under *Myers* and *Wetherhorn*, it was improper to even file the forced drugging petition before Bill had been committed. My second argument was the forced drugging petition was factually insufficient. Just as in the last case, the entirety of the forced drugging petition with respect to non-emergency drugging was a checked box in a pre-printed form stating:

> Petitioner has reason to believe the patient is incapable of giving or withholding informed consent. The facility wishes to use psychotropic medication in a non-crisis situation.

This just restated what the statute said, but in *Myers*, the Alaska Supreme Court had held it is unconstitutional to drug someone against their will in a non-crisis situation unless the state also proves by clear and convincing evidence it is in the person's best interests, and no less-intrusive alternatives are available. My position was, as I had raised previously, that API had to allege facts that, if they were true, would entitle API to a forced drugging order.

I asserted they had to say why it was in Bill's best interest, under the *Myers* criteria. In other words, my position was the forced drugging petition had to include factual allegations for all of the elements the *Myers* decision held were required before they could drug Bill against his will. I also argued the forced drugging petition did not satisfy Due Process, citing the United States Supreme Court in *Hamdi v. Rumsfield*:

> For more than a century the central meaning of procedural due process has been clear: "Parties whose rights are to be affected are entitled to be heard; and in order that they may enjoy that right they must first be notified." It is equally fundamental that the right to notice and an opportunity to be heard "must be granted at a meaningful time and in a meaningful manner."

In other words, Bill was entitled to know enough about API's case to give him a meaningful chance to fight it. It also meant Bill had to be given sufficient time to mount a defense.

Finally, I argued API had admitted Bill was competent to decide not to take the drugs. The statute said he had to be competent to agree to take the drugs as well as competent to decline the drugs. Even if he agreed to take the drugs, if he was not competent, API had to get a court order. So when they had given him the drugs when he agreed without going to court, they had admitted he was competent.

I had been filing similar motions for the last four forced drugging petitions, but because Bill had been let go the first two times, they hadn't been ruled on. The points on appeal for the forced drugging order then on appeal had this as one of its issues, but the appeal had not yet been decided. I didn't know whether the Alaska Supreme Court would rule on this issue in that appeal, so I wanted to have it available for a possible appeal in this case, if we lost. One never really knows what issues in an appeal will be decided, or at least I never do. The appellate court may decide on different grounds than the trial court did or than I might wish—and as a general principle, if it can avoid deciding a constitutional issue, it will. For these reasons, I would sometimes just appeal on the constitutional issue—which would tend to have the most systemic impact—to try and get a decision on it. I needed to make such motions each time because with rare exceptions, one can only appeal for reasons raised in the trial court. Thus, I filed many of the same motions in different cases, hoping to win at the trial court but also setting things up for an appeal if we didn't.

THURSDAY, OCTOBER 23RD, 2008

API's lawyer hadn't responded to my overture about trying to work something out and getting me Bill's medical records, so I e-mailed her at 10:00 the next morning, October 23rd, that I would just go ahead and subpoena them. I said if she wanted to provide any input about who I should subpoena for the records and when to conduct the deposition, she should let me know immediately. Still having received no response, I e-mailed her that evening, saying I would just go ahead and subpoena Bill's "treating" psychiatrist for a deposition to be conducted the next Wednesday.

FRIDAY, OCTOBER 24TH, 2008

The next morning, API's attorney called me to say they would just dismiss the forced drugging petition rather than have me depose Bill's "treating" psychiatrist. API filed the motion to dismiss the forced drugging petition later that day, saying Bill "has responded well to his care at API." This was without being drugged.

MONDAY, OCTOBER 27TH, 2008

Three days later, on October 27th, the court granted API's motion to dismiss the forced drugging petition, and the same day, API filed a new forced drugging petition. This one also included so-called emergency drugging as well as non-crisis drugging and did not say anything about why it was being filed three days after API had moved to dismiss the previous one. As with the first, API merely checked boxes on the pre-printed form reciting the statutory bases for obtaining forced drugging orders. There was absolutely no information in the forced drugging petition that might give a clue about what was going on. The probate master signed an order appointing the Public Defender Agency as Bill's lawyer, even though I already was his lawyer, making that appointment wrong. He also set a hearing before the Superior Court judge assigned to the case for October 29th, just two days later, which was the date he had set for a hearing on the earlier forced drugging petition dismissed that same day.

One might wonder how the court could screw up so badly about who was Bill's lawyer, as has been described for many of these cases. The reason is these petitions are handled robotically. The Public Defender Agency is appointed. No one looks at the file to see what might have gone on previously (usually nothing has). This demonstrates these cases are not considered true legal cases. People facing involuntary commitment have a constitutional right to a court hearing and lawyer, but things are just rubber-stamped, and the lawyers and court system just go through the motions of a legal proceeding. This tended to not be as true if one were able to have the hearing before the Superior Court judge assigned to the case, because these hearings are not so routine for them and they are used to conducting real cases. Normally, though, the Superior Court judges went along with whatever the probate master recommended.

The judge set a hearing for 9:00 a.m. the next day, October 28th, to figure out where things were and what to do. Later that day, I filed a motion to have the hearing in a real courtroom rather than the hospital. I also filed a motion for summary judgment that (1) the forced drugging petition should be denied because the forced drugging was not in Bill's best interest and (2) the court should order API to provide the less-intrusive alternative I had been advocating for the last few commitment cases. As I had previously, in support of this I filed affidavits from Robert Whitaker, Dr. Mosher, Dr. Jackson, Dr. Bassman, Paul Cornils, and Sarah Porter, as well as transcripts from previous trials of testimony by Dr. Mosher and Dr. Jackson.

A motion for summary judgment is another way to finish a case without going to trial. In a motion to dismiss, you are saying that even if the facts the other side alleges are true, they don't get to win. In a motion for summary judgment, you submit admissible evidence, primarily affidavits, about the facts. To defeat a motion for summary judgment, the other side has to present its own evidence—again, usually through affidavits—creating a factual dispute about something that makes a difference as to who wins. The rule phrases it as "a genuine dispute over a material fact."

TUESDAY, OCTOBER 28TH, 2008

Before the 9:00 a.m. hearing, I filed a motion to vacate (get rid of) the trial date, saying Bill was entitled to time for me to prepare and gather more information through discovery. At the hearing, API pushed hard to have the trial the next morning, but the judge set it for November 5th at 9:00 a.m. at API. This effectively denied Bill's motion to have the trial in a real courtroom, and I protested that in light of the trial being open to the public, it should be held in a real courtroom because it was not possible for a hearing to be truly public if it was held behind the locked doors at API. The judge was unpersuaded but willing to consider it if the trial went for more than one day. API tried to get the judge to rule I couldn't conduct any discovery, such as taking depositions, but the judge said Bill was entitled to learn API's case against him. I had my problems with this judge, but he was the most thoughtful of all the judges I had when representing Bill.

The judge said I would have to refile the motion to dismiss because the forced drugging petition to which that one was directed had been withdrawn, although he said it could just be a piece of paper saying I was refiling it. I refiled later that day, with an addendum saying API had admitted Bill was competent to decline the drugs because they let him decide to take the drugs.

WEDNESDAY, OCTOBER 29TH, 2008

On October 29th, API filed a witness list, naming fourteen witnesses to potentially testify at the forced drugging trial. In typical cases, API would call just one witness, maybe two, and the public defender wouldn't call anyone, except maybe their client.

THURSDAY, OCTOBER 30TH, 2008

On October 30th, I filed a motion to dismiss the emergency part of the forced drugging petition on the grounds it didn't allege any facts legally entitling API to drug Bill on an emergency basis. The petition didn't state any facts as to why emergency drugging was necessary "to preserve the life of or prevent significant harm to the patient or someone else," or what things API had tried first, both of which were required by statute. Instead, the entirety of the emergency drugging petition was just a checked box on a pre-printed form stating:

> There have been, or it appears that there will be,
> repeated crisis situations requiring the immediate use of

medication to preserve the life of, or prevent significant physical harm to, the patient or another person. The facility wishes to use psychotropic medication in future crisis situations.

This just parroted what was in the statute.

I also subpoenaed four API employees for depositions to be held November 3rd, including its CEO and the psychiatrist "treating" Bill. I subpoenaed the CEO to bring all policies, training materials, and other documents pertaining to emergency drugging. Since a subpoena is a court order, the CEO was required to bring these materials.

API filed an opposition to holding the trial in a real courtroom, saying, among other things, "API denies access to no one, unless there is a serious safety concern." The untruth of this was starkly illustrated during the trial. API also filed an affidavit about how dangerous it would be to take Bill into a courtroom, which was ridiculous because they had done it numerous times already that year, including for the hearing before the probate master just nine days before.

FRIDAY, OCTOBER 31ST, 2008

On October 31st, API filed (1) a motion to quash the deposition notices, seeking to prohibit me from taking any depositions, and (2) a motion for a protective order to prevent me from making the transcripts of any depositions public if they were held. It also filed an opposition to my motion for summary judgment and motion to dismiss. In this opposition, API stated, "[T]he petition includes all the factual reasons that administration of medication is necessary." I describe this sort of argument as "red is blue." Lawyers get up and just say blatantly untrue things, and they often get away with it. This is actually against lawyers' ethics rules, whether they're in court or not.

I replied to API's opposition to holding the trial in a real courtroom. The statute provides the trial should take place in "a physical setting least likely to have a harmful effect on the mental or physical health of the respondent [Bill], within practical limits." API asserted holding it at the "hospital" met this description, and I said Bill was entitled to a hearing on whether it was a physical setting least likely to have a harmful effect on him, because he disagreed with API on that point. I also said if API was so concerned about bringing Bill to the courthouse and back, I would be happy to do so.

MONDAY, NOVEMBER 3RD, 2008

The judge held a hearing first thing in the morning on November 3rd to rule on various pending motions. He denied Bill's motion to dismiss the emergency drugging order, despite having no understanding of what was going on. I suppose one could say it was my fault the judge didn't understand, but he wouldn't let me explain. He also denied the motion to hold the hearing at the courthouse, at least for the first day, but left open the possibility other days could be, depending on how things went. He denied API's motion to prevent me from conducting any discovery.

TUESDAY, NOVEMBER 4TH, 2008

November 4th started with the deposition of API's CEO, from whom I was trying to get information about their training and policies on emergency drugging. The CEO did not comply with the subpoena requiring him to bring documentation about API's emergency drugging policies and training. API's lawyer was obstructionist throughout the short deposition, objecting to the deposition even taking place, saying she was going to move for reconsideration of the judge's ruling that I could take depositions. The CEO was extraordinarily non-cooperative, at the urging of API's lawyer.

Next, I took the deposition of Bill's "treating" psychiatrist, who had signed the forced drugging petition. She testified she hadn't decided what drugs to force on Bill, even though API had to ask for approval for a specific drug or drugs at specific doses. When I pressed her on this, she testified she was focusing more on Risperdal, with Zyprexa as a second choice. She liked Risperdal because it was injectable and would last a long time in his system. She testified she wasn't more definitive because she liked to discuss the drugs with her patients. She obviously didn't have a clue about the requirements under the *Myers* decision for the forced drugging petition she'd filed against Bill.

My main objective in her deposition, though, was to reveal how API actually went about drugging someone for an "emergency." As set forth above, the legal requirements for emergency drugging are very strict, both in that (a) immediate use of the medication must be necessary "to preserve the life of, or prevent significant physical harm to, the patient or another person," and (b) the hospital must document the justification for the emergency drugging. Bill's chart said the emergency drugging was for "AAI," which the psychiatrist first testified meant "agitation, aggression, and insomnia." Then she testified it meant "agitation, anxiety, and insomnia," and when asked which it was, testified, "I look at it as agitation, aggression, and insomnia." The point, though, isn't how she looks at it, but what it means. If "AAI" had no set meaning, then it couldn't legitimately form the basis for emergency drugging. It was clear the psychiatrist also had no idea of the rules for emergency drugging.

API sent two lawyers to the deposition to be obstructionist, objecting to everything as irrelevant. For example, one of API's lawyers objected on the ground it was irrelevant for me to ask the psychiatrist whether the long-term use of the drugs might have caused brain damage, resulting in some of his symptoms. How could that not be relevant to whether the drugging was in Bill's best interest? The chart noted Bill had no teeth. The psychiatrist didn't know these drugs cause people to lose their teeth. I had found this out from my dentist when we were talking about the neuroleptics. Like everything else, Bill's loss of teeth was blamed on him rather than the drugs they'd forced on him for over twenty-five years. That same day, API filed a motion to forbid me from saying "forced drugging" and to prohibit Robert Whitaker, Dr. Jackson, and Dr. Bassman from testifying.

Bill's forced drugging trial was set to begin the next morning, and I had a lot of preparation to do. I was pretty sleep deprived from all this work that had to be done in a short time frame—not a good situation for me.

WEDNESDAY, NOVEMBER 5TH, 2008

API and the public defenders each had two lawyers at the beginning of the trial. I had my assistant. The public defenders were there because the judge had ordered them to attend, at least initially. One objected to me representing Bill only on the forced drugging petition, saying I had to be in for the whole case or nothing. The judge pointed out the court rules allowed limited representation, and the public defender said the judge in a previous case had not allowed it. The public defender complained I would not coordinate with them and I had submitted materials that were disparaging to the public defenders. That was probably fair enough. She also said Bill's choice of counsel was not completely clear. She asked the judge to ask Bill whether he wanted me to represent him, and the judge said he didn't think that was appropriate.

API brought up that it had moved to prohibit me from using the term "forced drugging." The judge said using the term "forced drugging" versus "involuntary administration of psychotropic medication" didn't cross the line into being disrespectful. Then, one of API's lawyers asked for a protective order against anyone publishing about the trial in a newspaper, because a member of the media was in the waiting room, wanting to attend. I suggested that API not allowing the reporter in was contempt of court because Bill had elected to have the trial open to the public. API told the court it was faxing a motion for a protective order. The motion sought to "protect [witnesses] from annoyance and harassment" by me. The motion protested that in the past, I had filed a civil rights complaint against an API psychiatrist, named him in court pleadings involving Bill, and tried to have criminal charges filed against him, which was now making it hard for him to get a job and for API to hire psychiatrists. My view was API's psychiatrists were committing assaults against the patients, and criminal complaints were completely justified. It is criminal assault to administer drugs to someone without legal authority to do so. Why should API and its psychiatrists be able to get away with assault? API's motion also cited the Zyprexa Papers injunction against me to try to establish I was untrustworthy.

I brought up that my summary judgment motion was pending, and the judge said he was denying it. I said I was entitled to oral argument, and the judge said, "We'll do that right now." So we had oral argument on the spot. I pointed out we had submitted affidavits and other testimony, and under the rules, API was required to submit affidavits or other proof to create a "genuine dispute of material fact" but had failed to do so. I said the proof we submitted established the drugs were reducing life spans by twenty-five years, are not effective for many people, and cause brain damage. I pointed out we had also submitted Dr. Jackson's expert opinion that Bill was suffering from dysmentia or dementia, and every dose would likely cause further damage. Dysmentia is psychiatric drug-induced instability in mood, behaviors, and interpersonal relations. I also said we had presented unrebutted evidence for an available and less-intrusive alternative. API argued it didn't need to present evidence on whether the drugs were dangerous. The judge said there were disputed material facts based on the entire file and Bill's history. In other words, he ignored the rule on summary judgment requiring API to submit affidavits or other admissible evidence to counter the evidence we submitted.

I then brought up it appeared API was illegally drugging Bill under the emergency drugging statute, but API said it was not subjecting Bill to emergency drugging. The court visitor then testified, including that Bill not wanting to take the drugs because it "kills his brain" was proof he was incompetent to refuse them.

API called a police officer, who testified the police had been called on Bill many times over the past few months, including by my office. This was true. Bill was scaring tenants in my office building, and I had to have him leave.

I called Dorothy Pickles, who had obtained her master's degree in social work after many years as a psychiatric patient, including being locked up in API a couple of times. Ms. Pickles had then worked at API and with Bill a few years earlier. She testified that in her opinion, Bill had at least four times expressed a desire not to have psychiatric medications when he was competent, and a couple of times when he was not competent. This was important because the statute didn't allow forced drugging if someone while competent had expressed their desire not to take the drug(s). This was specifically pointed out by the Alaska Supreme Court in *Myers*. The judge didn't allow Ms. Pickles to testify that API's medical records are slanted to support commitment and forced drugging, which she called "charting to the negative."

API then called a worker who had delivered psych drugs to Bill on a regular basis a number of years earlier when she worked for another agency, and she testified he had been reasonably pleasant and personable then. She was now working at API and said Bill couldn't even engage in a conversation off the drugs. When I cross-examined her, she said it would be good for someone to be with him all day in the community to, among other things, help keep him out of trouble. API questioned her again later, and she testified Bill had told her he wanted her to send him to Cuba. She then testified this wasn't Bill's true wish, demonstrating the contempt in which she held Bill.

The judge had other hearings that afternoon so he recessed the trial until the following morning. After 4:00 p.m., I received motions from API (1) to strike all the deposition testimony and (2) for a protective order prohibiting me from disseminating any of the deposition and hearing transcripts. In its motion to strike all the deposition testimony, API asserted API's policies and practices regarding "emergency" drugging were irrelevant, even though it had asked the court to approve such "emergency" drugging. API asserted the rest of the deposition testimony was irrelevant to its very limited view of what the court was to consider, which did not take into account the Alaska Supreme Court's rulings in *Myers*.

THURSDAY, NOVEMBER 6TH, 2008

The psychiatrist who was "treating" Bill was the only witness the next day, November 6th. The transcript of this day's hearing has 631 instances where the court recorder could not make out what was said. This raises Due Process concerns because Bill was entitled to an accurate transcript for possible appeal. Before I started taking cases, there had never been any appeals of involuntary commitment or forced drugging orders, and presumably no one had ever listened to the recordings to see how bad they were. By the time of this trial, however, they knew they had problems and were trying to fix them, but it clearly hadn't worked.

The psychiatrist testified she didn't try to discuss medications with Bill because he would get so angry about them. When she started to testify that not medicating Bill would cause him to deteriorate and there were studies to show this, I objected because she had not complied with the deposition subpoena to provide me with any studies she might rely on. She then changed her testimony to say she was relying on her experience.

Going back over the transcripts for writing this book, I was struck with how bad I am at cross-examination. I was never really a trial lawyer before I started taking these cases and can't say I really am now. In fairness to me, it is hard to accomplish much with the other side's witnesses. At least, that's what I tell myself. In any event, I didn't accomplish much in the cross-examination but did get the psychiatrist to admit that elements of my proposed less-intrusive alternative would be helpful to Bill. However, she was extraordinarily evasive.

The psychiatrist testified that when they were discharging him because he no longer met commitment criteria, they always offered to admit him voluntarily. One aspect of my proposed less-intrusive alternative was that Bill be allowed to stay at API if he wanted when he didn't have other housing. API said this was unacceptable, even though we were asking for virtually the same thing the psychiatrist testified they were already offering to him.

Just before finishing up for the day, API raised its motion to prohibit me from posting court filings on PsychRights' website. The judge ruled I could post any filing but reconfirmed I couldn't post deposition transcripts except to the extent they had been legitimately used in the trial. The judge set the next Monday, November 10th, as the last day of trial.

After the trial was over for the day, API filed a motion to reconsider the judge's ruling allowing us to take depositions, asserting that allowing Bill to obtain evidence from API pertinent to his attempting to prevent API from forcing unwanted chemicals into his body was "unduly burdensome."

FRIDAY, NOVEMBER 7TH, 2008

The next day, November 7th, 2008, the judge denied API's motion for reconsideration, which asked him to reverse his order allowing me to take depositions. Around 4:30, API filed objections to all the written testimony I had submitted. One of these objections claimed that a hearing on API's petition for an order that Bill be administered psychiatric drugs against his will was not a forum for challenging the appropriateness of psychiatric drugs to treat mental illness. This was beyond ridiculous because the *Myers* decision ruled the state could only drug someone against their will if the court found it was in the person's best interest.

I had occasion to e-mail the two API attorneys and concluded, "As always, I would very much prefer to work something out that is acceptable to everyone than litigate." One of API's attorneys wrote back that only the judge could decide, and it would be illegal to work something out. This is absurd.

MONDAY, NOVEMBER 10TH, 2008

First thing Monday morning, I filed a "Respondent's History," with exhibits, going through what psychiatry had done to Bill, starting in 1980 with his first breakdown. Looking back now, it seems to me the judge's view on Bill's history might have been much different from mine. I saw it as showing psychiatry had taken someone who'd had a natural reaction to a traumatic event and destroyed his life. I filed the history because I believed the judge would look at it the same way, but now I think he probably thought it just showed the severity of Bill's "mental illness."

API and I had stipulated that five of the witnesses for which I had pre-filed testimony—Dr. Loren Mosher, Robert Whitaker, Dr. Ronald Bassman, Dr. Grace Jackson, and Sarah Porter—had not examined or treated Bill, and the sixth, Paul Cornils, had not in the last twelve months. A stipulation is an agreement, in this case to certain facts. API had this theory that information about the drugs being very counterproductive and harmful was not relevant to the court's decision about whether they were in Bill's best interest, and this is what the testimony of these six was about. That is why API wanted the stipulation.

At the beginning of that day's trial, however, they said they wanted to cross-examine everyone even though we had already stipulated they had not treated Bill. I am sure they insisted on cross-examining these witnesses because they were hoping I wouldn't be able to arrange to get them on the phone, and the pre-filed testimony for anyone I wasn't able to make available for cross-examination would be thrown out.

The first witness called by API that day had worked for the Anchorage Mental Health Court and then, at the time of his testimony, was working for the Alaska Mental Health Trust Authority, which had some flexible funding it could provide. He testified there was so much concern about the problems Bill was creating in the community that a meeting had been called to see whether a services package could be put together to deal with the situation. The public defenders who had not been advocating for any particular services were invited to this meeting, while I, who had proposed specific service components based on my pretty extensive knowledge and understanding of Bill and had been representing him in quite a few cases, had not.

The next witness called by API was the person who had formerly been assigned as Bill's guardian, Steve Young. Citing Bill's eighty involuntary commitments, he testified Bill had been given excellent psychiatric care. Young testified Bill did better when he was on the drugs.

When I asked him whether he would force Bill to take drugs even if they would shorten his life, he testified, "We have to look at the quality of his life . . . that quality of life may even be more important than the quantity." When I asked him whether it was his decision to make, he said yes because Bill was incapacitated. Now, I don't necessarily disagree with the idea that quality of life can be more important than how long one lives. I feel that way to a certain extent, but what is so objectionable is they felt they got to overrule what Bill decided was a better quality of life. In reality, it wasn't about Bill's quality of life at all but about reducing other people's annoyance with him. This is an example of the power of a full guardian. *They can decide to shorten someone's life because he disturbs people.*

That morning, it had come out that API had refused to let a photographer from the local newspaper into the hearing. After the former guardian testified, the judge hauled in the head of API to interrogate him, at the end of which the judge said:

> In the future, the next time a reporter, member of the press, a photographer, a member of the public seeks access to the courtroom, that person is to be allowed access.

> I find it astonishing that API doesn't get it. I find it—I found it astonishing last time when the Department of Law precluded a reporter from coming into an open courtroom. I am astonished that it's happened again.

> I am not criticizing the two assistant attorney generals on this. I don't understand that you two have been involved.

> But API and the Department of Law have got to understand that if they are going to be allowed to have a facility within API, we deem it an open and public courtroom, that means that neither the Department of Law nor API can unilaterally deny a member of the public, including a member of the media, into the courtroom facility.

> I don't have any difficulty with API saying while you travel from the lobby into the courtroom, you cannot— the greater API rules apply. That's perfectly reasonable. But the use of [photographs or other media within what is effectively a public courtroom] is governed by court system rules, not API rules.

> Call your next witness.

API's next witness was a mental health clinician at the jail, who testified:

> [Bill] truly doesn't believe he should be incarcerated whatsoever, yelling, screaming, cursing, begging and pleading at the same time to be released and taken out.

In the witness' mind, this demonstrated Bill was very mentally ill, whereas I regard it as an admission of inhumane treatment in jail. He mainly testified Bill had gotten worse and worse in 2008, and that when they drugged Bill, he got better. Then he would be released, stop taking the drugs, and would get worse. He basically testified Bill was an out-of-control monster when not taking their drugs.

> I see Mr. Bigley when he comes into our institution, tormented thought, delusional content, ranting, raving, can't sleep because of the racing thoughts that are going through his mind.

> And then I see him get on medication, and I see the man able to rest, I see the man able to eat meals and not be afraid that we're poisoning him.

On cross-examination, I got him to admit Bill was actually pretty calm during the trial without being drugged. This was important because I had prevented them from drugging him for a considerable amount of time. This mental health clinician was API's last witness.

My first witness was the head of the local community mental health center. They had put together a proposal to provide Bill with intensive sixteen-hours-per-day services that could provide a less-intrusive alternative. My questioning was not very effective, but he did testify people taking psych drugs know better than anyone else how the drugs make them feel, and Bill should be given a chance to be successful in the community without being forced to take drugs.

My next witness was a long-time Alaskan psychiatrist, Aron Wolf, with whom I had worked a fair amount and who had been asked by the CEO of API to do an independent evaluation of Bill. Dr. Wolf testified that in general, he agreed with Robert Whitaker's affidavit. On cross-examination, though, Dr. Wolf testified he didn't think the drugs were killing Bill; he was going downhill, but whether due to the drugs or the natural course of the illness was an unanswered question.

I asked Dr. Wolf whether he thought it might calm someone down to be asked whether they would prefer medication or restraints, such as a being strapped to a gurney. He testified he hadn't really thought about it, and that was not the normal hospital protocol, but it might. I asked this question because I think when someone is having a meltdown, they can be approached and told, "Listen, we can't have you doing these things, because of _____, so if you don't calm down, we are going to have to inject you with Haldol or put you in restraints (strapped down) or seclusion (solitary confinement). Which would you prefer?" I think some people would prefer the restraints or seclusion over the drug, but I also think there is some chance that simply giving them the choice would allow them to calm down.

I called the CEO of API back to testify that API charged patients $1,018 per day for the privilege of being held there against their will. This was to show the less-intrusive alternative we had proposed was not as expensive as what they were doing.

Next were the cross-examinations of the people whose direct testimony I had pre-filed. First up was Dr. Grace Jackson. She testified there was so much information arguing against the use of neuroleptics she considered it both unscientific and, depending on the context, unethical to prescribe them. She testified she believed the Risperdal API wanted to force on Bill would kill Bill: "It's just a matter of time." During my redirect questioning, Dr. Jackson testified:

- If someone had managed to get off a neuroleptic, they should not be started back on them.

- Withdrawing from neuroleptics causes psychotic symptoms, manic symptoms, depression, and/or anxiety and agitation.

- It is important people be given an extended time off the neuroleptics, because it can take up to a year for the brain to "recalibrate" after the drug has been withdrawn.

Due to scheduling issues, the rest of the cross-examinations were put off a week until November 17th.

MONDAY NOVEMBER 17TH, 2008

The first witness API cross-examined on November 17th was Dr. Ron Bassman, from whom I had submitted an affidavit regarding less-intrusive alternatives. The cross-examination started as follows:

Q   Dr. Bassman, you are not a medical doctor, correct?

A   That's correct.

Q   So you are a psychologist, not a psychiatrist?

A   That's correct.

Q   You are not familiar with the standard of care for psychiatry in the State of Alaska, are you, Dr. Bassman?

A   No, I am not.

Q   You cannot offer any true alternative to medication for Mr. Bigley, can you, Mr. Bassman—Dr. Bassman?

A   Yes, I can.

Oops. API tried to clean this up by getting Dr. Bassman to testify he could not personally offer Bill a less-intrusive alternative in Anchorage, Alaska. Dr. Bassman's testimony lasted about two minutes.

Next up was Paul Cornils, whose erroneous testimony in May— that CHOICES would not work with someone who was not taking drugs—had been so devastating. One might wonder why I even included his affidavit this time after it had been such a disaster the previous time. That is a good question. First, and most importantly, he had worked extensively and successfully with Bill without the drugs, and I didn't have anyone else. Second, I thought I had gotten him straightened out that CHOICES would work with Bill even if he decided not to take the drugs. In the end, it didn't work out very well because he testified he didn't know any agency that would work with Bill if he wasn't taking the drugs.

Robert Whitaker's pre-filed testimony was the next to be subjected to cross-examination. He testified he was not a doctor and didn't know the exact drug regimen proposed for Bill. His testimony took just about five minutes.

I then called Susan Musante, who ran CHOICES. She testified that contrary to Mr. Cornils' testimony, CHOICES would work with Bill if enough staffing was funded, even if he chose not to take the drugs.

I thought I had arranged for Sarah Porter to be on the line from New Zealand, but I couldn't reach her. Even though the judge had said I needed to make everyone available for cross-examination that day, he gave me until the next day to get her on the line.

One of the things I have learned over the years is winning on these kinds of procedural points is not necessarily a good sign. Often it can mean the judge is going to rule against you on the main issue and doesn't want to give you a good appeal point.

TUESDAY, NOVEMBER 18TH, 2008

I did manage to get Ms. Porter on the line the next day for API to cross-examine. It lasted less than three minutes, and they accomplished nothing, but I had gotten her valuable testimony in the previous case into this one.

TUESDAY, NOVEMBER 25TH, 2008: TRIAL COURT DECISION

A week later, on November 25th, the judge issued a thirty-four-page written decision, granting the forced drugging petition but staying it (delaying the effective date) until December 15th to give me a chance to have the Alaska Supreme Court rule on whether the existing stay was still in effect. In approving the forced drugging, the judge held:

> The Court is willing to assume that past medications have damaged Bigley's brain. It is further willing to assume that additional brain damage will result if API is allowed to administer more psychotropics. But that does not end the analysis.

> The Court finds that the danger of additional (but uncertain) damage is outweighed by the positive benefits of the administration of medication and the emotional and behavioral problems that will escalate if Bigley is not medicated. Even if the medication shortens Bigley's lifespan, the Court would authorize the administration of the medication because Bigley is not well now and he is getting worse.

I guess judges decide who shall live and who shall die all the time, although the death penalty is not even allowed against murderers in Alaska.

To approve forced drugging under the Alaska Supreme Court's *Myers* decision, the court had to find there were no less-intrusive alternatives. With respect to this, the judge held:

> Even if Bigley were afforded the most protective
> wraparound set of services, such as a home and the
> team of attendants, the Court would authorize the
> medication.

Under the statute, to allow the forced drugging the court had to find Bill was not competent to decline the drugs. In support of his finding that Bill was not competent, he wrote:

> [Bill] does fear that he is being poisoned by medication
> that he has received in the past. But this is part of his
> delusional thought pattern and not an objection based
> upon his experience with or reaction to medication.

The judge had absolutely no basis for drawing this conclusion. Of course Bill's objections were based on his experience with the drugs. In fact, the material I presented included that Bill had been cooperative with the drugs during the first couple of admissions to API but started refusing when he decided they weren't helping and had terrible negative effects.

The judge did, however, criticize the lack of less-intrusive alternatives:

> There will be patients whose chronic illness and
> immediate needs are not as severe as Bigley's. For those
> patients it will be possible to identify less-intrusive
> means of protecting them than medication. But if API
> cannot deliver those means of treatment or array of
> services, is that failure to provide that less-intrusive
> means justification for the medication? That seems
> highly unlikely. The question that must be anticipated
> by API and other state agencies, is what responsibility
> or obligation does API or the state have to provide
> those services, whether by public facilities or by public
> funding.

MONDAY, DECEMBER 1ST, 2008

On December 1st, I filed an appeal of the November 25th forced drugging order. The points on appeal were that the Superior Court erred by:

1. proceeding on the forced drugging petition, in violation of the stay issued in Alaska Supreme Court Case No. S13116;

2. denying Bill's motion to dismiss for failing to state a claim upon which relief may be granted;

3. denying Bill's motion for summary judgment, there being no dispute over any material fact;

4. finding the course of treatment proposed by the Alaska Psychiatric Institute was in Bill's best interest;

5. failing to order the Alaska Psychiatric Institute to provide a less-intrusive alternative;

6. excluding the testimony of Dorothy Pickles;

7. concluding Bill was gravely disabled;

8. concluding there was no less-intrusive alternative to the forced drugging available; and

9. concluding no less-restrictive alternative to locking Bill up was available.

While similar, the rule is there must be no less-*intrusive* alternative available with respect to forced drugging and no less-*restrictive* alternative with respect to involuntary commitment. I also filed a motion in the trial court to modify the stay so it would last until the Alaska Supreme Court decided whether it should remain in effect. One of my reasons was that oral argument on the appeal of the May forced drugging order, which had been appealed and stayed, was set for December 16th, and the trial court's stay of the November 25th forced drugging order was set to expire the day before that. The judge extended the stay until December 17th.

WEDNESDAY, DECEMBER 3RD, 2008

On December 3rd, API filed a motion for clarification of the November 25th decision, asking whether it could drug Bill on an emergency basis in spite of the stay until December 17th, and threatening to release Bill because API could not "continue to house a patient who presents a danger to himself or to others with no appropriate method of treating that patient." That isn't the law. Bill's supposed extremely dangerous behavior, according to his "treating" psychiatrist, was "throwing himself up against a wall" and making threats. API's medical director said he was injuring his hand by punching the wall, and possibly suffering concussions by banging his head. It is interesting that Bill's "treating" psychiatrist did not say that. In any event, what this demonstrates clearly is API was incapable of treating people without using drugs. This was and remains basically true of psychiatric "hospitals" around the country. The judge granted the motion the same day without giving me a chance to respond, saying he should have been clearer in his November 25th decision.

DECEMBER 8TH–12TH, 2008

On Monday, December 8th, the public defender again moved to prohibit me from representing Bill on just the forced drugging petition, and I moved for a stay of the emergency drugging authorization.

On Tuesday, December 9th, API joined in the public defender's request to prohibit me from representing Bill, saying Bill had told its attorney he wanted her (API's attorney) to represent him and not me.

On Wednesday, December 10th, the judge denied the public defender's motion to remove me.

On Thursday, December 11th, Bill's guardian moved for reconsideration of the judge's denial of the public defender's motion to remove me and filed a motion to prohibit me from representing Bill. In it, the guardian asserted Bill had expressed he didn't want me to represent him anymore. I had informed the guardian that this was not my understanding, but if Bill told me he didn't want me to represent him, I would cease representing him.

On Friday, December 12th, the judge denied the guardian's motion to reconsider his refusal to prohibit me from representing Bill.

TUESDAY, DECEMBER 16TH, 2008

Oral argument on the appeal of the May forced drugging order was held before the Alaska Supreme Court in the morning of December 16th. The first thing I brought up was their May stay would be violated if they didn't take action by the end of the day. I spent the rest of my opening arguing for the less-intrusive alternative, because while some very important legal issues were involved, obtaining a less-intrusive alternative for Bill was the only thing that was going to actually help him personally. The other issues could establish good precedent and help other people in the future but wouldn't really help Bill. After API gave its argument, on rebuttal I stressed it was clear after twenty-eight years of forced drugging and seventy-five admissions that API's approach wasn't working, and Bill should be given a chance under the less-intrusive alternative he had proposed.

I had raised violations of Bill's right to Due Process in the briefing, and at the end of the argument, Justice Winfree asked me what I had requested from the trial court that I did not get and how that had prejudiced (harmed) Bill. I said I'd been denied time to prepare, denied discovery, denied Bill's chart until right before the trial started, and denied the right to know, before the hearing started, what case API was making. With respect to the last item, I said the petition should include information on all of the elements the *Myers* decision had required the court to consider. Recall, I had been making this argument at the trial court in a number of cases. This was the first case in which I had a chance to make the argument to the Alaska Supreme Court.

WEDNESDAY, DECEMBER 17TH, 2008

The next day, on December 17th, the Alaska Supreme Court denied the emergency motion to enforce the stay, thereby allowing Bill to be drugged into oblivion. Because of this I decided to drop the appeal of the November 25th forced drugging order. We already had the other one going on the constitutional issues, and since I had failed to prevent Bill from being drugged this time, the appeal wouldn't do him any good.

FEBRUARY 2009: BACK IN THE COMMUNITY

Bill was released from the hospital in mid-February 2009, and the types of social supports I had been trying to get him as a less-intrusive alternative were largely provided. A multi-agency team was formed to provide services to Bill, and a local agency called Assets assigned someone to help him meet his basic needs and avoid getting in trouble. I would have lunch with Bill fairly frequently. He stayed out of the hospital even though he had quit the drugs. This worked for months.

MAY 22ND, 2009: BIGLEY V. ALASKA PSYCHIATRIC INSTITUTE

During this period, on May 22nd, the Alaska Supreme Court decided *Bigley v. Alaska Psychiatric Institute*, the appeal of the May 2008 forced drugging order for which oral argument had been held the previous December 16th. We had a number of big wins, all based on violations of Bill's constitutional rights:

- If there is a feasible less-intrusive alternative, the state has to provide it or let the person go.

- A petition for forced drugging must include the factors the *Myers* decision required be considered. These are: the patient's symptoms and diagnosis; the medication to be used; the method of administration; the likely dosage; possible side effects; the risks and expected benefits; and the risks and benefits of alternative treatments and nontreatment.

- API had violated Bill's Due Process rights by not sufficiently notifying Bill of the nature of the treatment they were seeking to force on him and by not giving his lawyer (me) his hospital chart sufficiently in advance of the trial to allow for preparation.

The Alaska Supreme Court did rule Bill was not entitled to the less-intrusive alternative we had proposed, deferring to the trial court's factual determination that our proposal wouldn't work.

With respect to requiring the petition to include sufficient information, the court held:

> The right to refuse psychotropic medication is a fundamental right protected by the Alaska Constitution's guarantees of liberty and privacy. We held in *Myers* that such involuntary medication cannot be ordered unless a court finds by clear and convincing evidence that the treatment is in the best interests of the patient. Bigley asserts that the trial court erred in making this finding. We have determined in this case that Bigley did not receive adequate notice of the nature of API's treatment proposal and was denied access to information needed to prepare his case under the *Myers* best interests factors. While it is possible that these due process violations constituted harmless error, it is also

possible that they deprived Bigley of the opportunity to properly develop his case on best interests.

This is what I had said at the oral argument in response to the question from Justice Winfree. I have gone to seminars where appellate judges say oral argument doesn't matter, but there are three instances I can recall where my responses to questions made it into the appellate decision. I also recall when I blew a question that might have avoided a terrible loss if I had responded better.

JULY 2009: THE GUARDIAN PREVENTS ME FROM COMMUNICATING WITH BILL

Things were going relatively well with Bill until late June/early July 2009, when he vanished from my perspective. The guardian refused to provide me with any information, and it is clear they took steps to prevent Bill from communicating with me. The message on his cell phone had been changed and was no longer Bill's voice. It said Bill would return voicemail messages, but I left a couple and they were not returned. API wouldn't give me any information, citing confidentiality, even though I pointed out that under the recent *Bigley* Alaska Supreme Court decision, as his lawyer I was entitled to it. The guardian had told API and the court system I was no longer representing Bill, saying Bill no longer wanted me to represent him.

THURSDAY, JULY 16TH, 2009: MOTION TO DISMISS GUARDIANSHIP

On July 16th, because Bill had been doing so well, I moved to terminate the guardianship. This was probably a huge mistake. His guardian felt this was very irresponsible because they didn't think he could manage without their "help."

SATURDAY, JULY 18TH, 2009: ANOTHER TRIP TO API

Coincidentally or not, two days later Bill was hauled into API, purportedly because he was harassing his neighbors. API let him go two days later without filing a petition to commit him, presumably because he did not meet commitment criteria, even under their expansive view.

SATURDAY, JULY 25TH, 2009: YET AGAIN TO API

The next Saturday, July 25th, Bill was again hauled into API and then let out that Monday, again presumably because he didn't meet commitment criteria. Had he been brought in during the work week,

API probably would have immediately released him, but bringing him in on a Saturday meant API would not release him until at least Monday. This was no doubt known by the people having him hauled into API on Saturdays.

FRIDAY, JULY 31ST, 2009

The person from Assets who was supposed to be coordinating things for Bill and keep him out of trouble filed an *ex parté* petition on July 31st to have him committed. The grounds for the petition were that he was harassing and threatening neighbors, which put him in "grave danger of provoking violence against him."

SATURDAY, AUGUST 1ST, 2009

API filed a petition to commit Bill for thirty days on August 1st. The reasons given were that people were threatening violence against Bill for his behavior and that he was not eating. I didn't know about any of this at the time because API, the guardian, and the public defender were actively preventing me from finding out.

THURSDAY, AUGUST 6TH, 2009: THIRTY-DAY COMMITMENT HEARING

A hearing on the thirty-day commitment petition was held on August 6th before the probate master, who insisted Bill be represented by the public defenders even though they said Bill did not want them to represent him, and they didn't feel they could because he was refusing to communicate with them. The probate master wouldn't let the public defenders withdraw (quit representing Bill). The probate master recommended commitment, which the Superior Court judge granted the next day. Because of the active concealment by API, the guardian, and the public defender, I didn't know about this at the time either.

FRIDAY, AUGUST 14TH, 2009: A PLEA FROM BILL

Bill managed to get a call to me on August 14th from API and asked me to get him out of there. This was the first I had been able to talk to Bill since late June or early July.

MONDAY, AUGUST 17TH, 2009: HERE WE GO AGAIN

I entered an appearance in API's most recent case against Bill, this time not just for the forced drugging petition, which API had agreed to withdraw, but also for the involuntary commitment. API refused to recognize me as Bill's attorney, however, because his guardian was not allowing Bill to have me be his attorney.

MONDAY, AUGUST 24TH, 2009: API REFUSES TO LET ME VISIT BILL

I tried to visit Bill at API, but on the guardian's instructions, I was not allowed to see him.

WEDNESDAY, AUGUST 26TH, 2009

The probate master issued an order that I was not Bill's attorney, which I did not receive until August 28th.

THURSDAY, AUGUST 27TH, 2009: JURY DEMAND AND ITS REJECTION

On August 27th, which was before I had found out the probate master had ruled I couldn't be Bill's lawyer, I filed a demand for a jury trial in the event a ninety-day commitment petition was filed. Since there was no doubt the probate master and judge would order Bill committed, and Bill had won the last two jury trials, a jury trial was clearly the way to go. The next day, however, the probate master denied the demand for jury trial on the grounds that I was not Bill's lawyer, even though it was Bill's right to have one. It turns out the ninety-day petition was filed that same day, but I was not notified.

FRIDAY, AUGUST 28TH, 2009

I received an order from the probate master that I was not Bill's attorney because the public defender had not withdrawn. Keep in mind the probate master had refused to let the public defender withdraw.

MONDAY, AUGUST 31ST, 2009: MOTION FOR RECONSIDERATION

On August 31st, I filed a motion for reconsideration regarding the probate master's rejection of my representation of Bill.

WEDNESDAY, SEPTEMBER 2ND, 2009

The hearing on the ninety-day commitment petition was scheduled to be held in front of the probate master on September 2nd. API announced the idea was to get a forced drugging order so they could release Bill and drug him in the community against his will, with the support team that had been created the last time he was released. However, the public defender asked for a delay because Bill's representation was in question, and complained about my contact with

Bill. The probate master said in light of Bill's incompetence, he thought the guardian had the right to pick Bill's lawyer. This was an interesting concept since the guardian wanted Bill to lose. The probate master said the actual judge assigned to the case needed to decide the representation issue, and he was willing to delay the ninety-day commitment trial for a week to get it on the judge's schedule. The hearing was set for the following Thursday, September 10th.

API was concerned about not being able to drug Bill in the interim, and the public defender said it believed the judge's decision in the previous case ten months earlier, allowing emergency drugging, was still effective. Then the probate master said he was just going to recommend denying my motion for reconsideration about being Bill's lawyer so there wouldn't need to be a representation hearing. The probate master suggested I was violating the rules of professional conduct for lawyers and a report to the Bar Association might be appropriate. When API suggested the ten-month-old order on emergency drugging was not still in effect, the public defender just agreed to have Bill drugged on an emergency basis.

THURSDAY, SEPTEMBER 3RD, 2009

On Thursday, September 3rd, the Superior Court Judge in the case issued an order holding off, until the September 10th hearing, on deciding whether I was representing Bill, and directing that any objection(s) to the probate master's recommendations be filed by September 9th.

TUESDAY, SEPTEMBER 8TH, 2009

On September 8th, the day before I was to fly all night to a NARPA conference in Phoenix, where I was to give a talk, I filed an objection to the probate master's recommendation that I not be recognized as Bill's lawyer. In addition to making the arguments about why it was improper to deny my entry of appearance for Bill and to allow Bill's guardian to choose his lawyer, I made a number of arguments about why the forced drugging petition should not be granted, because I figured it might be my only chance. I pointed out it was improper for the public defender to agree to the so-called emergency drugging of Bill. I stated the ninety-day commitment petition was unconstitutional because it provided neither adequate notice of what Bill was being charged with nor facts sufficient to justify locking Bill up and drugging him against his will. I also argued forcing the drugs on Bill was not in his best interests. I also noted I was going to be out of state from September 9th to 12th to attend a conference at which I had a long-standing speaking engagement and requested they not hold the hearing during that time.

THURSDAY, SEPTEMBER 10TH, 2009

I was in Phoenix listening to a keynote address by Ira Burnim, the Legal Director of the Bazelon Center for Mental Health Law, about their great victory in New York City in getting the practice of institutionalizing mental patients in "group homes" declared a violation of the Americans With Disabilities Act, when I received a call from the court. I had to leave the presentation to take the call.

From reading the transcript I know that before they got me on the phone, the guardian said Bill had been saying for over a year that I didn't represent him. She said the guardian "wants to assure Mr. Bigley has appropriate legal representation, but that legal representation is not PsychRights." What "appropriate legal representation" meant apparently included the public defender agreeing to have Bill drugged against his will under phony emergencies. The public defender complained my piecemeal representation of Bill and sometimes critical statements about the public defender were problems.

When I got on the phone, the judge announced they were going ahead with the hearing on the ninety-day commitment petition and then would decide whether Bill was going to be represented by me. I said the representation issue needed to be decided first because Bill had the right to choose his own lawyer, and he would be harmed if he wasn't allowed to have me represent him. The judge said the guardian had filed three affidavits saying Bill didn't want me to be his attorney, and the court visitor reported the same thing. They also said Bill didn't want to look at the paperwork I had sent him, which were copies of all the filings I had made on his behalf. It is my practice to send my clients everything I file on their behalf.

I said Bill had never told me he didn't want me to represent him and had recently asked me to get him out of API. I then asked whether the judge had heard from Bill directly about whether he wanted me to represent him. I told the judge if he asked Bill, and Bill said he didn't want me to represent him, I'd withdraw. The judge asked, "You're prepared to do that here and now?" I said yes. Of course I wasn't going to represent Bill if he didn't want me to.

The judge then asked Bill whether he wanted me to be his lawyer, and Bill said, "Gottstein knows a lot about me. It's a Catch-22 in here all over," and then a bunch of stuff the court reporter didn't get. To both my and the judge's questions, Bill responded at least four times that he wanted me to represent him and then each time talked about other things he had on his mind, such as being the president.

So then the guardian argued Bill shouldn't be allowed to choose his lawyer because he was not competent to do so. When the public defender represented Bill, they almost always lost, whereas when I represented him, he won about half the time. What was incompetent about him choosing that? The guardian also said my representation of Bill had caused him substantial harm. In other words, having a lawyer actually try to enforce Bill's rights was wrong. The judge decided Bill was not competent to choose me as his lawyer, told me to get off the phone, and went on to conduct the ninety-day commitment hearing without me. He said I could have information relevant to appealing his decision to not let Bill choose me as his lawyer, but nothing else.

One of the interesting things the judge said in this hearing was that when the probate master makes a recommendation, the expectation is the actual judge in the case "will sign off on it immediately without a meaningful review of the underlying process and without waiting [for] the objection time." In other words, they weren't following the Alaska Supreme Court's ruling I described above about the judges being required to review a transcript of the hearing or at least listen to the recording of it. One of the interesting things the psychiatrist testifying against Bill said was that Bill saying *The New York Times* knew about him was a symptom of his mental illness. When it was pointed out there was a story about Bill in *The New York Times*, he just said, "Oh." The psychiatrist also testified Bill was delusional because he thought API was going to commit him.

The public defender did a pretty good job on cross-examination, but without calling witnesses it was hopeless to contradict the blatant lies to which the psychiatrist testified, such as that Tardive Dyskinesia was rare with the newer neuroleptics, being on the neuroleptics long-term doesn't increase the risk, and Tardive Dyskinesia, if caught in the early stages, can be reversed by stopping the medication. All of these statements are untrue. He also testified Ativan wasn't extremely addictive, which is untrue, depending on what "extremely" means. He also testified mental illness causes brain damage, which has never been proven and almost certainly is not true.

His community service provider was called to testify and said he didn't notice a difference in Bill on or off psych drugs. This was drastically different from the testimony of other API witnesses, almost all of whom were API staff. He also testified Bill had started cleaning his apartment and had kept it clean and become less paranoid about services during the February–June 2009 period, when he had been out of API and not on psych drugs.

THURSDAY, SEPTEMBER 24TH, 2009

On September 24th, the judge issued an order granting the ninety-day commitment and forced drugging petitions. The order also prohibited me from making any unsolicited contact with Bill, which was pretty upsetting to me because I felt it would make Bill think I had abandoned him.

BILL'S LAST TRIP TO THE ALASKA SUPREME COURT

Bill did still come by. I asked him whether he wanted me to appeal the denial of his right to choose me as his lawyer. He said he did. Therefore, on Monday, October 5th, 2009, I filed an appeal to the Alaska Supreme Court on behalf of Bill, saying he should have been allowed to pick his attorney. The public defender tried to get the appeal dismissed, saying PsychRights had no right to appeal. However, I never asserted I or PsychRights had the right to appeal the court's denial of Bill's choice of lawyer. Instead, I was appealing *on Bill's behalf* over the court's denial of his right to choose his lawyer. That is the way it works. The lawyer appeals on behalf of the client.

On January 7th, 2010, the Alaska Supreme Court put the appeal on hold and sent the case back to the trial court to determine whether Bill was competent to decide who he wanted to represent him, whether he wanted me to represent him, and whether he wanted to appeal the denial of his right to choose his lawyer.

On January 12th, the trial court judge issued a decision that Bill was not competent to choose his lawyer, and on January 20th, the Alaska Supreme Court dismissed the appeal (threw it out). The Supreme Court said I had the right to file an original application, on my own behalf, that I had the right to represent Bill. Since it was never about *my* right to represent Bill, I did not. So from that point on, API and the guardian had their way with Bill, drugging him without any real constraint.

On May 14th, 2007, Dr. Jackson had testified Bill would be dead within five years if they continued to drug him. She was off by a few months. Bill died on November 21st, 2012 at the age of fifty-nine.

Ch. 12.   Ruminations

One of the things that struck me while writing this book was that people of good intentions (I am not referring to Eli Lilly and its lawyers) had such diametrically opposed beliefs. To me, it is crystal clear locking people up and drugging them against their will is not "for their own good" but instead very harmful to them. One of my goals in writing this book is to show this truth. The totally unproven and almost certainly untrue notion that what gets diagnosed as mental illness is some kind of brain defect has many horrific results. Chief among these is it is used to justify drugging millions of people with ineffective, counterproductive, and harmful drugs. People diagnosed with serious mental illness in the public mental health system are now dying twenty-five years earlier than the rest of the population. In the early 1900s, before the introduction of these so-called "treatments," people diagnosed with serious mental illness had normal life spans.

The credence given to the notion that what gets diagnosed as mental illness is a brain defect dehumanizes those so diagnosed. Bill is a classic example. His experience and desires were irrelevant to "The System" because they were considered just manifestations of misfiring neurons. Bill's periodic belief he was Jesus Christ, for example, was considered proof he was a raving lunatic. What these people don't understand is by believing he was Jesus Christ, the suffering—even torture—inflicted upon him by the mental health system gave meaning to his life. It was his cross to bear. His other beliefs, such as being or knowing the president and being very wealthy had a similar function.

Most people faced with the unrelenting psychiatric force inflicted on Bill would have been beaten into submission. Bill never was. During the forced drugging fight in September 2007, a "Pickles" cartoon came out that I thought was perfect, and I asked Bill whether it was okay to put it on his PsychRights webpage. He said it was.

Bill was proud of being in *The New York Times*. He wanted to be important, and I think he was. The 2009 Alaska Supreme Court decision in *Bigley v. Alaska Psychiatric Institute* is very important, and it wouldn't have happened without Bill. And of course, his role in getting the Zyprexa Papers released was also very important.

In the end, how important was the release of the Zyprexa Papers? The most obvious long-term benefit from their release was the public exposure of Zyprexa's harm. The release of the Zyprexa Papers has saved many lives, possibly tens of thousands or more, and helped reveal the abuses of the drug industry. At the same time, it is still being used on hundreds of thousands of people, including being forced on many. The same is true of the other neuroleptics.

Also, at least for a while, Bloomberg News was intervening successfully in similar lawsuits to unseal documents. This included *Alaska v. Lilly* as well as the multidistrict lawsuit over Seroquel, another second-generation neuroleptic that also causes metabolic and other problems.

My sense is that as a result of the Zyprexa Papers, there was a short period of time when lawyers were less willing to keep such information secret. However, things seem to have gone back to normal, with damning documents being kept secret as a matter of course. When lawyers are faced with companies telling them they won't settle unless everything is kept secret, the lawyers almost always advise (insist) their clients agree. Illustrating this, after seeing the first *New York Times* front-page story, which identified me as the source of the Zyprexa Papers, Ellen Liversidge, whose son had been killed by Zyprexa, wrote me about her settlement with Lilly:

While the attorneys were negotiating with Lilly on the 8000 plaintiff settlement, my attorney said there were many incriminating documents, and they would all be revealed once the agreement was reached. WRONG. The attorneys, allegedly representing our interests, signed an agreement of confidentiality with Lilly. Then my lawyer lied to me, saying "all the information had been revealed."

This is a situation where the benefits accrue to one group and the detriments to another. In other words, their clients are not harmed by keeping the information secret, but the public is harmed. Their clients only get benefits, i.e., money. This is also true of the lawyers, who get paid (a lot) if the case is settled but don't get paid if they lose. The judges are supposed to allow the secrecy only if it is in the public interest, but in practice, they don't. The secrecy greases the wheels of settlement as well as litigation, and judges want to have cases resolved and off their docket. So the incentives are all pushing towards keeping things secret. Normally, no one is representing the public interest.

I think it is fair to say that by issuing the secrecy order, the Zyprexa MDL court was complicit with Lilly in hiding the great harm being done to people as a result of Zyprexa. If this information had become public earlier, thousands of lives could have been saved, and hundreds of thousands of people would probably not have taken Zyprexa, avoiding the less than fatal but still serious detrimental effects of Zyprexa.

With all due respect, I believe the Zyprexa MDL court had blinders on when considering my subpoena and release of the Zyprexa Papers. It felt I had violated its Secrecy Order, and never gave serious consideration to the possibility I had not. Protecting its authority was really the court's only consideration in my view—that and greasing the wheels of settlement. It did not give fair consideration to PsychRights' legitimate interest in the Zyprexa Papers. It did not give fair consideration to the fact that PsychRights followed the Secrecy Order's rules in obtaining the Zyprexa Papers. Dr. Egilman was allowed access to the documents only for the purposes of the Zyprexa MDL and may have violated that by calling me. Once he had, though, I had my independent and proper reasons for subpoenaing them, including alerting the public to the great harm caused by Zyprexa.

I can see how the courts interpreted my actions as aiding and abetting Dr. Egilman's violation of the Secrecy Order, but I considered it his obligation to comply, and I had repeatedly told him he must. I thought Lilly would object before I received the documents, and I would be arguing against Lilly in the Alaska court as to why I was entitled to obtain and use them in Mr. Bigley's case. It was only because Dr. Egilman determined Lilly had been given a reasonable opportunity to object that I received them. I believed I had received them under the Secrecy Order's rules and at that point, they lost their secrecy.

I have written some harsh words about the public defenders, saying their function is not to adequately represent their clients but to check the box off that people facing psychiatric imprisonment and forced drugging have had a lawyer before they were locked up and drugged against their will. This is not meant as criticism of any individual public defenders. I actually like the ones I have dealt with. It is "The System" to blame. The public defenders have too many cases to do any adequately. When I represented someone in these cases, it was the only case I had, and I devoted everything I could to it. In light of the ridiculously short time frame in which to conduct such an important legal proceeding, I think this is the only way to adequately defend such a case. The public defenders are simply not allowed to do the same.

Having said this, ineffective legal representation is the lynch pin for the massive harm being done to people through psychiatry. If people were being represented effectively, the current system would be unable to lock up the legions of people and drug them against their will, and would have to find some other way to deal with people who are diagnosed with mental illness and being disturbing. If PsychRights had the resources to employ just two or three lawyers full time in Anchorage, Alaska for such representations and to pay for expert witnesses, I believe PsychRights could break the system and force the provision of different approaches that have been shown to work and help people get through the problems they are having.

I try not to ascribe bad motives to people. So I wonder how psychiatrists and the other people in our mental illness system, or general health system, for that matter, can push these counterproductive and harmful drugs, let alone force them into someone who doesn't want them. I used to believe these people just didn't know, but that is no longer a viable defense because the facts about the harms caused by the neuroleptics, and the harms caused by the other psychiatric drugs with no real benefit, are very well established. It is hard not to conclude they are society's enforcers against people who are disturbing, merely pretending to be operating in those people's best interests and in accordance with law. I just don't think most of them see themselves that way, though, and I wish I understood their thinking.

It is easy to simply conclude that companies like Eli Lilly and the lawyers they hire are just evil. It is easy to ascribe it to the same motive Willie Sutton gave for robbing banks: "That's where the money is." No doubt needing to pay the bills and wishing to be wealthy are contributing factors, as is the natural tendency to go along with authority. But as Maya Angelou said, "Throughout our nervous history, we have constructed pyramidic towers of evil, ofttimes in the name of good." Similarly, Joseph Brodsky said, "What we regard as Evil is capable of a fairly ubiquitous presence if only because it tends to appear in the guise of good." I think both of these are applicable to our mental illness system and describe what Hannah Arendt termed "the banality of evil." I can only hope this book in some way combats the banality of evil which is coercive psychiatry, enabled by the fraudulent promise of magic potions.

People who have been on the wrong side of the locked door and the pointy end of a needle—psychiatric survivors—are the most knowledgeable about the horrors of coercive psychiatry, but there are other people of good character who also know, such as Dr. Grace Jackson, Robert Whitaker, Vera Sharav, and Dr. David Cohen. I have written a little bit about the psychiatric survivors who got involved in the Zyprexa Papers affair, but I didn't do justice to any of them. Each deserve book-length treatment to document the incredible things they have done.

Acknowledgments

There are many people who helped me write this book over the two years it took, most of them in the last few months.

My beloved wife, Nancy, was there from the beginning, supporting the effort and encouraging me. Nancy has been steadfast even though she is concerned this book will provoke the wrath of Eli Lilly and possibly crush us financially. She has always believed in the book's importance. My sister Sandy also gave me early encouragement and offered suggestions on the manuscript. Robert Whitaker also encouraged me from the beginning to write this book and offered invaluable suggestions.

Ron Bassman told me the editor for his terrific book, *A Fight to Be: A Psychologist's Experience from Both Sides of the Locked Door*, was Dania Sheldon. He put us in contact, and Dania agreed to be my editor. She has been a huge help. Dania really believes in this book. Then, her beloved cat, The Curl, got sick and passed away, and another beloved cat, Socrates, got deathly ill. In spite of her intense sadness, she continued to help, always delivering her edits within the time frame she promised, and I will be forever grateful. She is the consummate professional. Any mistakes are no doubt my fault because I cannot type three letters without getting one of them wrong and couldn't help tinkering with the manuscript to the very end.

John McKay was very generous with his time in reviewing and commenting on my manuscript even though he is always very busy. In addition to editorial suggestions, which were remarkably similar to Dania's, he had very insightful comments and suggestions from being a participant as well as a superb lawyer.

From Holland, Mira DeVries, an amazing advocate against the abuses of psychiatry, also offered valuable suggestions.

Dick Reichmann, a local playwright and actor, gave me some early suggestions, which I greatly appreciate.

The marvelous dedication photograph of Bill, which I think really captures him, was taken by my terrific then-assistant, Lisa Smith, who spent many, many hours with Bill—mainly listening. Speaking of photographs, my step-daughter, Jaclyn Delguidice, took the photo of me that became the silhouette on the cover.

Finally, I want to thank Bob Parsons for agreeing to do the cover, even though it was outside his comfort zone. I have known Bob since elementary school, have always loved his drawings, and really wanted him to do the cover. I had a concept of Bob drawing the courtroom scene with Vera Sharav, of which I have a vivid visual memory, but Bob is such a professional he didn't feel that would be the best for the book and came up with the marvelous cover design we have. If this book is a sales success, I will give a lot of the credit to the cover Bob conceived and implemented, which doesn't demonstrate his gift at drawing. I want you to know the talent that you would otherwise miss:

About the Author

Jim Gottstein grew up in Anchorage, Alaska where his father was a prominent businessman and his mother one of the most beloved women in town. Jim was on track to go into the family grocery and real estate empire, studying for a business degree at the University of Oregon when the law found him during his required Business Law class. He didn't miss a question the entire class and realized law was a good fit. He managed to get into Harvard Law School as the only sky-diving applicant from Alaska that year.

After graduating from law school in 1978, Jim went into private practice in Anchorage with Robert M. Goldberg, primarily representing Alaska Native organizations. In 1982, he experienced a psychotic break due to sleep deprivation and was introduced first hand to the mental illness system. He was told he would be permanently mentally ill and to forget about his law career. Luckily, he escaped psychiatry and the experience led him to legal representation and other advocacy for people diagnosed with serious mental illness not as lucky as he. Jim opened his own law office in 1985, generally focused on business matters, and is now mostly retired from the private practice of law. In 2002, Jim founded the Law Project for Psychiatric Rights (PsychRights) to mount a strategic litigation campaign against forced psychiatric drugging and electroshock, and to inform the public about the counterproductive and harmful nature of the drugs and shock.

1/26/2020

Made in the USA
Middletown, DE
30 January 2020